Maxwell Anderson and the Marriage Crisis

Fonzie D. Geary II

Maxwell Anderson and the Marriage Crisis

Challenging Tradition in the Jazz Age

palgrave
macmillan

Fonzie D. Geary II
Batesville, AR, USA

ISBN 978-3-031-13240-7   ISBN 978-3-031-13241-4   (eBook)
https://doi.org/10.1007/978-3-031-13241-4

© The Editor(s) (if applicable) and The Author(s), under exclusive license to Springer Nature Switzerland AG 2022
This work is subject to copyright. All rights are solely and exclusively licensed by the Publisher, whether the whole or part of the material is concerned, specifically the rights of translation, reprinting, reuse of illustrations, recitation, broadcasting, reproduction on microfilms or in any other physical way, and transmission or information storage and retrieval, electronic adaptation, computer software, or by similar or dissimilar methodology now known or hereafter developed.
The use of general descriptive names, registered names, trademarks, service marks, etc. in this publication does not imply, even in the absence of a specific statement, that such names are exempt from the relevant protective laws and regulations and therefore free for general use.
The publisher, the authors, and the editors are safe to assume that the advice and information in this book are believed to be true and accurate at the date of publication. Neither the publisher nor the authors or the editors give a warranty, expressed or implied, with respect to the material contained herein or for any errors or omissions that may have been made. The publisher remains neutral with regard to jurisdictional claims in published maps and institutional affiliations.

This Palgrave Macmillan imprint is published by the registered company Springer Nature Switzerland AG
The registered company address is: Gewerbestrasse 11, 6330 Cham, Switzerland

For Laura

Acknowledgments

My first experience attempting meaningful research in the field of theatre occurred in the first semester of my master's program at the University of Kentucky in 2004. There I found myself enrolled in a course entitled *20th Century Plays of War* taught by Dr. Rhoda-Gale Pollack. Dr. Pollack introduced the class to *What Price Glory*, a play that enraptured my attention. She made a point of emphasizing Maxwell Anderson's former prominence as well as the paucity of recent research into his work. This incongruity combined with my admiration for the play inspired my curiosity and provoked my eternal sympathy for underappreciated figures. I immediately determined to make Anderson my project for that course. He then remained ever present for me throughout two years at UK, with my master's thesis coming under the direction of Dr. Geraldine Maschio, then five years at the University of Missouri while earning my Ph.D. under the guidance of my dissertation chair, Dr. Cheryl Black. These formative years spent learning from these scholars were incalculable in the creation of my subsequent publications on Anderson's work and, of course, in the ultimate completion of this book.

I owe thanks to several individuals and institutions for their vital assistance in bringing this book to fruition. First, my utmost gratitude to Maxwell L. Anderson for granting permission from the Anderson Estate to quote from his grandfather's works. The Harry Ransom Center at the University of Texas at Austin proved both generous and immensely helpful in providing access to key Anderson papers and manuscripts held in its repository. The Billy Rose Theatre Collection at the New York Public Library went above and beyond in facilitating my access (when it appeared my opportunity was lost) to the only available typescript of Anderson's unpublished play, *Gypsy*. The interlibrary loan department of the Mabee-Simpson Library at Lyon College in Batesville, Arkansas did a remarkable job tracking down key materials. Lyon College also provided a generous research grant, which defrayed the cost of my travel to Austin, Texas. My thanks to Dr. Stuart Hecht, editor of the *New England Theatre Journal*, who granted permission for me to use significant portions of an article I published in said journal related to Anderson's play, *Saturday's Children*. I would also like to express my gratitude to Dr. Heather Nathans who selflessly gave of her time and expertise as an editor in assisting me in the development of my book proposal.

Many thanks to my children, Fonzie III, Isabelle, and Sophia, who all love their father very much and found bearing with his absences and research distractions a monumental task. Lastly, but most important of all, my sincerest gratitude to my wife, Laura Geary, who has enriched my life in ways beyond quantification and who, for me, forever and always remains a source of love, inspiration, and strength. This book would never have happened without her.

Contents

1 Jazz Age Theatre and the "Marriage Crisis" — 1
2 *White Desert*: Marriage as Manifest Destiny — 37
3 *Sea-Wife*: Marriage and Superstition — 67
4 *Saturday's Children*: Love Before Marriage — 97
5 *Gypsy*: Love After Marriage — 129
6 Maxwell Anderson Reassessed — 159

Index — 185

CHAPTER 1

Jazz Age Theatre and the "Marriage Crisis"

Maxwell Anderson's contribution to American drama, particularly as revealed in his marriage plays of the Jazz Age, has never been fully appreciated by critics or scholars. Recent research on Anderson has been scant and evaluations of his work published in the twentieth century tended to center on his aesthetic use of verse drama during the 1930s. This book attempts to alter the lens in which Anderson's reputation is viewed by focusing on the 1920s and examining Anderson's plays as social critiques of an important, pervasive facet of American life and culture. Throughout the Progressive Era and into the Jazz Age, many Americans either lamented or welcomed (depending on their perspective) the notion that what was perceived as traditional marriage was embroiled in an existential crisis. In the last hundred years the institution of marriage in the United States has certainly evolved, but those in the 1920s who feared a "crisis," who fretted over marriage's imminent disintegration, underestimated the weight the institution bears in American culture. The plays of Maxwell Anderson covered in this book represent, therefore, an important resource for helping us better comprehend the nuances of the marriage debate during the Jazz Age and, in turn, aid in a more complete understanding of how marriage and gender roles in the United States have evolved.

© The Author(s), under exclusive license to Springer Nature Switzerland AG 2022
F. D. Geary II, *Maxwell Anderson and the Marriage Crisis*, https://doi.org/10.1007/978-3-031-13241-4_1

Case Study #1

In his 1927 book, *The Companionate Marriage*, Judge Ben B. Lindsey relates a remarkable true story of three young adults he identifies pseudonymously as Esther, Archie, and Bob. Esther married Archie who was, in Lindsey's estimation, an upstanding young man. Archie worked hard, provided well, and had an easy, kindly temperament. However, Esther soon discovered after their marriage that, despite all of Archie's positive qualities, she shared little in common with him. A mutual friend of theirs, Bob, was nothing like Archie in the way of reliability, work ethic, or charm, but Esther found herself wanting to spend more time with Bob than with her husband. Archie noted his wife's attitude and frankly inquired if she would be happier with Bob. When Esther replied in the affirmative, Archie immediately and amicably suggested divorce. The law at the time stipulated a six-month waiting period upon filing for divorce. During this time Esther and Bob, with Archie's knowledge and consent, lived together. By the time the six months had ended, thus finalizing the divorce, Esther was already pregnant. Shortly afterward she married Bob. Just before the birth of their child, Esther and Bob were treated to a dinner party given by Archie in celebration of their blissful union.[1] According to Lindsey, "It was a thoroughly amicable occasion."[2]

Case Study #2

In this case, Judge Lindsey conveys his experience with a married couple he identifies as Mr. and Mrs. Blank. The Blanks were both well-educated people occupying the upper echelon of society. They were, as far as Lindsey could tell, in love and devoted to each other. They were also keen to explore sexual satisfaction outside of their marriage. Both knew of and consented to the other's myriad love affairs. However, their marriage did not begin with such an arrangement. As is so often the case, the Blanks began in complete monogamy and their union was nearly torn asunder when Mrs. Blank discovered her husband was carrying on an extramarital relation. After an initial bout of outrage from Mrs. Blank followed by a bitter confrontation with her husband, the Blanks mutually decided their marriage would work better if sexual freedom were permitted for both of them and so codified their agreement. Given the time period, one might have expected Lindsey to have gleaned this story from the husband. However, all of his information in this case came out of a long and detailed conversation with the wife.[3] When Lindsey expressed surprise, Mrs. Blank retorted, "What's the harm—aside from the fact that we have always been told that it was wrong?".[4]

The Crisis Defined

While the above stories from Judge Lindsey are anecdotal and, one imagines, not at all typical, they do emblematize, at a micro level, the radical attempts at work in the 1920s at re-framing the institution of marriage. For many people, even in the twenty-first century, such marriage scenarios as Lindsey describes would be unthinkable. However, for Lindsey the matter was quite straightforward. In the first case, Archie had simply "*accorded to another human being the freedom of action we should all be prepared to accord to other human beings, so long as such freedom does not infringe on other people's rights*" (emphasis in original).[5] Thus, the reasonableness of Archie's position, as Lindsey viewed it, was a matter of common human decency and there existed no constructive need for rash emotions, such as jealousy or rage, to interfere. In the second case, Lindsey attributes the working relationship of the Blanks to "a daring reasonableness" and chalks up any moral judgment leveled against them as symptomatic of "a world where the vast majority of persons don't seem to use any rationality at all."[6]

The idea of evolving human rights, subverting gender roles, and challenging conventions were part and parcel of the discourse in 1920s America. Dramatic cultural sea changes occurred in the wake of World War I. Women, of course, finally achieved the right to vote, thus expanding the potential of their political voice. New dance crazes such as the fox trot and the monkey glide evoked animalistic sexuality,[7] which served as "part of the rebellion against the older sexual mores."[8] Flapper dresses, sleeveless with short hem lines, exposed more of a woman's skin to the public than ever before, thus subverting traditional ideas of modesty and scandalizing conservative society. Though Warren G. Harding won election to the presidency on the promise of returning America to "normalcy," radical develops of the 1910s insured a new normal for the 1920s. Among the ideals garnering the most virulent criticism, the most intense interrogations, was that of traditional matrimony. As in any culture war, there existed vociferous arguments on both sides of the coin and plenty of waffling in the middle. There were those who sought to adhere to tradition, those who sought to modify it slightly, and those who sought to turn it on its head and set it on fire. However, many people agreed, rightly or wrongly, that the institution of marriage in the United States had come under closer scrutiny during the 1920s than it ever had in previous generations.

In 1925, psychiatrist Beatrice Hinkle observed, "Among the many subjects agitating the minds of the people of the United States to-day [*sic*] none compares in its insistence and acuteness with the question of the future of the institution of marriage."[9] The title of Hinkle's article referred to marriage as "chaos." Sociologist Ernest Groves preferred the term "crisis" for his 1928 book studying the vicissitudes of modern American marriage.[10] In 1924, the *Nation* published a series of articles entitled "New Morals for Old," which focused on issues of marriage and male/female relationships written by intellectuals of diverse backgrounds such as British philosopher Bertrand Russell,[11] American anthropologist Elsie Clews Parsons,[12] literary critic and occasional playwright Floyd Dell,[13] and novelist and social reformer Charlotte Perkins Gilman.[14] As the title of the *Nation*'s series suggests, these critics were not advocating a reckless descent into hedonism, but rather a reframing of morality better suited to the modern American temper. The focus of this series of articles lends weight to Hinkle's suggestion that the fate of marriage as an institution in the United States was, indeed, a major subject of discussion in the Jazz Age.

Statistics offered some support for those fearing, if not a crisis, at least a seismic shift in attitudes toward matrimony. The overall marriage rate per 1,000 unmarried females plummeted from 92 in 1920 to 79.2 in 1925 and then to 67.6 by 1930.[15] While divorce rates held steady throughout the 1920s at a national level,[16] one finds significant increases when comparing to previous generations. On a micro level, in their famous study, *Middletown*, Robert and Helen Lynd reported that divorce rose 622% in Muncie, Indiana from the early 1890s to the early 1920s.[17] On a broader level, only 1 in 21 American marriages ended in divorce in 1880 with 1 in 12 resulting in divorce in 1890.[18] By 1924, the divorce rate reached 1 in 7.[19] The broadening of education for women was also seen as a factor affecting marriage. Between the 1870s and 1920s anywhere from 40–60% of female college graduates remained single compared to only 10% of women as a whole throughout the nation.[20] Moreover, attitudes about sex were shifting as well. Noted American sexologist Alfred Kinsey found that 36% of women born after 1900 reported having engaged in premarital sex as opposed to 14% of women born pre-1900.[21]

While sexual promiscuity was still frowned upon, young women of the 1920s often found premarital sex acceptable if the two partners were in love.[22] Thus the 1920s witnessed a clear shift in cultural attitudes about marriage, sex, and gender roles in the United States. However, challenging a tradition as old as matrimony represented a monumental task in the 1920s and continues to challenge Americans in the twenty-first century. As Groves stated, "This marriage ideal is too thoroughly intertwined with social experience to be easily or lightly thrown aside."[23]

The Marriage Institution & Protestant Victorianism

Marriage represents one of humanity's oldest, most steadfast institutions. One of the earliest references to its importance in Western culture occurs in Plato's *Republic* when Socrates stresses the need for society "to make marriage as sacred as possible."[24] What, exactly, constituted sacredness in a marital arrangement has varied widely over time. Historically, many Americans have tended to view a monogamous union between a man and a woman, with the husband functioning as sole breadwinner while the wife tended domestic duties, as the norm. However, the concept of the male breadwinner/female housewife did not take hold in the United States until the nineteenth century.[25] This was in part, due to wage disparity between genders. As one historian notes, working women of the nineteenth century "generally earned only one-third the wages of a man," which rendered her work within the home a far more valuable asset to the family.[26] The male breadwinner model was, therefore, a matter of necessity for most middle class and working-class American families in the 1800s. In the 1700s, marital norms varied by class. Working-class men often sought marriage early because their "earning power" reached its zenith in their late teenage years. Thus, it could behoove them to have children early so that the children may sooner start working themselves and contribute to the family's income. For middle class families, however, marriage was often delayed due to the need for men to devote long periods of their lives either to formal education or mastering a craft. Consequently, not only did middle class Americans of the late eighteenth century marry later in life than their working-class contemporaries, but they, by extension, had children later in life.[27] Prior to the twentieth century marriage in America served utilitarian purposes and its shape was often contingent upon the circumstances into which one was born.

Utilitarian purposes, however, do not account fully for the power the institution of marriage holds in American society. Regardless of what shape it takes, matrimony endures, arguably, because it strikes at two primal human desires: the need for companionship and the instinct to extend the species. Over the course of millennia, as human civilization advanced and populations exploded, the instinct for procreation eventually became subverted to an instinct for sex. As British physician and sexologist Havelock Ellis observed, without even a hint of romance, "Marriage in the biological sense, and even to some extent in the social sense, is a sexual relationship entered into with intention of making it permanent."[28] In referencing marriage first in the "biological sense," Ellis narrows the institution to its lowest common denominator: sexual hunger. Groves basically agreed, with perhaps a tinge of sententiousness, when he characterized marriage as society's "attempts to stabilize the union of male and female, and to protect society from the menace of unrestrained and irresponsible sex behavior."[29]

Groves's moral tint alludes to two factors impacting conceptions of marriage in American culture. First, in speaking of marriage in terms of stabilizing monogamous male/female unions, Groves's assertion could be read as a veiled reference to the intertwining of marriage with religion. For Americans that religion was Christian and predominantly Protestant. One cannot understate the importance of Protestant Christianity in informing American cultural character. As historian Warren Susman asserted, in America "the role of religious ideology in the shaping of other ideological positions is key."[30] Feminist historian Nancy F. Cott connects monogamous marriage to prevailing Christian culture dating back to Revolutionary America, noting its importance in the founders' "moral and political philosophy."[31] Second, in referencing the need to protect society at large from the consequences of unbridled sexual promiscuity, Groves hints at conventions of social control brought about by the onset of the Victorian era. America, it seems, had not culturally divorced itself from England. Charles Dickens noted this peculiarity when he observed several taverns decorated with portraits of both George Washington and Queen Victoria.[32] When discussing the evolution of matrimony in modern America, the complex relationship between Protestantism and Victorian principles become crucial.

The Protestant Victorian ethos centered on the veneration of personal industry and self-control. The avoidance of idleness through hard work served to enhance both the individual and the broader world by "curbing men's animal passions, which if left unchecked would bring about social collapse."[33] Balance was achieved through the idea of separate gendered spheres. According to this model, men were thought most capable of engaging in public matters such as "politics and the economy" while women were viewed as best suited to ruling over "the private world of the home."[34] Within the home, women were expected to foster a "noncompetitive and nurturing environment," and to behave in a manner "refined" and "controlled," which was the opposite of men, who were viewed as naturally aggressive.[35] However, men were expected to rein in their baser instincts in the same way one "would build a muscle, through repetitive exercises of control over impulse."[36] Ralph Waldo Emerson put the matter succinctly when he defined women as "the civilizers of mankind."[37] Men existed to conquer and achieve; women existed to temper and reproduce.

Protestant Victorianism created a notoriously strident atmosphere around the baser aspect of companionship: sex. Sexual talk was typically prohibited, often on moral grounds. Theatre director/producer George Abbott testified to his own experience growing up in the late nineteenth and early twentieth centuries: "In those days sex was a sin and something you didn't talk about."[38] Playwright Elmer Rice, born around the same time as Abbott, recalled having "never heard the subject referred to, even indirectly" within his family.[39] There were, of course, other conduits of information. Despite reticence within Rice's home, he reports having gleaned significant knowledge of sex by the age of twelve through "the conversation of older boys, supplemented by graphic and literary material."[40] Talking was one thing, but any indulgence in sex by men was regarded as a failure of self-control, which often led to feelings of shame, guilt, or self-abasement. Max J. Exner, who became something of a specialist in sex education in the early decades of the twentieth century, conducted a study of 948 college males born in the 1890s. Exner's research revealed that most of the young men characterized their own sexual behavior using terms such as "vicious," "evil," "vulgar," and "degrading."[41] Most of the young men in Exner's study "viewed their sexual behavior as a problem, as a sign of moral weakness and a failure of manly self-mastery."[42] However, though undesirable, men were expected to succumb to pleasures of the flesh due to their naturally primal instincts. Rice provides an instructive example. Having attained the age of sixteen, Rice's uncle took him aside, declared that he was now "old enough to 'have a woman,'" and agreed to finance the transaction. Rice declined the offer, but later surreptitiously arranged to lose his virginity to a prostitute.[43] While men were expected to backslide in such ways, women, by contrast, were expected to remain chaste in order to preserve their moral superiority. Charlotte Perkins Gilman spoke to the idea of a woman's chastity representing her most prized asset: "She might be a liar and a coward, lazy, selfish, extravagant, or cruel, but if chaste these traits were overlooked. If unchaste, no array of other virtues was enough to save her."[44] Men might suffer personal guilt from their sexual escapades, but women risked comprehensive societal animosity.

The sexual ethics and gender roles imposed by Protestant Victorian society received further reinforcement from the scientific community in the nineteenth century. Many physicians of the time subscribed to the nerve energy theory, which held that the human body was driven by finite energy diffuse across bodily organs.[45] American physician George M. Beard coined a term for the diagnosis of a nerve energy deficiency, neurasthenia. Beard postulated that neurasthenia resulted from the loss of too much nerve force, which caused a person to behave "like an uncharged electric battery."[46] The female body's energy, so the theory goes, was centered in her reproductive organs[47] whereas the male body collected its energy in the heart and brain.[48] Therefore, in theory, a woman exercising her brain would draw vital energy away from her ovaries, running the risk of sterility.[49] Likewise, a man engaging in masturbation or excessive amounts of sexual activity deprived his brain of its vital energy, thus resulting in supposedly consequent health issues.[50] Sexual restrictions and gender roles, therefore, were not simply moral or social imperatives; they represented matters of health and sickness not only for the individual, but for humanity as a whole. The neurasthenia theory implied that a woman who spent time reading, attending college, or otherwise developing her mind, was imperiling her responsibility to propagate the species. It was best for her to conserve her nerve energy until the right man came along.

Progressive Era Challenges to the Protestant Victorian Ethos

The Progressive Era, beginning in the 1890s and carrying through World War I, witnessed myriad challenges to traditional Protestant Victorian mores, particularly as related to sex, gender roles, and marriage. Among the most significant group pushing these challenges was the "new woman." While often associated with the Jazz Age, the first "new women" emerged as early as the 1890s and were characterized by women seeking higher education and trickling into the workforce.[51] According to historian Lois Rudnick, there were at least two incarnations of the new woman. Progressive new women grounded their rationale for reform upon the Protestant Victorian idea of female moral superiority.[52] As such, these women promoted the idea that America needed feminine moral guidance outside the home as well as inside,[53] thus challenging the notion of separate spheres while adhering to traditional values. In essence, one might say progressives were attempting to usher in change while working within the cultural system. Progressive new women tended to focus their efforts in areas such as social work, education, and public policy. Ida Wells' advocacy for anti-lynching laws and Jane Addams' push for child-labor reform were among the more notable examples.[54]

By contrast, radical new women injected more iconoclastic notions into their advocacy for feminine equality. These women drew inspiration from European socialism and sought to challenge sexuality directly, a subject progressive new women tended to avoid.[55] Swedish feminist writer and activist Ellen Key linked sex to physical and spiritual health and advocated women dissolving marriages that failed to produce sexual fulfillment.[56] Nancy Cott writes that Emma Goldman stood among the radicals who connected "sex oppression to class oppression," thereby consolidating feminine subjugation with both the personal (sex) and the economic (work). Influenced in part by Key, Margaret Sanger attacked marriage laws and venerated female sexual independence as essential to equality. For Sanger and many other feminists of the 1910s, birth control represented the most fundamental aspect of a woman's freedom. By gaining control over when pregnancy occurred without resorting to abstinence, women could both express their individual sexuality and stand a better chance of securing economic autonomy.[57] Historian Mari Jo Buhle writes that the radical new women "sought in sexual liberation the key to future social revolution, the destruction of 'bourgeois' values in general. They therefore linked sexual repression to the spiritual barrenness of middle-class society, its conventions and artificialities."[58] Cott echoes Buhle when she observes that feminists viewed "Victorian marriage as hierarchal and emotionally barren, based on dominance and submission."[59]

Advocacy of sexual liberation inevitably stretched into criticism of Protestantism's moral codes, which sometimes produced unlikely allies for women. Sigmund Freud, who was certainly no feminist, argued that marriage led to unsatisfactory sexual relations precisely because prevailing Christian mores limited intercourse to procreation, which normally occurred in the first few years of the union. This sexual restriction, Freud asserted, produced ill-health particularly for women because they were held to a stricter moral code than men.[60] Havelock Ellis added to the debate, arguing that the religious conception of marriage as a "sacred duty" was "antiquated."[61] Ellis advocated trial marriage before full commitment in order for couples to better test the waters of sexual compatibility, which he regarded as crucial to both good health and a successful union.[62] Bertrand Russell repudiated the sexual shaming of women, striking at Protestantism on its own turf by contrasting Christ's conduct toward the adulterous woman[63] with religious leaders who "have shown themselves invariably willing to cast the first stone."[64] Emma Goldman struck a more revolutionary tone, in concert with her anarchist philosophy, calling the Christian church "a stumbling block to progress"[65] and labelling marriage as little more than "an economic arrangement...furnishing the woman with a life-long life insurance policy."[66] Goldman further set her sights on the admixture of American Protestantism with American law as a principal reason for female sexual repression.[67] These and other critics espoused various remedies for the inequities and general dissatisfaction that were often byproducts of traditional marriage, from the adoption of so-called trial marriages to the complete abolition of marriage altogether.

However, some scholars have questioned the veracity of the entire Protestant Victorian ethos. Historian Ann Douglas has persuasively argued that the "Victorian matriarch" became a symbol of oppressive moralizing, which the "modernists" in 1920s New York, both men and women, were united in opposing.[68] Douglas connects this reaction to the obsession, prevalent in the 1920s, with masculinizing American culture. Psychologist John B. Watson, taking Freud as a guide, blamed mothers for sublimating their dissatisfaction with marital sex into selflessness with respect to their children. Watson went so far as to label mothers as little more than "adult murderers of a child's disposition."[69] Watson was not alone in his thinking. In 1899, another noted psychologist, G. Stanley Hall, advocated against the rectitude instilled by Victorian mothers as too effeminate and encouraged more rough-and-tumble-play for boys.[70] The attitudes of learned men such as Watson and Hall bear out Douglas's notion of the Victorian matriarch as something of a convenient scapegoat of societal inequities. Historian Christina Simmons takes the matter a step further. Simmons argues that 1920s proponents of sexual equality actually created a "myth of Victorian repression" in order to facilitate their reform ambitions.[71] The purpose of the Victorian myth, as Simmons labels it, was a need for 1920s activists to generate "a broad generalization of Victorian culture" so as to "rhetorically distance themselves from the past and present themselves as pioneers of a modern way."[72] The truth, Simmons argues, is far more complicated as evidenced, in part, by the endurance of systems of inequality and repression for women. Sex and marriage are facets of life the morals, conventions, and attitudes of which are "conditioned and constructed." This fact, Simmons argues, remains as evident in the twenty-first century as it did in the Victorian period.[73]

Irrespective of how one characterizes the Victorian ethos, be it as a symbol, myth, or reality, one cannot deny the impact its perception made on Americans in the 1920s. Americans in the 1920s were experiencing and, in many cases, actively perpetrating dramatic cultural shifts. These shifts required accounting. Human beings are, after all, naturally driven to make sense of their world. Many 1920s Americans perceived, rightly or wrongly, that the institution of marriage was under assault. Some welcomed this assault while others fought against it with each camp searching out their own justifications. The Protestant Victorian ethos may have presented a convenient scapegoat for those seeking radical changes to the social order or a buoy for those intent on preserving "tradition," but one must bear in mind that most writers, artists, and intellectuals of the Jazz Age, including Maxwell Anderson, were products of the late nineteenth century. While many challenged or outright rejected the Protestant Victorian ethos, they also could not help but be inculcated with it. We see this dissonance at work in examining how the alleged marriage crisis was addressed. It also seems important to recognize that the intentionality Simmons applies to activists in creating the Victorian myth almost certainly did not apply to Anderson himself. Unlike many playwrights of his generation, such as John Howard Lawson, Anderson was not one to write with a specific agenda for social change. He seems to have come to playwriting quite by accident and, by his own admission, was spurred, at least initially, by pecuniary motives rather than activism.[74] As we shall see in analyzing his marriage plays of the 1920s, Anderson never directly advocates for any specific system or alternative to traditional marriage. He confronts his audience with dramatic conundrums, but, like any Socratic gadfly, he never tries to convert them to a solution.

The Crisis Addressed

There existed in the 1920s no shortage of theories and opinions about reasons for the alleged decline of marriage. Popular magazines such as *Ladies Home Journal* and *Good Housekeeping* were rife with advice columns offering counsel on the subject. One such advice-giver, Ruth Scott Miller, observed in 1925 that the rise in divorce had been attributed to myriad reasons ranging "from ease of marriage and lack of religion to installment-house [sic] furniture and sexual incompatibility."[75] Miller's somewhat sardonic comment hints at two broad, overarching culprits often cited by social critics of marriage: economics and sexual morality. Of these, Miller centered her criticism upon the evolution of social economics. Statistics bear out Miller's assertion. By the mid-1920s, 60% of all furniture sold was purchased on an installment plan,[76] which must have placed a strain on the economic stability of many married couples attempting to adhere to the nineteenth century male breadwinner ideal of marriage. Men, Miller argued, had failed to evolve past the nineteenth century whereas the woman has developed "twentieth century standards" powered by her evolution as "a wage earner and a voter."[77] The power endowed women by their earning potential means they were no longer required to accept a husband's unwavering authority.[78] Another critic, William Johnston, agreed that male dominance over the economy left women in subjection, which led to unhappy unions.[79] Johnston's proposed solution was to pay wages to wives for their contributions, but only if she continues "faithfully performing her duties in homemaking."[80] While Miller and Johnston imply the onus for divorce lay in patriarchal authority over wage-earning, Clara Savage Littledale (yet another advisor from the popular magazines), placed the blame on women seeking "perpetual lovers" rather than husbands.[81] "No woman married," Littledale declared, "without hoping that, in her case, the lover-like solicitude, the love-making, the almost absurd devotion of the lover during courtship, will go on forever."[82] Littledale's advice was for women to adhere to the traditional Victorian morality, simply accepting their husbands' foibles and trusting his supposed innate ability to function as an "executive" within the marriage.[83]

The subject of evolving sexual mores seemed a chief concern among those taking a more social scientific approach to the marriage conundrum. Ernest Groves tended toward more traditional morality. Apt to defend the vitality of marriage as an institution in society, Groves deflected his criticism away from marriage and onto arguments of culture. Groves asserts that the marriage crisis stemmed not from the strictures associated with marriage itself nor from feminine economic equality, but rather from a failure of individuals to cultivate and maintain relationships.[84] Groves attributed this failure to the "pleasure philosophy of life" permeating 1920s society.[85] The emphasis on pleasure was in turn, according to Groves, spurred by the advent of birth control, which served to alter marriage into little more than "a sex union...devoid of social obligations."[86] Groves further cites a lack of preparation and instruction for marriage in formal education as a significant contributing factor.[87] When life becomes "a hard struggle and survival difficult...the solemn duties of endurance, self-discipline, and self-denial" come to the forefront.[88] In Groves' estimation, the 1920s had simply grown too hedonistic to support the virtues a successful marriage required and demanded. Society could restore traditional marriage with an alteration of the cultural mindset. Groves encapsulates his veneration of matrimony when he writes, "Wholesome marriage has long been one of the most beautiful achievements in the life of men and women."[89]

However, many among the intelligentsia argued that it was, in fact, the institution of marriage itself spawning the shifting landscape of male/female relations. Often this opinion varied by degrees. A superior court judge in Illinois, for example, held that while the state of matrimony was not "obsolete," some traditions associated with it, such as the custom of transferring a young female from one family to another, are "archaic."[90] Bertrand Russell, however, took an even less compromising stance, stating, "The belief in the importance of rules of conduct is superstitious."[91] Floyd Dell tended to agree, writing, "Conventions are, doubtless, always rather ridiculous, inevitably a shackle upon the free motions of the soul, being imposed by fear."[92] Moreover, while Groves attributed the supposed marriage crisis in part to a lack of education, there is evidence to suggest otherwise. One observer in 1925 reported that the number of women enrolled at institutions of higher education increased sevenfold from 1890.[93] Therefore, increased divorce rates positively correlate with an increase in higher education for women.

Few made such concerted efforts to completely redefine marriage as the aforementioned Judge Ben Lindsey, a family court jurist from Denver who, along with Wainwright Evans, published *The Companionate Marriage* in 1927 (just a year before Groves published his study on the "crisis"). In contrast with Groves, the iconoclastic Lindsey took the view that a traditional marriage did nothing to signify a higher moral standing. "We ought always to be conscious," Lindsey wrote, "that mere subjective habit is not genuinely ethical; that it travels in a rut of tradition; that *conduct determined by it is not thought-out conduct*. What it prescribes may, or may not, be wise and expedient; but whichever it is, it involves no moral decision or rational choice" (emphasis in original).[94] Lindsey (who speaks in first person throughout the book) tackles issues of sex and what he views as the oppressive dynamics of marriage with frankness no doubt shocking for many of his readers at the time. His conversation with Mrs. Blank offers one such example. Lindsey reports Mrs. Blank opining that permitting open marriages would result in fewer dissolutions.[95] Lindsey paraphrased her sentiments without sententiousness, "So you recommend adultery as a cure for divorce."[96] Such observations pervade Lindsey's elucidation of what makes marriage work and not work. Simmons credits Lindsey with popularizing "the essential elements" of companionate marriage, summarizing said elements as "1) easier divorce, especially for childless marriages; 2) legalization of birth control; 3) provision of sex education for youth."[97] Interestingly, both Groves and Lindsey, standing at opposite ends of the poles philosophically, advocate for better education. However, Groves pushed for education about marriage whereas Lindsey stresses education about sex. Lindsey's promotion of companionate marriage, his candor in evaluating sex, and his advocacy for birth control place him closer to the spirit of radical new women of the Jazz Age. With the onset of the 1920s, the idea that men and women existed in "separate spheres," which was "so critical in the construction of nineteenth-century sexual mores, had collapsed."[98]

Setting the Stage: Jesse Lynch Williams's *Why Marry?*

American theatre proved itself in step with the cultural moment regarding marriage even before the dawn of the 1920s. Perhaps nothing epitomized this trend more than Jesse Lynch Williams's aptly titled 1918 hit comedy, *Why Marry?*, which holds the distinction of winning the inaugural Pulitzer Prize for Drama. The title itself could stand as the emblematic question of the age. Williams opens the preface of his published version of the play with an anecdote relating an interaction he had with "a most estimable lady." The woman inquires as to what his new play is about to which Williams replies, "*Why Marry?*...tells the truth about marriage." Apparently surprised, the woman asks him why anyone would choose to write such "unpleasant plays." Perhaps feeling somewhat defensive, Williams informs her that his play is not "unpleasant." The woman retorts, "Then it isn't true!"[99] Williams does not tell us whether or not this woman was married, but one can easily suspect she probably was and, perhaps, had been for a long time.

Williams continues his preface by discussing reactions to his play and offers some revelatory insights into the ethos of the late 1910s, which would carry over into the 1920s. First, he defines marriage as "our fundamental institution."[100] He then remarks upon the expectation different generations had of the play based on its provocative title. Young people, Williams surmised, would be disappointed if they went to the play expecting to be "shocked." The older generation, however, were less likely to attend the play in the first place. Williams reports having heard of two people "scandalized" by the play. Both were "old people" and neither of them had actually watched the play all the way through. One was a woman who only read the title and responded by sending Williams "several indignant letters." The other was "an elderly bachelor" who took his niece to see the play and, at the end of Act II, became fearful of what Act III would hold and promptly whisked the young lady away to presumable safety. According to Williams, the young lady returned the next day with a number of her peers. He inquired as to whether any of them had been "shocked" by the content. The young lady replied, "Oh, no…we are too young to be shocked." The playwright asserted, "There never were two generations inhabiting the same globe simultaneously with such widely separated points of view."[101] Williams's conclusion certainly bears all the marks of hyperbole. However, the essence of his thought speaks to the truth of an age when the generational gap with regard to perceptions of "our fundamental institution" was dramatically widening.

As Williams alludes in his preface, *Why Marry?* makes no bones about its intentions from the outset. This play, in no uncertain terms, dramatically represents the fundamental debates pertaining to Progressive Era marriage. Williams's characters are more akin to Jungian archetypes than flesh and blood human beings. Helen, the principal female character in the play, is a *bona fide*, college-educated, unapologetic "new woman" (a term directly used to describe her throughout the play). Her love-interest, Ernest, is a renowned scientist, intellectual, and humanitarian who openly espouses progressive ideas about gender equality. Three of the supporting characters serve as representatives from different facets of conventional morality: (1) John, a wealthy, pragmatic capitalist who uses marriage to enhance social status and maintain family respectability; (2) Theodore, a clergyman speaking for the religious tenets of matrimony; (3) Everett, a judge who sees, through his legal insight, the evolving nature of matrimonial connections. Each of these men have a vested interest in the relationship of Helen and Ernest. John is Helen's brother and thus feels compelled to tamp down her rebellious spirit for the sake of appearances. Theodore, a cousin of the family, waffles between his need for John's financial support and his genuine conviction that marriage is a sacred matter. Finally, Everett, uncle to Helen and John, seeks to steer the family conflict toward a moderate compromise.

The main thrust of the play's conflict centers on Helen's desire to travel with Ernest to Paris as his assistant, a position she has held for some time. John, however, balks at allowing her to accompany the scientist for fear of how society would perceive such a trip between an unmarried couple. Ernest works for an institute that John finances, which permits the latter a significant degree of influence over the situation. John does everything in his considerable financial power to permanently separate his sister from Ernest's attention. Failing in this endeavor, he then attempts to force the couple to marry. If they insist on being together, John reasons, then they must render their union respectable. Helen and Ernest are genuinely in love with each other. However, they steadfastly refuse to submit to marriage. The terms Helen and Ernest do agree upon rattles every character espousing conventional morality. To the chagrin of John and every other establishment character in the play, the couple announces their intention to maintain both a love and work relationship while living apart and continuing to eschew legal matrimony. Everett attempts to play the mediator throughout the play, struggling in vain both to quell John's rage and reason with the obstinate couple. When all else fails, Everett concocts a trap. Playing to the couple's religious sensibilities, the wily judge extracts an acknowledgment from both Helen and Ernest that they are, in effect, accepting each other as husband and wife in the eyes of God. Immediately upon the couple's verbalizing this fact, Everett uses his legal authority to pronounce them married and the play abruptly ends.

The success of *Why Marry?*, which premiered Christmas Day, 1917, and ran for 120 performances,[102] belies the apparent trouble it initially faced in finding an audience. Though originally published in 1914, according to Williams, "no theatrical manager on Broadway would produce it" until late 1917.[103] On the other hand, reviews of the play ranged from tepid to laudatory. A historian for the Pulitzer Prizes said little of substance regarding the first winner for drama, simply recalling it as "a slender, but agreeable comedy."[104] An unsigned critic for the *Brooklyn Dailey Eagle* noted rather blandly that "the production was in good taste."[105] The critic for the *New York Times*, however, was much more effusive, declaring the play "perhaps the most intelligent and searching satire on social institutions ever written by an American."[106] Several critics praised the acting company, often singling out Nat Goodwin (in role of the judge) for the highest praise, and noted Williams's debt to Shaw insofar as his use of satire.

One of the most striking aspects of *Why Marry?* for the purposes of this analysis lay in the abrupt conclusion. Williams has his main couple stand strong all the way till the end, only to have them humbugged by a clumsily contrived trick imposed by the judge. Helen and Ernest, who had spoken of their convictions at length over the course of the drama, then remain silent throughout the short time remaining in the play. Moreover, one of the play's subplots involves Everett's impending divorce from his wife, who has absconded to Reno, Nevada for the purpose. Just before Everett tricks the young couple into matrimony, he receives a telegram from his wife wherein she repents her decision and states her resolve to remain married. Thus, Williams avoids a potentially shocking ending through a pair of brusque *deus ex machina* devices that serve to uphold, however tacitly, the status quo. This adherence to convention would pervade many of the marriage plays to follow as the Progressive Era gave way to the Jazz Age.

Marriage Plays of the 1920s

American theatre has often been recognized as coming into its own as a cultural institution in the 1920s. Scholars have often connected this cultural maturation with the advent of Eugene O'Neill, who kicked off the decade by winning his first Pulitzer Prize for *Beyond the Horizon*. However, the genesis of New York's emergence as a cultural Mecca began at least a decade earlier. Broadway's preeminence was already growing exponentially by the end of the nineteenth century. In 1900, New York held more theatres than either Paris or London. Broadway impresarios Marc Klaw, Abe Erlanger, and Charles Frohman, along with the Shubert brothers, formed a partnership in concert with theatre producers across the United States to effectively control the bulk of the nation's theatre business. As historian Ann Douglas tells us, "by 1910 or so, a successful production was by definition a New York one."[107] This reality clearly impacted Maxwell Anderson's thinking throughout his career. While O'Neill cut his teeth in the "little theatre" of Provincetown, Anderson only ventured off the Great White Way once in his career.[108] For Anderson, theatre was almost always a Broadway or bust proposition (*Sea-Wife* stands as a rare exception, as we shall see). However, in 1920, Anderson had not yet discovered playwriting as a career. But marriage remained at the forefront of the cultural debate as the new decade dawned.

Frank Craven's *The First Year* (1920) both picked up where Jesse Lynch Williams left off and established a new tone for marriage plays in the Jazz Age. That Craven's play proved one of the most popular hits of the decade lends credence to the notion that marriage remained an attractive subject for many Americans in this era. *The First Year* centers on a young couple, Grace and Tommy, struggling to adjust to their initial year of married life. Passion fades after the wedding bells, and the relationship degenerates into daily squabbles over bills and other mundane aspects of domesticity. Matters come to a head when Grace leaves her husband, but in the final confrontation all is made well with the announcement of her pregnancy.[109] Contrary to the ending of *Why Marry?*, in this case the wife was cleansed not by marriage per se, but by that other sainted aspect of womanhood: maternity. Craven further alters the avenue of approach to marriage by avoiding specific political language. Unlike in *Why Marry?*, the term "new woman" never comes up nor do any of the characters openly debate issues of inequality. *The First Year* is, quite simply, a domestic comedy about a young couple's struggles in love and matrimony.

A survey of other critically acclaimed plays of the 1920s further exemplifies the pervasiveness of marriage as a theme. Zona Gale's *Miss Lulu Bett* (1921) required an alternate ending wherein her independent-minded heroine ultimately accepts traditional marriage in order to placate audience sensibilities of the time.[110] In *Anna Christie* (1922), Eugene O'Neill relates the story of a former prostitute who finds redemption in marriage after having been rejected by both her father and lover.[111] Owen Davis's *Icebound* (1923) depicts a wayward man reformed by the civilizing force of a woman whom he agrees to marry in the end.[112] Sidney Howard's *They Knew What They Wanted* (1925) portrays a woman surrendering to adulterous temptation, but gaining forgiveness from her husband, which deepens her devotion to him.[113] In 1926, George Kelly achieved fame with *Craig's Wife* wherein the titular character views marriage as a means to an end. Mrs. Craig seeks security in her husband and employs incessant manipulation over him and everyone else in the play to insure her position. In the end, her scheming ways are discovered and her husband abandons her to the desolation of the house.[114] All of the plays aforementioned, with the exception of *The First Year*, were Pulitzer Prize winners. This distinction is important for this analysis because, as noted, the dominance Broadway wielded over American theatre in the 1920s was almost unquestioned. Furthermore, once Anderson made his name as a playwright, he was almost uncompromising in his aim for success in New York. Therefore, examining plays that achieved either popular success, as in *The First Year*, or critical success, as in the various Pulitzer winners, on Broadway offers the clearest barometer of the world in which Anderson was trying to make his way. For the most part, this world tended toward conservative agreeableness as it concerned the status quo in regard to sex, marriage, and gender roles.

Of course, not all theatre artists sought to remain within the comforts of convention where marriage and/or sex was concerned. The 1926–1927 Broadway season proved a particularly contentious one. According to Burns Mantle, complaints of immorality on the stage compelled New York's district attorney to assemble a pool of jurors drawn from the citizenry whose job it was to view and judge allegedly offensive dramas.[115] The result of this effort culminated in police raids of three productions deemed sufficiently lascivious to warrant suppression: Mae West's hit play, *Sex*, depicting the adventures of a prostitute; William Francis Dugan's *The Virgin Man*, about a virgin college boy defending himself against the temptations of "three wild women,"[116] and Arthur Hornblow Jr.'s *The Captive*, which dramatized a lesbian relationship. Mantle reports that all three acting companies as well as the producers of the three plays were arrested.[117] For some the police action was insufficient. Two months after the raids one such critic bemoaned the indifference of public authorities toward the stage, complaining that public controversy often erupted, but substantive action was seldom taken.[118] Barrett H. Clark, however, assailed what he regarded as excessive action taken with respect to the three plays raided. In an age where moralists amended the Constitution to forbid alcohol, Clark sardonically suggests the need for additional amendments to include "stage censorship; then book censorship; a censorship of thought, and finally of sex itself."[119]

Theatre, by its very nature, differed significantly from other creative forms in terms of how marriage was treated. On the literary scene, novelists such as Sherwood Anderson created "dark, brooding stories dealing with marriage, morality, and individuals destroyed by success."[120] The poet Edna St. Vincent Millay "flouted convention in her personal life and in her poetry expounded on women's sexual freedom and equality."[121] By contrast, the successful marriage plays achieved success, for the most part, by having their female characters conform to conventional matrimony. Of the two examples that edged toward challenging convention, *Miss Lulu Bett* was given an alternate ending to conform to the status quo and *Craig's Wife* depicted a heroine so unsympathetic as to leave the audience feeling she deserved ostracism. On the other hand, the plays that were blatantly nonconformist were shut down. Exploring female motives pertaining to sex and marriage without risking public condemnation proved a tricky business in the theatre. Unlike literary prose or poetry, the theatre must satisfy a finite audience in a public way. Whereas one could purchase a copy of Millay's poetry and squirrel it away for personal perusal, attending the theatre demands public exposure. A playwright tackling controversial themes had to walk a fine line between promoting radical ideas and catering to public taste. Numerous playwrights emerged in the 1920s who pushed the envelope in terms of aesthetic experimentation. However, when considering playwrights in connection with the "marriage crisis," Maxwell Anderson emerges as one with a particular skill for expressing social commentary in his plays that, while not artistically experimental or the most socially radical, nevertheless effectively and provocatively reflect an important cultural moment in American history.

THE EMERGENCE OF MAXWELL ANDERSON

Maxwell Anderson's aesthetic critiques of marriage were incubated during a youth steeped in literature and personal conflict with the Americanized version of Protestant Victorianism. Born 15 December 1888, Anderson was the second child of eight and the son of an itinerant fire and brimstone preacher.[122] Anderson would later testify of his upbringing: "Church was a pretty constant factor, and we got to know the Bible well by just listening."[123] However, despite his father's efforts at inculcating the Protestant faith into his son, Anderson grew to distrust religion from an early age. He later characterized his father's preaching as akin to "salesmanship"[124] and reportedly refused baptism when he was only eight-years-old.[125] Such marked defiance at such a tender age foreshadowed Anderson's steadfast resentment toward almost all institutionalized traditions, ceremonies, and conventions.[126] The traveling nature of his father's evangelism rendered it difficult for Anderson to establish roots. From the year of his birth to 1908, Anderson recalled living in thirteen different locations across Pennsylvania, Ohio, Iowa, and North Dakota.[127] In part a consequence of this nomadic existence, Anderson escaped into literature and poetry, cultivating a lifelong adoration of William Shakespeare.[128] His love of reading paid dividends in young adulthood when he was able to pass enough coursework through examination to graduate from the University of North Dakota a year early with a degree in English.[129] Thus, Anderson's background was not naturally theatrical, as was O'Neill's, and he never resided in or near locations given to rich theatrical activity.

However, it was Anderson's good fortune to have studied at the University of North Dakota during the tenure of Professor Frederick Koch. When first offered the job at UND in 1905 the Harvard-educated Koch viewed moving to the prairie as a kind of exile.[130] Once arrived, however, Koch became a dynamic leader at the university, inspiring students with productions of classical plays, which they would then tour to various towns up to 800 miles across the state.[131] Koch's success led him, in 1910, to founding the first organized theatrical society at UND, which counted Anderson among its charter members.[132] Influenced by playwriting professor George Pierce Baker and drawing inspiration from the Irish Renaissance, Koch began focusing on methods of developing dramas centering on facets of American life,[133] ultimately gaining fame as a progenitor of American folk drama.[134] Anderson's reticence about revealing personal information[135] renders it difficult to discern any influence Koch may have had on his writing. In a 1927 letter to critic and scholar Arthur Hobson Quinn, Anderson comments that while he "studied Shakespeare under Prof. Koch," Koch "had not yet begun his classes in playwriting" while Anderson was attending UND.[136] Furthermore, Anderson seems not to have carried a strong impression of Koch's theatrical club. Toward the end of his life, in recalling his time at UND, Anderson omits any mention of Koch.[137] However, the potential imprint of Koch's folk influence manifests in Anderson's early work of the 1920s in such works as *White Desert* and *Sea-Wife*, as we shall see.

During his time at UND another significant event occurred that likely influenced his marriage plays. Anderson fell in love with one of his classmates, Margaret Haskett. In many ways Margaret was everything Anderson was not. According to Anderson's biographer, Alfred S. Shivers, Margaret, who was two years older than Anderson, was known as a "witty...clever, vivacious, free-spirited" woman, yet mostly "conventional in outward behavior."[138] Like Anderson, Margaret was unafraid to rub against the grain of social norms. For example, when an African-American was denied admission into her sorority, Margaret withdrew her own membership.[139] Unlike Anderson, Margaret was raised Catholic and came from a wealthy family.[140] Anderson would marry Margaret, to the indignation of their respective families, shortly after both graduated from UND in 1911.[141] Both the Andersons and Hasketts were resentful of each other's religion and Margaret's father held the further animus of his daughter marrying a man, in his view, beneath her status.[142] The marriage, as it turned out, was doomed.

Anderson's first serious foray into playwriting did not come until over a decade after his college graduation and marriage. In the interval, Margaret surrendered her pursuit of a graduate degree at Stanford University in deference to her husband's own academic work.[143] She had also born Anderson three sons.[144] Anderson, meanwhile, labored as a journalist at various newspapers, first in California and then in New York. However, the future dramatist found no alacrity in journalism. He became intrigued by playwriting upon hearing a reading of John Howard Lawson's *Roger Bloomer*. Anderson did not think much of Lawson's play and believed he could write a better one.[145] His transition from journalist to playwright was a natural one at the time. Historian Christine Stansell notes that, though rare in the nineteenth century, "[t]he trajectory from journalist to writer...was common by the 1910s."[146] Following an abortive attempt at historical verse drama that never saw the stage,[147] *White Desert* would bring Anderson his first taste of Broadway in 1923[148] and represents his initial effort at wrestling with male/female relationships, gender roles, and the supposed marriage crisis. Over the next six years Anderson would write three more plays dealing explicitly with the challenges, frustrations, and inequities imposed upon human life by the institution of marriage as defined and codified by American culture. During this same period, his own marriage was collapsing. Though details are sketchy, Anderson and Margaret had grown apart, the gulf accelerating when Anderson began an extramarital affair.[149] It seems more than reasonable to assume that Anderson's education and experience, both formal and personal, likely impacted the content of his dramatic creations.

The Plays

Anderson drew from a well close to home for *White Desert*. Set on the North Dakota prairie in 1888 (the year of Anderson's birth), the drama centers on two married homesteading couples and their struggles against the constraints of traditional matrimony. Anderson employs the isolated landscape and the harsh, unforgiving North Dakota winter (hence the title) to his dramatic advantage. The principals, Michael and Mary Kane, are newlyweds just arrived to stake their claim and build their life together. However, the combination of cabin fever and the sensual allure of Sverre Peterson, the only other man in the area, feed Michael's rabid jealousy. For her part, Mary questions the wisdom of why she should have married in the first place when she knew it meant forfeiture of her individual freedom. Her questions about marriage further deepen Michael's suspicions about her fidelity. He engages in what one could argue amounts to psychological abuse as he presses her for details of her sexual past as well as what he sees as her attraction to Sverre. Mary ultimately asserts her independence and resolves to break away from Michael, but with tragic consequences.

In 1924, Anderson would revisit similar themes from *White Desert* in a play entitled *Sea-Wife*. This time employing nineteenth century New England for his backdrop and taking inspiration from Matthew Arnold's poem, *The Forsaken Merman*, Anderson blends poetic tragedy with fantasy. The protagonist, Margaret, has mysteriously returned to her husband after reportedly spending several years at sea with a powerful merman, by whom she bore two children. The merman has permitted her only a brief sojourn, however, insisting she return to him within a certain amount of time or he will murder her children. The townspeople, steeped in New England's puritanical religious culture, assail Margaret as nothing more than a fallen woman (and perhaps a witch to boot) and seek to brand her and ostracize her husband. When her husband fights back, the violence intensifies. The script, as produced by small companies outside of New York, indicates Margaret is afflicted by mental illness connected with postpartum depression and child loss rather than a supernatural merman. She ultimately dies under mysterious circumstances. Sexuality and gender inequity pervade the play as Anderson emphasizes the lustful hypocrisy of the men juxtaposed with Margaret's undeniable innocence.

White Desert and *Sea-Wife* represent two of Anderson's early efforts, but neither placed him on the rolls of successful American playwrights.

He would soon place his name among theatrical elites later in 1924 when he teamed with journeyman writer Laurence Stallings to pen *What Price Glory*, which ran for over 400 performances and was hailed as one of the great plays of the season. Following two more efforts in collaboration with Stallings, neither of which was successful, and a solo effort that achieved a modest Broadway run,[150] Anderson returned to the subject that seemed to preoccupy him throughout the 1920s: the vicissitudes of love and marital relationships. In 1927, Anderson achieved his first meaningful solo success as a playwright with *Saturday's Children*.

Unlike *White Desert* and *Sea-Wife*, Anderson centers the action of *Saturday's Children* in his own time and place, attempting to replicate the lifestyle and traditions of the typical New York middle class family. The protagonist, Bobby Halevy, represents a woman of the modern temper weighted down by the conventions of the past. Though she lives with her parents, she supports herself in a clerical job, has no serious prospect of marriage, and does not manifest a keen desire to attain a husband. However, her younger sister, Florrie, who is married with a child, persuades her to find a man. Bobby feels conflicted, but she agrees to an arranged meeting with her casual boyfriend, Rims O'Neil. Finding herself swept up in the literal romantic script Florrie has written down on paper for her, Bobby impulsively seduces Rims into marriage. The romance, however, quickly flames out and Bobby finds herself miserable in domestic drudgery. Her overwhelming sense of buyer's remorse, in a manner of speaking, spurs her to leave her husband. The play ends with Bobby and Rims reaching an understanding. They will continue to live apart and lead their own lives, but will occasionally meet for sexual encounters. On this note, the play ends in ambiguity, but one thing is clear: Bobby has no plans to resume traditional married life.

Two years later, Anderson would once more revisit themes of marriage and gender roles. *Gypsy*, produced in 1929, adds a touch of popular psychology into the fray as the female protagonist, Ellen, wrestles with the impact of her mother's past upon her own current motivations. Ellen is married, but fiercely independent. She and her husband maintain separate finances. She remains open about her past sexual history with various men. Her husband, David, touts himself as a man of modern temper and supports Ellen's autonomy. When Ellen becomes pregnant and does not want the child, he supports her decision to have an abortion. When he offers to pay for the procedure, she steadfastly refuses, insisting on paying the bill herself. Ellen's flirtatiousness with other men and her flagrant disregard for marital conventions that interfere with her happiness and individuality strain David's devotion despite his overtures of supporting female equality. Ellen leaves her husband for her lover, but finds little contentment. The play's original ending proved controversial. Ellen, having banished her lover, attempts suicide by turning on the gas. A phone call from another lover interrupts the attempt. Rejuvenated by the new lover's invitation, Ellen ventures out happily on her way to another sexual liaison with yet another man. Something, however, happened after opening night. What that something was is unclear, but we know that Anderson felt compelled to rewrite the ending so that Ellen completes her suicide attempt instead.

Anderson's Limitations

Given everything we know of Anderson's background, education, and philosophical bent, it becomes crucial to note and recognize the cultural limitations inherent within the scope of his work. Historian Ann Douglas observes that the nineteenth century Protestant ethos, grounded as it was in Calvinist theology, did not bear as strong a presence for African Americans as it did for White Americans in the 1920s. Douglas postulates this divide derives, in part, from the difference between written versus oral religious traditions. White American Protestantism is imbued with an extensive written theology dating back to seventeenth century Puritans. In other words, Douglas notes, one must be "literate" in order to receive it and literacy was "a privilege [Puritan descendants] did not extend to America's enslaved black population."[151] Growing up the son of a Protestant minister, Anderson possessed firsthand knowledge of Calvinistic theology. Furthermore, being raised in Midwestern rural settings would have placed him, for the most part, amidst a predominantly White population. According to the 1910 census, for example, the population of North Dakota (where Anderson graduated college) was over 98% White.[152] Anderson's upbringing, therefore, inculcated him not just with Protestant traditions, but with distinctly White traditions.

Anderson's privileged status manifests in other aspects of his life and experience as well. Though not born into wealth, Anderson graduated from a state university and completed a master's degree at Stanford. Such opportunities were largely denied to African Americans in the first decades of the twentieth century. Furthermore, for most of his adult life Anderson existed in the middle class or higher (once playwriting made him famous). His eventual privileged socioeconomic status combined with his extensive education thus widens the gulf between himself and the traditions of lower classes and nonwhite populations. Adding to these points, Anderson's personal attitudes about women tended to affirm tradition. Whereas many married intellectuals of the period experimented with gender equality in marriage, the Andersons did not. Despite graduating from college and gaining admission to Stanford along with her husband, Margaret Anderson ultimately surrendered her educational goals in favor of devoting herself to being a wife and mother. Despite the fact that she was highly regarded for her intellect at the University of North Dakota, Margaret would never attain an independent career of her own.[153] Finally, as previously mentioned, Anderson wrote for Broadway and while Broadway represented the grandest stage, it did not, necessarily, constitute the most diverse. Later in life, Anderson would extoll the theatre as a truly democratic art form.[154] However, to paraphrase critic John Mason Brown, theatre is only a democratic art form for people who can afford it.[155] In writing for Broadway, Anderson, by default, wrote for a predominantly White middle to upper class New York audience. His plays were invariably populated by White actors. In effect, Anderson did not have to worry about inflaming racial tensions because he never attempted to characterize racial issues during the 1920s. He wrote about what he knew and understood: White Protestant literati. In analyzing these plays, one must always bear in mind that Anderson's Whiteness inevitably narrows his frame of reference.

Anderson was a mass of contradictions. He was the son of a preacher imbued with biblical teachings who rejected his father's faith at an early age. Yet, he kept a Bible by his bedside and was reportedly quite fond of reading Ecclesiastes and the Sermon on the Mount.[156] He was an unabashed pacifist during World War I, yet publicly encouraged American intervention in World War II three years before the attack on Pearl Harbor.[157] He railed against government overreach all his life, yet supported blacklisting during the anti-communist movement in the 1950s.[158] He often and vehemently pushed ideas of individual liberty while scorning obedience to convention, but married twice and had an extended relationship that functioned, for all intents and purposes, as a traditional marriage.[159] He loftily described the theatre as "a cathedral," and "a religious institution devoted entirely to the exaltation of the spirit of man,"[160] yet confessed he was mainly drawn to write plays in order to make money.[161] Despite his avowed atheism, he wrote several essays and plays emphasizing the need for humankind to adhere to faith of some kind.[162] Anderson often seemed restless, almost at war with himself. In one of his more argumentative essays, he declared, "Personally I don't trust any critic—or anybody else, including myself" when it came to evaluating the worth of any play.[163] One longtime associate characterized him as "mercurial."[164] George Abbott believed he held a deep-seated sense of romanticism despite his "stolid" demeanor[165] while a journalist who worked with Anderson in the 1920s found him argumentative and pessimistic.[166]

Anderson's inscrutable personality in some respects mimics the incongruities of broader American culture. The United States has, throughout its history, often found itself at odds with the ideals it extolls versus the realities it perpetuates. The presence of slavery represents the most obvious example, leading as it did to America's internecine war. However, the subjugation of women ranks high as well. From its conception to its ratification to its implementation, the American Constitution was not understood as guaranteeing the same rights to all citizens. The unamended Constitution, for example, does not specify criteria for voting rights. Qualifications to vote were left for individual states to codify. Yet it was not until 1890 that the first state (Wyoming) granted women the right to vote. By 1900, only four states permitted women full suffrage rights.[167] In addition, the Comstock Law of 1873 rendered the dissemination of birth control across state lines a federal crime. Twenty-four states subsequently passed localized variations of this so-called "anti-obscenity law."[168] The power brokers within each state were almost exclusively male and so women possessed little voice in making or influencing the law. The Constitution, despite purporting to, among other things, "promote the general welfare," was not construed by men in power as permitting women a voice at the ballot box nor allowing women the right to protect themselves from pregnancy. Social activists of the first decades of the twentieth century would consequently view suffrage and birth control as lynchpins of equality. Given the immense focus that feminists would place on birth control, subversive critiques of marriage became inevitable.

Rationale

Aside from *What Price Glory*, Anderson has generally not been recognized for his work in the 1920s. This lack of recognition stems, in part, from the fact that Anderson had yet to come into his own as a playwright. Of the eight plays he wrote for Broadway in the 1920s, four were collaborations and one was adapted from a book.[169] Having not been born into or trained for the theatre, Anderson, who did not take up playwriting until his thirties, seems to have come by his craft slowly. Alfred S. Shivers, who counted himself among Anderson's "devoted admirers,"[170] nonetheless characterized the 1920s as an "apprentice period" for the playwright.[171] Another reason for the dearth of attention given to Anderson's work in the Jazz Age lies in his enormous success of the 1930s. The Depression era saw Anderson parlay his love of Shakespearean verse into his most critically and commercially successful dramas. Plays such as *Elizabeth the Queen* (1930), *Mary of Scotland* (1933), *Winterset* (1935), and *High Tor* (1936) were hailed at the time and, along with winning a Pulitzer Prize (for his prose satire, *Both Your Houses*) and two New York Drama Critics Circle Awards (for *Winterset* and *High Tor*), helped solidify Anderson's position as a noteworthy dramatist in his time. These successes naturally led scholars to center the bulk of their critical evaluations upon Anderson's Depression era plays while largely ignoring the 1920s.

Any rehabilitation of Anderson's Jazz Age dramas was further hampered by the overall decline of Anderson's reputation. As early as 1953 one scholar remarked on how Anderson had slowly fallen out of favor.[172] As one would expect, this decline continued following the playwright's death in 1959. Whereas Eugene O'Neill enjoyed a Renaissance after his death and has since become a cottage industry among many theatre scholars, Anderson's contribution to American drama has remained dubious at best and, at worst, forgotten. This disparity exists, in part, because scholars have tended to focus their attention with an eye toward his aesthetic use of classical style dramatic verse.[173] Examinations of Anderson as a social critic have been wanting and, when they have occurred, have tended toward his work in the 1930s. Moreover, focusing on dramatic verse may have further accelerated Anderson's decline as this angle of evaluation inevitability led to comparisons of Anderson's work to that of noteworthy tragedians throughout history. Such comparisons would place most any writer at a marked disadvantage. John Gassner, a prolific critic and theatre scholar, was not alone among critics when he asserted Anderson sometimes devolved into "a mere echo of the great writers of the past."[174] The critical consensus seems to have Anderson chalked up as an imitator rather than an innovator.

That Anderson did not excel in creating fresh dramatic forms should not disinherit him from a place of appreciation in the annals of American drama. Content and social reflection, when skillfully crafted and thoughtfully reasoned, often confront audiences with powerful moments in the theatre. The content of Anderson's dramas, particularly his marriage plays of the 1920s, reflect critical cultural moments in American history the effects of which ripple into the twenty-first century. Furthermore, these plays under consideration separate Anderson from many of his peers, who tended toward affirming the status quo through the assertions of male protagonists. In fact, amidst the male-centric nature of American theatre throughout much of the twentieth century, Anderson stands apart from most of his contemporaries in terms of his portrayal of women. In a career spanning over thirty years and over thirty produced plays, nearly one-third of Anderson's total Broadway output depicted females in leading roles.[175] All four plays under consideration in this analysis center on female protagonists. Shivers dismissed *White Desert*, *Saturday's Children*, and *Gypsy* as "surely minor when they are measured by any sound standard of judgment."[176] However, these three plays from the Jazz Age, along with *Sea-Wife*, represent important reflections upon marriage, gender roles, sexual mores, and the ongoing struggle toward individual equality in American culture.

Anderson taps into tensions between men and women in ways both nuanced and provocative. In so doing, he explores how the strictures of one of society's most ancient institutions feed the prevailing view of gender roles, which in turn perpetuate gender inequality. This book examines these four plays with an eye toward Anderson as both critic and artist who employs various elements to extract revelatory insight into the tradition of marriage in American life. In each play Anderson weaves folk elements with contemporaneity as well as incorporating, perhaps subconsciously, facets of his own troubled relationships with women. The result brings us somewhere between George Bernard Shaw and Eugene O'Neill, providing a fresh and long overdue reevaluation of Anderson's standing in the annals of American theatre. These four plays stand apart from the more well-known efforts at wrestling with marriage and sexuality on the 1920s American stage in two important ways. They do not pander to the status quo as did the more popular successes such as *The First Year*; nor do they overtly provoke the audience as did more radical efforts such as *Sex*. These four plays represent thoughtful dramatic portrayals of women evolving independent identity while struggling to negotiate the primal needs of companionship with the societal strictures imposed by institutional marriage.

NOTES

1. Ben B. Lindsey and Wainwright Evans, *The Companionate Marriage* (Garden City, NY: Garden City Publishing, 1927), 83–84.
2. Lindsey and Evans, 84.
3. Ibid., 21–31.
4. Ibid., 23.
5. Ibid., 85.
6. Ibid., 33.
7. Ann Douglas, *Terrible Honesty: Mongrel Manhattan in the 1920s* (New York: Farrar, Straus and Giroux, 1995), 52.
8. Lewis A. Erenberg, *Steppin' Out: New York Nightlife and the Transformation of American Culture, 1880–1930* (Chicago: University of Chicago Press, 1981), 154.
9. Beatrice M. Hinkle, "The Chaos of Marriage," *Harpers* 152 (1925): 1.
10. Ernest R. Groves, *The Marriage Crisis* (New York: Longmans, Green, 1928).
11. Bertrand Russell, "Styles in Ethics," *Nation* 118 (30 April 1924): 497–499.
12. Elsie Clews Parsons, "Changes in Sex Relations," *Nation* 118 (14 May 1924): 551–553.
13. Floyd Dell, "Can Men and Women be Friends?" *Nation* 118 (28 May 1924): 605–606.
14. Charlotte Perkins Gilman, "Toward Monogamy," *Nation* 118 (11 June 1924): 671–673.
15. *Historical Statistics of the United States: Colonial Times to 1970, Part 1, Bicentennial Edition* (Washington: Government Printing Office, 1975), 64.
16. Ibid.
17. Robert S. Lynd and Helen Merrell Lynd, *Middletown: A Study in Modern American Culture* (New York: Harcourt Brace, 1929), 121.
18. Lynn Dumenil, *Modern Temper: American Culture and Society in the 1920s* (New York: Hill and Wang, 1995), 130.
19. Ibid.
20. Carroll Smith-Rosenberg, *Disorderly Conduct: Visions of Gender in Victorian America* (New York: Oxford University Press, 1985), 253.
21. Dumenil, 136.
22. Ibid.
23. Groves, 4.

24. Plato, *Republic*, trans. by G.M.A. Grube, revised by C.D.C. Reeve (Indianapolis: Hackett Publishing Company, 1992), 133.
25. Stephanie Coontz, *Marriage, a History* (New York: Viking, 2005), 8.
26. Ibid., 174.
27. Ibid., 158.
28. Havelock Ellis, *Psychology of Sex* (New York: Ray Long, 1933), 256.
29. Groves, 172.
30. Warren I. Susman, *Culture as History: The Transformation of American Society in the Twentieth Century* (Washington: Smithsonian Institution Press, 2003), 56.
31. Nancy F. Cott, *Public Vows: A History of Marriage and the Nation* (Cambridge: Harvard University Press, 2000), 9.
32. Charles Dickens, *American Notes* (New York: Modern Library, 1996), 117.
33. John F. Kasson, *Amusing the Million: Coney Island at the Turn of the Century* (New York: Hill and Wang, 1978), 4.
34. Erenberg, 7.
35. Ibid.
36. Gail Bederman, *Manliness and Civilization: A Cultural History of Gender and Race in the United States, 1880–1917* (Chicago: University of Chicago Press, 1995), 11.
37. Ralph Waldo Emerson, "Woman," in *Emerson: Political Writings*, edited by Kenneth Sacks (New York: Cambridge University Press, 2008), 159.
38. George Abbott, *Mister Abbott* (New York: Random House, 1963), 12.
39. Elmer Rice, *Minority Report: An Autobiography* (New York: Simon and Schuster, 1963), 57.
40. Ibid.
41. John D'Emilio and Estelle B. Freedman, *Intimate Matters: A History of Sexuality in America* (New York: Harper and Row, 1988), 180.
42. Ibid., 180.
43. Rice, 83–84.
44. Gilman, 671.
45. Bederman, 83.
46. Ibid., 85.
47. Smith-Rosenberg, 258.
48. Ibid., 261.
49. Ibid., 258.
50. Ibid., 261.
51. Dumenil, 99.
52. Lois Rudnick, "The New Woman," in *1915, The Cultural Moment: The New Politics, the New Woman, the New Psychology, the New Art, and the New Theatre in America*, edited by Adele Heller and Lois Rudnick (New Brunswick: Rutgers University Press, 1991), 75.

53. Ibid.
54. Ibid.
55. Ibid.
56. D'Emilio and Freedman, 46.
57. Nancy F. Cott, *The Grounding of Modern Feminism* (New Haven: Yale University Press, 1987), 48.
58. Mari Jo Buhle, *Women and American Socialism, 1870–1920* (Urbana: University of Illinois Press, 1981), 260.
59. Cott, *Modern Feminism*, 157.
60. Sigmund Freud, *Sexuality and the Psychology of Love* (New York: Macmillan, 1963), 31–33.
61. Ellis, 273.
62. D'Emilio and Freedman, 224.
63. Gospel of John 8:1–11, *King James Bible*.
64. Russell, 498.
65. Emma Goldman, *Red Emma Speaks: An Emma Goldman Reader*, edited by Alix Kates Shulman (Amherst: Humanity Books, 1998), 56.
66. Ibid., 57.
67. Ibid., 155.
68. Douglas, 6–9.
69. Ibid., 43.
70. Bederman, 77.
71. Christina Simmons, *Making Marriage Modern: Women's Sexuality from the Progressive Era to World War II* (New York: Oxford University Press, 2009), 6–7.
72. Ibid., 7.
73. Ibid., 11.
74. Shivers, *Life*, 79.
75. Ruth Scott Miller, "Masterless Wives and Divorce," *Ladies Home Journal* 42 (January 1925): 20.
76. Douglas, 192.
77. Miller, 20.
78. Ibid.
79. William Johnston, "Should Wives be Paid Wages?" *Good Housekeeping* 80 (March 1925): 30.
80. Ibid.
81. Clara Savage Littledale, "So This Is Marriage!" *Good Housekeeping* 80 (January 1925): 115.
82. Ibid.
83. Ibid.
84. Groves, 12–13.
85. Ibid., 32.
86. Ibid., 44–45.

87. Ibid., 20–21.
88. Ibid., 34.
89. Ibid., 26.
90. Miller, 20.
91. Russell, 498.
92. Dell, 605.
93. Charles A. Selden, "Sex and Higher Education," *Ladies Home Journal* 42 (February 1925): 39.
94. Ben B. Lindsey and Wainwright Evans, *The Companionate Marriage* (Garden City, NY: Garden City Publishing, 1927), 10.
95. Ibid., 27.
96. Ibid.
97. Christina Simmons, "Companionate Marriage and the Lesbian Threat," *Frontiers: A Journal of Women Studies* 4 (Autumn 1979): 55.
98. D'Emilio and Freedman, 233.
99. Jesse Lynch Williams, *Why Marry?* (New York: Charles Scribner's Sons, 1918), ix.
100. Ibid.
101. Ibid., x.
102. *The Best Plays of 1909–1919*, edited by Burns Mantle and Garrison P. Sherwood (New York: Dodd, Mead, and Company, 1933), 315.
103. Williams, x–xi.
104. John Hohenberg, *The Pulitzer Prizes* (New York: Columbia University Press, 1974), 43.
105. *Brooklyn Dailey Eagle*, 27 December 1917.
106. *New York Times*, 26 December 1917.
107. Douglas, 60.
108. Anderson produced *The Golden Six* off-Broadway in 1958, shortly before his death. The play quickly failed. See Alfred S. Shivers, *The Life of Maxwell Anderson* (New York: Stein and Day, 1983), 260.
109. Frank Craven, *The First Year* (New York: Samuel French, 1921).
110. Zona Gale, *Miss Lulu Bett* (New York: D. Appleton, 1921).
111. Eugene O'Neill, *Anna Christie* in *O'Neill: Complete Plays 1913–1920* (New York: Library of America, 1988).
112. Owen Davis, *Icebound* (Boston: Little, Brown, 1923).
113. Sidney Howard, *They Knew What They Wanted* in *Sixteen Famous American Plays*, edited by Bennett A. Cerf and Van H. Cartmell (New York: Modern Library, 1942).
114. George Kelly, *Craig's Wife* in *Three Plays by George Kelly* (New York: Princess Grace Foundation-USA, 1999).
115. Burns Mantle, *The Best Plays of 1926–1927* (New York: Dodd, Mead, and Company, 1927), 3.
116. Ibid., 463.

117. Ibid., 4.
118. Frederic F. Van de Water, "The Obscene Drama," *Ladies Home Journal* 44 (April 1927): 8.
119. Barrett H. Clark, "Some New York Plays Not Yet Stopped by the Police Censors," *Drama* 17 (1927): 199.
120. Dumenil, 153.
121. Ibid., 155.
122. Shivers, *Life*, 1–5.
123. Maxwell Anderson, "Memoir," in *Dramatist in America: The Letters of Maxwell Anderson, 1912–1958*, edited by Laurence G. Avery (Chapel Hill: University of North Carolina Press, 1977): 304.
124. Ibid.
125. Shivers, *Life*, 7.
126. Ibid.
127. Robert Rice, Interview with Maxwell Anderson for *PM's Sunday Picture News* (29 November 1942): 23.
128. Anderson, "Memoir," in *Dramatist in America*, 304.
129. Ibid., 304–305.
130. John P. Hagan, "Frederick H. Koch and North Dakota: Theatre in the Wilderness," *North Dakota Quarterly* 38, no. 1 (1970): 76.
131. Ibid., 78–79.
132. Ibid., 80.
133. Ibid., 79–80.
134. Ibid., 75.
135. Shivers, *Life*, xx.
136. Maxwell Anderson to Arthur Hobson Quinn in *Dramatist in America: The Letters of Maxwell Anderson, 1912–1958*, edited by Laurence G. Avery (Chapel Hill: University of North Carolina Press, 1977), 29.
137. Anderson, "Memoir," in *Dramatist in America*, 304–305.
138. Shivers, *Life*, 35.
139. Ibid.
140. Ibid., 36.
141. Ibid., 45–46.
142. Ibid.
143. Ibid., 47.
144. Ibid., 354.
145. Ibid., 59–83.
146. Christine Stansell, *American Moderns: Bohemian New York and the Creation of a New Century* (Princeton, NJ: Princeton University Press, 2000), 152.
147. Anderson wrote his first play, entitled *Benvenuto*, in 1922 based off of the recently published biography of Benvenuto Cellini. Disliking the result and not inclined to rework it, he abandoned the play. See Shivers, *Life*, 79–80.

148. Shivers, *Life*, 81.
149. Ibid., 104–111.
150. The other plays Anderson collaborated on with Stallings were *First Flight*, which closed after 12 performances, and *The Buccaneer*, which closed after 20 performances. Both plays were produced in 1925. Also in 1925, Anderson achieved a modest run of 113 performances with his solo play, *Outside Looking In*, which was based off the book *Beggars of Life* by Jim Tully.
151. Douglas, 92.
152. U.S. Census Bureau, *1910 Census, Volume 3* (Washington: Government Printing Office, 1913), 341.
153. Shivers, *Life*, 47.
154. Maxwell Anderson, *Off Broadway: Essays About the Theatre* (New York: William Sloane Associates, 1947), 33.
155. John Mason Brown, *Two on the Aisle: Ten Years of the American Theatre in Performance* (New York: W. W. Norton, 1938), 199.
156. Shivers, *Life*, 267.
157. Ibid., 182.
158. Ibid., 55–56; 237–238.
159. Shivers, *Life*; Also see Hesper Anderson, *South Mountain Road: A Daughter's Journey of Discovery* (New York: Simon & Schuster, 2000). A touching memoir from Anderson's daughter, this book relates Hesper's eventual discovery that her mother, Mab (Anderson's second "wife") never legally married her father. The two lived as a married couple and projected the image of a traditional union with Anderson the breadwinner and Mab his helpmeet. The relationship dissolved when Anderson discovered Mab was having an affair. She subsequently committed suicide when he steadfastly refused to take her back. The dynamic offers a telling picture of Anderson's attitude toward women, but as his relationship with Mab began in the 1930s, it falls outside the parameters of this study.
160. *Off Broadway*, 28, 51.
161. Shivers, *Life*, 79; Rice, 24.
162. See *Off Broadway: Essays About the Theatre*; for Anderson, faith was a secular matter, emphasizing the theatre itself as well as the system of democracy as the greatest hopes for humankind. Later in his career he wrote two plays centering on Christian figures: *Journey to Jerusalem* (1940) centering on the life of Christ and *Joan of Lorraine* (1946) depicting Joan of Arc. Other plays, such as *Winterset* (1935) and *Key Largo* (1939) emphasize faith as a conduit for personal morality, but in secular philosophy rather than religious doctrine.
163. *Off Broadway*, 11.

164. John F. Wharton, *Life Among the Playwrights* (New York: Quadrangle, 1974), 27.
165. Abbott, 104.
166. Bruce Bliven, *Five Million Words Later: An Autobiography* (New York: John Day Company, 1970), 120.
167. "Map: States Grant Women the Right to Vote," *National Constitution Center*, Content Copyright 2006, https://constitutioncenter.org/timeline/html/cw08_12159.html.
168. "The Pill: Anthony Comstock's 'Chastity Laws.'" PBS, American Experience, Accessed 4 May 2022, https://www.pbs.org/wgbh/americanexperience/features/pill-anthony-comstocks-chastity-laws/.
169. *What Price Glory*, *First Flight*, and *The Buccaneer* were written with Stallings; *Gods of the Lightning* was written in 1928 with Harold Hickerson; *Outside Looking In*, written in 1925, was adapted from *Beggars of Life* by Jim Tully.
170. Shivers, *Life*, xviii.
171. Alfred S. Shivers, *Maxwell Anderson* (Boston: Twayne, 1976), 10.
172. Patrick J. Rice, "Maxwell Anderson and the Eternal Dream," *Catholic World* 177 (1953): 364.
173. See Allan G. Halline, "Maxwell Anderson's Dramatic Theory," *American Literature: A Journal of Literary History, Criticism, and Bibliography* 16 (1944): 63–81; Howard D. Pearce, "Job in Anderson's *Winterset*," *Modern Drama* 6 (1963): 32–41. Arthur M. Sampley, "Theory and Practice in Maxwell Anderson's Poetic Tragedies," *College English* 5 (1944): 412–418; Harold H. Watts, "Maxwell Anderson: The Tragedy of Attrition," *College English* 4 (1943): 220–230.
174. John Gassner, *Dramatic Soundings* (New York: Crown, 1968), 149.
175. Arthur T. Tees, "Maxwell Anderson's Liberated Women," *North Dakota Quarterly* (Spring 1974): 53.
176. Shivers, *Maxwell Anderson*, 10.

CHAPTER 2

White Desert: Marriage as Manifest Destiny

Maxwell Anderson's first produced play, *White Desert*, was an abysmal failure on the commercial stage. The production no doubt faced competition as would any New York premiere, but a quick glance at Broadway in the 1920s bears out the stark competitive reality. Burns Mantle counted 196 productions during the 1923–1924 season,[1] which was not necessarily atypical for the time, but certainly demonstrates Jazz Age audiences had greater options than do twenty-first century theatre-goers. Furthermore, Mantle asserts unequivocally, based both on his own judgment and a survey of other critics, that "the general quality of drama was higher than it ever has been before."[2] The subjectivity of such a statement goes without saying, but nevertheless the consensus among critics (or at least the ones Mantle surveyed) classified the 1923–1924 Broadway season as particularly strong. Finally, October 1923 (the month *White Desert* premiered) saw 26 new productions hit the boards.[3] With so many established productions already playing and more than two dozen new offerings in a single month, Anderson's four act verse drama about a married couple struggling in the frozen prairie of North Dakota faced an uphill battle in drawing crowds. According to box office receipts from the Princess Theatre, only 65 people viewed the production on opening night, 18 October 1923. Attendance dropped to 16 just six days later and never rose above 72.[4] The production closed after only 12 performances.[5]

© The Author(s), under exclusive license to Springer Nature Switzerland AG 2022
F. D. Geary II, *Maxwell Anderson and the Marriage Crisis*, https://doi.org/10.1007/978-3-031-13241-4_2

While *White Desert* failed to find an audience, Anderson hastened its descent into theatrical obscurity. All indications point to the fact that the playwright bore no sentimentality for his maiden Broadway effort. In a 1927 letter, Anderson confided that he had "several opportunities to publish it [*White Desert*] and at least two to revive it on Broadway," but believed the script "was in such poor shape that it needed complete revision," a task for which he could not muster the necessary energy.[6] These sentiments did not sweeten with old age. In a retrospective a few years before his death, Anderson remained dismissive of *White Desert*: "That play lasted a couple of weeks. It was a poetic tragedy, and didn't deserve to last that long....I didn't know why anybody produced it."[7] Consequently, *White Desert* has never seen publication.

Determining how to proceed with a close analysis of a play never formally codified in print represents a terrific challenge. The Maxwell Anderson Papers, held by the Harry Ransom Center at the University of Texas at Austin, houses the bulk of known material related to *White Desert*. This material includes various drafts of entire acts and a mass of corrected fragments for a total of over three hundred individual leaves. There exist typescript and handwritten versions and fragments. A published inventory of the collection indicates two complete drafts, one in verse and one in prose.[8] However, upon multiple visits I discovered these drafts had apparently been reorganized. One folder consists of all the acts and fragments written in verse. Rather than keeping the draft in order and the fragments separate, the fragments for Act I, for example, are all together with the draft of Act I. Then the draft and all fragments for Act II follows next in the folder and so on. Another folder contains prose drafts and fragments, but seems much less organized and it becomes difficult knowing what goes where. Yet a third folder contains an individual draft of Act V (the play was originally conceived in five acts) in verse. Finally, there exists a typescript reconstruction of the play by Alan Anderson, one of the dramatist's sons, which was placed in 1984, years after the publication of the original inventory.[9]

In examining *White Desert*, I have endeavored to consider every piece at my disposal, but certain assumptions were made for the sake of clarity. Principally, I concluded that the typescripts likely represent more polished versions of anything handwritten. The only discernible variance between the verse and prose drafts lay simply in presentation. As Anderson scholar, Laurence G. Avery, notes in the published inventory[10] and I have confirmed through personal observation, the dialogue of both drafts is essentially identical. Anderson's producer had the script typed to look like prose for fear the actors would balk at having to enunciate poetry.[11] The verse folder contains what appears to be a full draft of the script in four acts. This fact can be ascertained by the pagination included within the individual acts.[12] On Broadway, the play was presented in a prologue and four acts.[13] Alan Anderson reconstructed the play in prose and conflates the original structure to two acts comprising of five scenes because the two-act structure "seemed a more familiar form for the present day."[14] Alan reported in his introduction that he did not attempt retaining Anderson's verse form "because much of what has been left to us is not in verse form."[15] However, this assertion is simply not true as an entire draft in verse exists. Alan's scenes basically correspond to the dialogue of the original acts in the verse typescript. Out of deference to Anderson's devotion to verse drama, I have centered my analysis on the verse typescript and utilized Alan's reconstruction for purposes of cross-reference.

Rationale

Unlike contemporaries such as O'Neill and Tennessee Williams, Anderson tended to avoid anything resembling autobiographical facets. He once demurred on a request from his sister to contribute to a family history[16] and rebuffed two potential biographers seeking personal information.[17] Many of the plays that earned him success were personally distanced by factors such as history and geography (*Elizabeth the Queen*), adaptation (*Bad Seed*), or fantasy (*High Tor*). Moreover, aesthetically speaking, Anderson often expressed a loathing for realism as evinced in his admonition to critic Heywood Broun: "A great play cannot deal with ordinary people speaking commonplaces. It cannot deal with ordinary life."[18] However, in establishing the setting for *White Desert*, Anderson clearly hearkened to his roots. The play opens in December 1888 (the month and year of the playwright's birth) and takes place on the plains of North Dakota (the state in which Anderson graduated college). Furthermore, Anderson gained inspiration for the plot from his wife, Margaret, who told him of her parents' early struggles in North Dakota.[19] One also suspects the folk influence of Prof. Frederick Koch, who long championed writing plays with distinctly American settings and themes.[20]

Placing the action in 1888 adds an important distinction for our analysis. North Dakota did not achieve statehood until 1889. Thus, Anderson places his characters onto a vast, but barren landscape wherein land was subject to seizure by claimants in accordance with the American idea of Manifest Destiny. The Clayton-Bulwer Treaty with England in 1850, which halted American expansion to the south, is credited with slowing the progress of Manifest Destiny.[21] However, the hunger for property among ordinary Americans did not diminish and many Americans turned north and west for more land. This hunger was rooted in the philosophy of John Locke, who ranked property on par with life and liberty in terms of essential human rights.[22] Thomas Jefferson channeled Lockean ideas into the Declaration of Independence, transposing "property" with "the pursuit of happiness," but nonetheless aligning with "America's emerging capitalist mentality."[23] America added enormous quantities of territory throughout the first half of the nineteenth century, principally at the expense of Mexico.[24] These acquisitions lured pioneers westward in search of supposedly "free land." Frederick Jackson Turner famously theorized that the challenges faced by pioneers trekking across the untamed wilderness led to the construction of a unique brand of American individualism.[25] This westward migration coincides with the formation of the male breadwinner concept of marriage, which marriage historian Stephanie Coontz argues did not take hold until the nineteenth century.[26] Therefore, Anderson's backdrop for *White Desert* places his female protagonist in a time and place wherein both the nation and the institution of marriage were undergoing immense transformation. Furthermore, the connection of property ownership to the pursuit of happiness extends the play's critique into the Jazz Age. In Meyer v. Nebraska (1923), the year *White Desert* premiered, the United States Supreme Court held "the right of the individual...to marry, to establish a home and bring up children...as essential to the orderly pursuit of happiness." The Court's argument was not uncommon for Americans in the 1920s. In 1928, Ernest Groves echoes the Supreme Court's language, conflating love and landownership when he points out that, historically, institutional marriage served to protect three primary rights: "property, sex, and affection."[27] It is unlikely Anderson was aware of the Supreme Court case when writing the play. However, that the Court felt a need to include such a provision in a case wherein marriage was not the principal question represents another example of how debates about marriage pervaded America in the 1920s.

White Desert offers a view of two marriages. The primary focus centers on Mary and Michael Kane, two newlyweds who have just staked their claim in the frigid North Dakota territory. Sverre and Annie Peterson, living on a nearby claim, represent the secondary marriage. The analysis of this chapter will naturally center on Mary's journey from infatuated bride to disillusioned wife and, finally, to tragic heroine. Throughout the play, Anderson layers in imagery, themes, and symbolism connecting the institution of marriage to ideas of the frontier and property ownership. *White Desert* echoes the doctrine of Manifest Destiny and America's historical veneration of property ownership as a means of reflecting and critiquing the oppressive consequences women often faced when submitting to the institution of marriage.

Prologue: Are You Sure This Is Still the Earth?

White Desert opens with a brief prologue wherein Anderson establishes the stark barrenness of the landscape and casts marriage into the realm of unreality. Various fragmentary incarnations of the prologue exist. For the sake of clarity, I have opted to adhere to Alan's prose reconstruction. We begin with Michael and Mary Kane standing outside their claim shack in the North Dakota territory. The prairie is covered with snow glistening in the moonlight. Mary manifests all the glow and optimism of a young, blushing bride. Staring at the meager shack and spartan conditions, she can hardly believe it: "Are you sure this is still the earth? We've been so long coming, and it's all so smooth and white. I begin to think it's the moon. Why, that's the earth out there that shines like the moon!"[28] Mary's moon metaphor equates marriage with what would have seemed an impossible fantasy to an audience in 1923, over 40 years before the first moon landing. Mary extends this idea moments later when she refers to their new home as a "very frigid satellite,"[29] once again associating her situation as disconnected from the grounding of earth. While the script offers no hint of from where the Kanes travelled, Mary's observations indicate a long journey in distance, time, or both. Her poetic allusions to the moon reflect a sense that she has entered not merely a new normal, but a new reality not of this world. Marriage for her, at this point, represents an idealized adventure in much the same way pioneers idealized westward expansion, seeing opportunity while almost blind to risk; leaving behind whatever ground once possessed and breaking new ground. Mary has surrendered her old ground (single woman) for what she perceives as an exciting new frontier (marriage).

Michael strikes a palpable contrast to his wife, laying the foundation for the conflict to come. First, he dismisses Mary's romantic allusions in language lacking both poetry and imagination: "Anyway, here's a house. If we're on the moon, why then there's a house in the moon."[30] Second, he mocks Mary's poetical bent. When she inquires as to what people eat in the territory, Michael responds with "Why, naturally, green cheese. The place is made of it."[31] Third, he questions Mary's sanity or, at least, her intelligence, when he says, "I'm afraid your brain is going."[32] Finally, when Mary persists in her giddiness, Michael shuts her down: "Don't be so damn symbolic."[33] One might interpret Michael's reactions as playful teasing. But Michael garnered little sympathy from the critics. Arthur Pollock, for example, described him as "strong, slow-witted, none too intelligent."[34] Furthermore, when keeping in mind a married couple standing on the threshold of their honeymoon, the progression he makes from dismissing to mocking to insulting to shutting down, particularly in light of Mary's obvious alacrity, presages a sense of incompatibility. In the opening minutes *White Desert* confronts the audience with a façade. A young honeymoon couple composed of two characters who are not made for each other.

Despite Mary's romantic notions in these early moments of the play, she soon reveals herself a contemplative woman as well and not a shallow, naïve girl one might have expected on a 1923 stage. She confides to Michael that her incessant discourse results from trepidation about what happens when she crosses the threshold of the shack: "But I'm really lingering on this side of the sill because I'm a free, wild girl until I cross it, and after that I'm a man's woman, tamed, broken to the yoke—children, dishes and dustpans—captured by the enemy, hobbled, a ring in my nose, wings clipped—."[35] Mary makes pointed reference to the sacrifices women were expected to make, characterizing marriage as submission not unlike imprisonment or the plight of farm animals. In so doing, Mary echoes criticism by Emma Goldman, who argued that matrimony "prepares the woman for the life of a parasite, a dependent, helpless servant, while it furnishes the man the right of a chattel mortgage over a human life."[36] When Michael facetiously suggests they can call the whole thing off, Mary acknowledges both the inequity of the arrangement and the sheer absurdity of wanting it: "But that's the worst of it! I don't want to go. I want to be a slave. I know I'll get tired of cooking breakfasts for you and yet I sign up for a life job of it and jump at the chance."[37] This passage represents the genesis and paradox of Mary's struggle. Throughout the play she wrestles with the contradictions inherent in the supposed ideal marriage; women are expected to want marriage even though they recognize its resultant dissolution of her identity.

In the final moments of the prologue, Mary observes the pressures of matrimony, in certain respects, cut both ways: "Here I am forever round your neck like a thousand brick[s]. You'll never get away again, never be free, never tear loose down the pasture again—poor boy!"[38] Michael, in submitting to marriage, sacrifices to some degree, his personal freedom. However, as Goldman noted, the husband's power in relation to the world stands much stronger than his wife's. Thus, while marriage does place a strain on him, that strain does not squeeze as tightly for him as it does for her.[39] Anderson effectively establishes his critique of marriage in these opening moments, thus setting up the disaster to come.

Act I: A Marriage, Not a Purchase

The tension between Mary and Michael escalates throughout the course of Act I, where Anderson also introduces us to the secondary married couple in the play, Sverre and Annie. The action opens on the two couples in a game of Pedro, a popular nineteenth century card game somewhat akin to bridge. Michael, partnered with Annie in the game against his wife and Sverre, continues his belittlement of Mary. He criticizes Mary for playing the wrong card and complains of her having a short memory.[40] This complaint echoes his assertion in the prologue about her "brain going," thus establishing a pattern for Michael mistrusting Mary's mental state. Mary attempts to defuse the situation with sarcasm, but at the same time makes her displeasure known: "Don't reprove me, my lord. You make me feel the way I used to when my mother told me to pull down my dress."[41] Michael, in other words, makes her feel like a child and Mary resents his paternal air. When Mary and Sverre wind up on the winning side of the game, Michael attributes the victory to "fool luck," thus once again diminishing Mary's intellect as well as her ability. Mary, however, chalks the win up to her "cold intellect."[42] The competition between Mary and Michael strikes at something deeper than a mere card game. Sverre ultimately becomes Michael's competitor for Mary's affection. Therefore, he grows morose not only over his inadequacy as a man losing to his wife in a game of cards, but also as a man about to lose his wife's loyalty to him. In the harsh, competitive nature of the frontier, Michael struggles for firmer footing. For her part, Mary subverts the dominant culture's conception of womanhood. Women were not considered effective as cerebral calculators. Such skill was thought to reside strictly within a man's domain.

Sverre and Annie Peterson, while not the focus of the play's critique, serve to reinforce much of the play's theme in these early moments of Act I. Unlike Mary and Michael, the Petersons did not even know each other prior to arriving on the prairie. They each staked out individual, adjoining claims. "The rest," Sverre declares, "was what they call propinquity. Here we were, alone in the middle of the wild west without a chaperone. You can imagine what happened."[43] "Propinquity" (meaning simply the close proximity of one thing to another) was a key term often employed by advocates of Manifest Destiny.[44] Nineteenth century leaders tended to view the map in terms of "natural borders." The Louisiana Purchase as well as the annexations of Texas and Florida were justified by many as the natural right of the United States given the territorial proximity of the land.[45] Sverre's use of the term "propinquity" thus directly equates marriage with imperialism. Annie was not so much married as she was conquered. Edna St. Vincent Millay invokes a similar stand in her use of the term propinquity in one of her early sonnets: "I, being born a woman and distressed/By all the needs and notions of my kind,/Am urged by your propinquity to find/Your person fair, and feel a certain zest/To bear your body's weight upon my breast." Millay, however, ends the poem with the woman asserting her independence.[46] Anderson presents a woman unable to resist annexation by a man due to the absence of a "chaperone," driving sexual hunger, and the isolation imposed by the desolate, frigid terrain. Marriage, then, becomes what Havelock Ellis observed: a merely legal arrangement to civilize the permanency of sexual relations.

As Act I progresses, Anderson again utilizes the Petersons to advance the theme of isolation. Sverre and Annie offer a host of tribulations encountered over five years on the prairie. These include the vicissitudes of weather, the fluctuation of crop prices, incessant chores, and, according to Sverre, the boredom that develops from not having "another man's wife to look at."[47] Sverre's jocularity leads Annie to overlook this slight. However, other comments from Sverre about the nature of marriage challenge the idea of a permanent love relationship. When Mary idealistically hopes her and Michael's honeymoon will continue indefinitely,

Sverre counters that the honeymoon "ends the first time the fire goes out in the range—especially if your wife lets it out by forgetting to put coal on it."[48] Sverre refers, literally, to a fight he and Annie had over the stove losing heat, but the sexual metaphor seems obvious enough. Marriage, like life on the prairie, represents an arduous, thankless existence a couple performs cut off from the rest of the world. Moreover, if the fire in the home dies, the fault lies principally with the wife rather than the husband. Anderson's metaphor, within the context of frontier theory, paints a picture of marriage as a wilderness to be conquered and tamed.

After the Petersons exit, Act I concludes with a dramatic confrontation wherein Mary renders her first serious stand for independence. Mary, sensing a sudden surliness in her husband, probes Michael for the cause of his abrupt mood shift. Though reticent at first, Michael confesses he found Mary's behavior with Sverre inappropriate when, after the card game, Sverre pretended to steal a ball of yarn from Mary and then coaxed her to fish it out of his pocket. Mary enjoyed the joke and thought nothing of it. Moreover, this flirtation occurred while Mary and Sverre were sitting on her and Michael's marriage bed,[49] which suggests an adulterous act. Mary, in a manner of speaking, invited another man to share the marriage bed. Reaching into Sverre's pocket for the spool of thread symbolizes her succumbing to another man's sexual charm. Michael's jealousy percolates, which may have spurred one reviewer's somewhat chiding observation that he "was more madly given to jealousy than Othello, with absolutely no reason or motive."[50]

Michael's motive, however, becomes quite evident when Mary disabuses him of the realities of women. He comforts himself by assuming that Mary does not "know men"; meaning that as a woman she is naturally unaware of the subtle sexual machinations men engage in. In this sense, he reflects the typical Victorian attitude, which held women to be sexless, passionless creatures. Mary, however, offers incisive correction:

> But I do know. How could a woman
> Grow up anywhere and never once
> Find out for herself what a man is made of, or
> Learn how to judge what a man says and does?
> How did I choose you, Michael, if I had no
> Mind of my own? And is a woman so different
> From a man?[51]

Mary thus renders a bold assertion for a nineteenth century American woman. Stating she knows "what a man is made of" teases the possibility of prior sexual knowledge. Moreover, Mary places herself in a position of both power and intellectual independence. She chose him, not the other way around, because she possesses her own mind. When Michael expresses hope that a woman would, naturally, hold higher morals than a man, he again expresses a common Victorian idea. Mary, however, openly challenges his assumptions: "I think the two/Are very much alike, myself; they both/Fall in love, they're both passionate, both jealous."[52] For such a man as Michael, Mary's assertions would confront him with a worldview entirely foreign to everything he had been taught to believe about male/female relations.

Mary's brazenness nearly overwhelms Michael as the first act draws to a close. In a flurry of indignation, she levels three more dramatic salvos at Michael's assumptions about women. First, she demands equality in marriage:

> Michael, if I'd known
> You thought me a sort of inferior animal
> I'd never have married you, and never come out here
> To live with you. Either you speak to me
> As an equal or we'll end this thing at once.
> I'm a free agent. I can go away.[53]

Anderson seems to present us with a Jazz Age woman trapped in a Victorian age. Indeed, Mary's conception of marriage as essentially a contract made between two equal parties prompted critic Anita Block to label Mary "an intensely modern young woman."[54] Mary extends her independent streak when she next rails against Michael for presuming to teach her as if she were a child:

> I know Sverre and his kind. I grew up with boys
> Just like him. He'd go as far as a woman would let him,
> And so would nearly every other man.
> If I'd wanted to be untrue to you I could have done it
> Long before I knew you. I saved myself
> For my husband---and now my husband begins to teach me
> How to take care of myself. It's an insult![55]

Finally, she directly challenges the sexual double-standard by demanding of Michael, "Did you save yourself for me? Answer that!/Tell me the truth and I'll tell you the truth."[56] Michael never answers that question. Instead, he fixates on the possibility of her having premarital liaisons with other men. His response once again echoes the typical moral elevation Victorians accorded women: "I set you apart,/Mary, I didn't think of you as having—" and here he stops, presumably unable to say the word "sex." Mary finishes his line with "Been alive?".[57]

Michael's doubts bring to mind the fact that he and Mary had engaged in premarital sex with each other. This remembrance stokes his jealousy and he presses to know "all/We were before."[58] Mary, her ardor cooled, tries to assuage him into bed for the night, but Michael refuses to cease the pursuit. In terms of the frontier symbolism in the play, it is as if Michael's claim to a property has been challenged and he resolves to know what his rights to that property actually are. Mary stirs to anger once again and, in the process, reinforces the frontier theme. Deciding to go for a walk, Mary rejects Michael's attempts to hold her in the shack: "I need/No man's permission to do what I please.../It was a marriage, remember, not a purchase."[59] She exits and thus closes Act I.

Mary's door slam of Act I does not carry the same finality as Nora's door slam in Ibsen's *A Doll's House*, but it symbolizes a rejection of a principal frustration for many married women of the time: the equating of marriage to possession. In his experience serving in Denver's family court system, Judge Lindsey cited "jealousy, taking the form of a claim to the exclusive ownership and possession of a mate" as "the cause of most divorce litigation whenever such litigation is based on a failure in the sex life of the parties involved." Lindsey adds, "I am sure, too, that it is, directly or indirectly, the cause of ninety per cent of the unhappiness in married life."[60] Lindsey's observations precisely reflect Michael's conflict. For Michael, sexual purity was the issue, not marriage. He evinces no qualms about having had sex with Mary before marriage because he assumed he was the only man to issue a claim on her chastity. Far from motiveless, as one reviewer complained, Michael finds himself consumed with jealousy precisely because he doubts his sense of ownership over Mary's body. Mary, for her part, insists that the idea of ownership should never factor into a marriage. Anita Block praised Mary as a woman "who alone owns herself and owes explanations to no man."[61] Mary's rabid sense of independence, however, is plagued by her idealism as evoked in her poetic rhapsodizing in the prologue. The action of Act I permanently fractures that idealism.

Act II: Beware of Me

Act II[62] opens on a scene of fragile marital bliss. A few days have elapsed since the action concluding the first act. Tempers have cooled and Mary resumes her efforts at maintaining her idealism. In so doing, the play extends its themes of marriage as forms of imperialism, ownership, and isolation associated with the Manifest Destiny model. Preparing for breakfast, Mary revels: "Why, Michael,/Think of it, half a section of land all ours,/Three hundred and twenty acres free and clear,/Ours to the center of the earth and ours to the stars—."[63] As was her wont in the prologue, Mary once again rhapsodizes about married life in connection to the possession of land. Her romanticization of property ownership makes it seem almost as if marriage would not exist in its completed form in the absence of land. Yet as the title of the play implies and as we know from the struggles enumerated by Sverre and Annie, the land itself lacks fecundity. Making the land work demands immense sacrifice and incessant effort, which few prove strong enough to stand. The land, therefore, becomes a metaphor for marriage itself. Land ownership and marriage are ideal conditions dictated by American culture. People rush to lay hold of them because of the idealization of simply laying hold of them. Once in possession, however, the harsh and isolated landscape suffocates, suppresses, and leads one to question why they ever sought possession in the first place.

In the interval between Act I and Act II, the newlyweds have engaged in extensive conversations regarding their sexual past. Both acknowledge numerous infatuations prior to marriage, which leads Michael to muse on the role chance plays in love: "one little turn the wrong way/Might have sent me east, you west, never to meet,/Or I might have come to this place with another woman/Or you with another man."[64] Michael's emotional separation becomes all the more evident. The notion of true love seems little more than a myth to him. He does not see destiny in marriage, but rather the circumstance of propinquity. Mary's proximity was enough to justify his pursuit. Mary, on the other hand, rejects this unromantic idea. She makes plain she would have come to the prairie with "no other man alive. It's heresy, blasphemy,/Sacrilege."[65] Mary's religious rhetoric reinforces the philosophical gulf between her and Michael. Furthermore, this rhetoric underscores the impact of religion, particularly Christianity, on American marriage, an aspect more fully discussed when we come to *Sea-Wife* in the next chapter.

2 WHITE DESERT: MARRIAGE AS MANIFEST DESTINY   49

Talk of previous infatuations rekindles Michael's jealousy. He ratchets up the pressure on Mary to reveal the "truth" and "facts" about her past and openly doubts her forthrightness. Mary renders several efforts at polite evasion, but finally relents:

> They were such bits of trifles, the kind of trifles
> Children brood over and accuse themselves—there was once
> I went to church with a boy, I don't know why;
> I didn't like him—he was coarse somehow—
> When we knelt down his thigh touched mine and I
> Was thrilled, and didn't move away. I cried about it
> Afterward. I didn't tell that, Michael,
> Because it still makes me uncomfortable.[66]

Mary's discomfort with this fairly mild confession speaks volumes about the sexual mores, gender roles, and double-standards in nineteenth century America. As one critic put it, Mary's attitude that women are no different from men threatens Michael's "masculine complex on the subject of female chastity."[67] Michael's jealousy intensifies, turning him, as another critic observed, into a combination of Iago and Othello, "diffusing his own ugly venoms and imbibing them with gloomy gusto."[68] Michael demands first to know if Mary, prior to her meeting him, had ever had sexual intercourse with another man. Mary replies, "Only—in imagining." Still unsatisfied, Michael next demands to know if Mary since has extinguished all fantasies about other men. This question proves a significant turning point as Mary concedes:

> I ought to
> Say yes, for I know you'll dislike it, but if it's the truth
> We want, and nothing less—I can't say yes—quite—
> For there was once I passed a man in the street
> And he looked at me and all at once I was dreaming
> That he took me in his arms—I dreamed it all out—
> All that morning I think I was dreaming about him—
> Don't you day-dream, Michael?—but you were always there
> At the back of my mind—safe—and I was safe, too,
> Because I knew I had you.[69]

The assertion of having "dreamed it all out" leaves no doubt that Mary's sexual desire burns as hot as any man's. Anderson presents a subversive portrayal of woman as not merely susceptible to, but willingly in pursuit of, sexual fantasy as a means of feeding her natural carnal hunger. This portrayal runs against the grain of Victorian ideals of feminine purity and casts women equally in the role of seeking conquest. Mary tries to defend herself by appealing to his fantasies, but true to form and double-standards, he ignores the question. Instead, he continues the dogged pursuit of his claim over Mary's body and we soon learn the crux of his suspicion when he asks her is she ever fantasized about Sverre. At this point, right on cue, Sverre enters.[70]

Sverre's entrance results in both reinforcement and subversion of the separate gendered spheres idea. As Michael makes plans to leave for town to purchase supplies, Sverre volunteers to do the farm work in his absence. When Mary objects, insisting she can perform the tasks herself, Sverre notes the lack of callouses on her hands and proclaims her the "aristocracy" of the prairie.[71] With that, the men ignore Mary and begin making plans about the work. Mary resents their presumptions: "But just because I'm a woman any man can walk in and take my job from me? It isn't fair."[72] Sverre jokingly replies that Mary would do the same to him if she found him "feeding a baby or making a bed."[73] Sverre's assertions amount to chauvinism cloaked in chivalry. As a man, he naturally expects to take possession of Mary, tend to her, and protect her as one would a propertied claim. Mary challenges the status quo, but her attempted subversion meets with dismissal. Moments later, however, Michael leaves the shack and, once alone with Sverre, Mary muddies the waters of separate spheres even further. She refuses Sverre's overtures to help her clean the breakfast dishes, insisting he "mustn't waste time" on such domestic chores.[74] In effect, then, Mary behaves precisely as Sverre predicted she would if she found him attempting tasks normally assigned to women. These moments reflect the dissonance traditional gendered roles impose when men and women wrestled over what actions were most appropriate for their designated realms.

At this point, Anderson introduces us to a new character, Dugan, who represents the archetypal American rugged individualist. He has arrived to serve as Michael's guide through the treacherous terrain into town. Following some raucous banter with Sverre, Dugan soon finds himself alone with Mary in a brief scene demonstrating another example of traditional American masculinity. Mary obviously feels a certain emotional kinship with Dugan for, unlike Sverre, she manifests a willingness to confide in him about the trouble in her marriage. Also unlike Sverre,

Dugan encourages her candor without any hint of ulterior motives. There is no indication that Dugan views Mary as a potential conquest. However, Dugan's benignity, while well-intentioned, masks a complete lack of true empathy. When Mary divulges Michael's jealousy, Dugan tries to assuage her: "Jealous? If that's all, little one, you can thank your lucky stars. We're all jealous, every fool alive. There's nothing really wrong till he's jealous of somebody else."[75] Dugan's tone and action seem paternal and condescending, particularly his reference to Mary as "little one." Moreover, in dismissing Mary's palpable fear, Dugan minimizes her agency as an individual to process her own feelings. This moment serves, yet again, to emphasize Mary's total isolation. She has no one in whom she may truly confide.

Michael re-enters as Dugan comforts Mary, once more stirring his jealousy and setting up the final confrontation in Act II. Though Michael finds the pair in an embrace, the stage directions indicate Dugan responds to Michael's entrance "quite unembarrassed,"[76] thus emphasizing Dugan's intentions are not lascivious. Once alone with Mary, Michael demands she confess her conference with Dugan. When she demurs, he continues harassing her in dogged pursuit. Mary attempts to brush him off: "Michael, it was nothing./I hardly remember."[77] At this Michael launches into a tirade with blind ferocity:

>   Not three minutes ago,
> You easy woman, he had his hand on your head—
> And you sit there and say you don't remember,
> Do you call that nothing? Is that the kind of thing
> You have such difficulty bringing to mind?
> Well, I don't wonder. Let me tell you something;
> The last two nights I haven't slept; I've lain there
> Beside you trembling all night long, wondering,
> Wondering, doubting—Hell knows what I haven't dreamed,
> And God, now I know it's true. You're the kind, the kind,
> You've got the taint in you—you slept, you were quiet,
> You dreamed—oh, you breathed quietly all night long---
> Yes, your mind's easy—you've fooled me, you'll fool me again;
> You whore, you bitch—What were you saying to Dugan?[78]

Here again we see the parallels with the American emphasis on private property noted earlier. Michael reacts rather like a man subjected to invasion, as if something has been stolen from his possession. Moreover, his use of the words "whore" and "bitch" was guaranteed to ruffle sensibilities. Americans in the first two decades of the twentieth century were more committed to sanitizing language than were the British or Europeans.[79] George Abbott affirms that "the language [of *White Desert*] was very daring" and recalls his wife objecting when he belted out those two words while reading the play to her in their small apartment. Mrs. Abbott was terrified the neighbors might overhear.[80]

Mary keeps her cool despite the onslaught and continues trying to placate talk Michael. Notably, she never cowers or manifests fear of him. Her sense of control, particularly in the face of his animus, reinforces Victorian notions of brutish men and civilizing women. Mary attempts to bring Michael back to order by insisting she never loved anyone else. When he again remarks about her evasiveness, she almost scolds him with "But you aren't quite inviting/Confidences just now."[81] But the final straw for Mary in Act II lands when Michael questions whether their marriage can continue with her looking over every man she meets, "Noting his points, experimenting with him,/Fitting yourself to him, anticipating, acting the deed."[82] This insinuation proves too much for Mary's patience. She orders Michael to leave, but before he departs she strikes her own blows. She taunts him for insinuating her to be "a very common slut,/Free to your friends, open to any man.../Why, then, perhaps you are right."[83] After goading him thus, she concludes: "But now before God,/Whatever I am, we shall be even, Michael,/You and I; you have hurt me here; you have hurt me/Till nothing will ever hurt me anymore./Beware of me."[84] With that threat, Michael exits and Act II concludes.

Whereas Act I ended with Mary's rejection of marriage as property ownership, Act II ends with an even stronger stance of her clearly drawing lines of battle. Ultimately, Mary stands strong for her individuality and agency. All efforts to adhere to convention have failed, but not because of her. They have failed because of the pressure imposed upon their marriage by nineteenth century ideals of marriage as a matter for possession by the man of the woman. Being that Michael and Mary are newlyweds, we can speculate that they are driven by hormonal forces if not beyond their control, then certainly, given the time period, beyond their comprehension. Though standing at opposite sides of the question in terms of how to reform marriage, both sociologist Ernest Groves and Judge Ben Lindsey agreed that a lack of education stood among the preeminent reasons for marital troubles. Lindsey, in particular, bemoaned "the scores, the hundreds of marriages that ought never to have contracted," chief among them being "marriages made in the heat of passion."[85] While we never learn the full circumstances of Michael and Mary's union, Anderson's depiction evinces the earmarks of a marriage not well considered beforehand. The result becomes Michael falling further and further into the pit of jealousy, but in Act III Mary begins to fully discover and assert her identity.

Act III: An Old Law of Sex

Act III[86] opens in a literal snowstorm, physicalizing the metaphorical storm that has grown between Mary and Michael. The action resumes with Sverre carrying Mary's lifeless body into her shack. As warmth slowly restores her to consciousness, she reports that she intended to commit suicide by exposure. Isolation seems to have accelerated her mental deterioration.[87] She confides, "I have been pacing this cage since yesterday/Thinking how a woman's little risk/Goes down on the red and if it comes up blue/That ends it. She's out of it./From now on I'm/A looker-on at the game."[88] Mary turns marriage into a gambling metaphor, presumably roulette (though there is some confusion as roulette tables are traditionally red and black). When women engage in marriage they must bet it all on red (the color of passion). She becomes beholden to her husband for security. If her gamble fails, she has no recourse as men tended to view divorced women as damaged goods.

Moreover, Mary has become despondent over Michael's assault of her womanly identity. She relates to Sverre her last confrontation with Michael, fixating on the word "whore" and reveals profound psychological effects: "When I close my eyes/I can read what he said written out in fire/On darkness; when I open them I can hear it/Chanted like a ritual in church,/Back and forth; I shall go mad, I suppose,/But I would rather die."[89] Beginning in the nineteenth century, chastity came to represent the essence of womanhood as defined by patriarchal culture.[90] Mary's anguish at being labelled a whore embodies Charlotte Perkins Gilman's observation that if a woman lacked chastity "no array of other virtues could save her."[91] Even though Mary has not, in reality, ceded that virtue, the mere insinuation that she has presents a significant threat. Yet again we see the parallels between men seeking exclusive rights to feminine purity in marriage and the excitement associated with the acquisition of "virgin land" that drove the ideology of Manifest Destiny.

The prairie's isolation contributes to Mary's mental breakdown when alone, but generates a different effect when confined with another man. That the flirtation from Act I leads to an affair in Act III may not surprise anyone, but the manner in which the affair comes about represents a deviation from standard theatrical tropes. As Sverre comforts Mary, the shack's confinement, exacerbated by the blizzard, prove too much for his masculine instincts. He soon begins waxing poetic over how much he loves Mary, how he will whisk her away from her unappreciative husband, and they could live together in bliss:

> We could drift in a canoe through forests
> No man has ever walked in, and for winter
> Go on snowshoes; I've lived the life, Mary,
> I tell you it's good, if you would only come.
> When it's cold we'll have a high wood fire;
> We'd lie warm in each other's arms when it storms;
> There's a whole world out there nobody wants,
> Ours for no more than taking it.[92]

Sverre's plan, if one could call it such, exudes romance and youthful impracticality reminiscent of Mary's moon metaphor from the prologue. His rhapsodizing represents the sort of thing a young woman in a traditional story might go in for, dashing off with her knight in shining armor to a more adventurous life. Mary, however, stuns Sverre with her answer: "But I don't/Want to go." When Sverre asks if she loves him, she flatly replies, "No."[93] Mary now evinces maturity and agency in the face of a man trying to sweep her off her feet, an attitude divergent from one she manifested at the beginning of the play.

Mary's reaction leaves Sverre both confused and contrite, but she soon unveils her true purpose. Having been branded a whore by her husband, Mary means to indulge herself with another man as punishment to Michael. She reveals to Sverre that she had not really intended on suicide after all. She sought one chance to engage in an adulterous affair. When she noticed Sverre near the shack, "the occasion offered." She thus exposed herself to the storm as a means of luring Sverre into a rescue and bringing the two of them the cabin.[94] This moment seems unbelievable for it suggests Mary imperiled her life to entice Sverre, which seems an incredible extremity. Furthermore, it also makes Mary seem ruthlessly calculating and almost predatory, which does not fit with her overall character. However, when one considers the mental trauma, the assault on her identity as a woman followed by prolonged isolation in a barren landscape, it becomes easier to comprehend why she suddenly behaves as she does. Mary's change is not sudden, but rather represents an evolution of her character in response to the dramatic circumstances she has endured.

Once again Anderson plays to isolation combined with the primitive backdrop of the North Dakota prairie to intensify the drama. Sverre refuses to accede to Mary's frank request for an affair. He finds it inconceivable she would "dirty" herself just to hurt Michael. Mary, however, speaks to the inequality of gender roles when she retorts:

> I will, by God, I will!
> But you will never know how hard it is.
> You can take pleasure anywhere and forget it,
> Being a man. You can love anywhere,
> And somewhere else tomorrow; it's as easy for you
> As eating a new dish at a new table.[95]

Mary thus completely abandons her romantic idealism. By equating sexual intercourse with eating, sex becomes little more than a physical drive demanding satisfaction. When Sverre remains steadfast in his refusal, Mary reminds him of the natural realities:

> You don't know yourself.
> Was there ever a man strong enough to refuse
> A woman's invitation on any ground
> Whatever? There's an old law of sex that's bigger
> Than your will. The night will be long. I promise you
> You'll think better of it.[96]

Sverre threatens to leave, but exiting the shack risks death when considering the blizzard. And the shack, of course, is a confined space. Mary therefore believes she only needs to bide her time and let nature take its course. Sverre, for all his posturing, cannot resist the urge and the act ends with the two engaged in a kiss.[97] Anderson plays against the common tropes insofar as Sverre does not romance, seduce, or rape Mary. Quite the contrary, Mary demonstrates full agency over her sexual behavior and embodies a woman who hungers for physical passion. Sverre represents the Victorian notion of a man struggling and failing to control his supposed natural primitive instincts. In *White Desert*, sex on the prairie lacks any romantic idealization. Rather sex represents little more than raw lust, a biological function pursued equally by men and women; a function closer to breeding than anything resembling idealistic love codified by marriage.

Act IV, Scene 1: Guilty or Innocent, It's All the Same

The first scene of Act IV[98] takes place the next evening when Michael returns, advancing the crisis and establishing the grounds for the climax. The action opens on Mary and Sverre in the shack with Mary packed up and ready to venture out on her own. Sverre makes one last attempt to persuade Mary to abscond with him, but she remains steadfast in her refusal. Desperate, Sverre moves in for a kiss, which Mary rebuffs. Recognizing the futility of further pursuit, Sverre respects Mary's wishes and exits without animosity.[99] Anderson thus provides a striking foil for Michael. Sverre, while certainly no saint, proves much more amenable to acknowledging Mary's independence as a woman than does her own husband. This point, however, raises the question as to what effect the institution of marriage plays in influencing the degree of respect he shows for her. After all, propinquity aside, Sverre loved Annie once upon a time, or at least believed he did, but that relationship grew cold post-marriage. Annie confides as much to Mary moments later when she laments Mary's leaving: "It's much homier when there's a woman nearby. I've felt so alone, you know." She then inquires if Mary told Sverre of her departure, to which Mary cryptically replies: "He knows, I think." Annie then declares, "Life is so strange, isn't it? I wish I were—beautiful."[100] Though never explicitly revealed, one imagines Annie has guessed the truth about the affair. For Annie, once a schoolteacher with an independent streak, marriage has winnowed away her sense of self, thus prognosticating what Mary might become should she remain with Michael.

The high point of this scene arrives when Michael returns and attempts reconciliation. Taking a conciliatory tone, he insists he will no longer dictate to Mary. However, he weaponizes love to justify his egregious behavior, claiming he only acted as he did "because I'd loved so unreasonably."[101] Anderson, a great admirer of Shakespeare, here echoes Othello's plaintive defense of "one who loved not wisely but too well."[102] At this point, however, Mary has yet to apprise Michael of her affair. Instead, she attempts to extricate herself without disabusing him, prompting Michael to shift his tone back to possessiveness: "You can't go. I won't have it! You're mine!"[103] Mary reiterates her sentiments from the end of Act I: "That's an old mistake of yours. I'm not a slave or chattel. You didn't buy me. I can go when I please."[104] Michael's rabid obsession and Mary's striking audacity reflect Judge Lindsey's admonition against viewing marriage as a form of ownership. But despite Michael's reprehensible behavior and despite Mary's bold stand, she nevertheless makes one last effort to persuade him to "just take each other as we are."[105] The power institutional marriage possesses in terms of tradition and law are on full display. Mary has a strong bent toward independence, yet she cannot quite bring herself to make a clean break from her matrimonial commitment.

Mary's desperate attempt to save her marriage leads to her finally confessing to her extramarital affair. First, however, she extracts a promise from Michael to accept her "even if I were a strumpet."[106] Michael vows that he will, but the promise proves hollow. Upon hearing the details of the affair, he launches into a rancorous verbal assault. When Mary reminds him of his promise, he accuses her of tricking him into promising. He not only views her as a whore, but as a conniver as well.[107] Michael's characterization of her as not only loose, but dishonest, cements her status as a low woman in the eyes of Victorian patriarchy. Mary notes the irony that Michael was just as enraged when she had done nothing as when she had actually committed adultery: "Guilty or innocent, it's all the same."[108] A woman thus faces double jeopardy. She must protect herself against actual temptation from men, but also shield herself from even the insinuation that she may have acted against propriety. Seeing no other recourse, Mary resolves, finally, to leave her marriage.[109]

Act IV, Scene 2: Something Wrong from the Beginning

White Desert concludes with one brief scene representing the culmination of the tragedy presaged in the Prologue.[110] As Mary prepares to leave the prairie and her marriage behind, Sverre attempts once more to convince her to run away with him. She, however, remains steadfast in her refusal, asserting that she "must get clear of this altogether or it will kill me!" But she bears no ill-will toward Sverre, pointing out the dissolution of her marriage was inevitable and that their affair only "hastened the process."[111] The action intensifies once Michael enters and begins antagonizing first Sverre, then Mary. When Mary tries to leave, Michael taunts Sverre to travel with her because he has "earned the right." Mary responds with her ultimate rejection: "But I don't want him, Michael; I don't want him along; do you understand? I've never wanted any man in the world, seriously, but you. And now that's finished. I was right to betray you, right to drag down our love. For you'd have failed in the end as you have failed me now. Now we know it. There was something wrong from the beginning."[112] This moment of recognition speaks powerfully to the theme of the play. It also runs against one critic's assessment that perhaps Michael's "morbid jealousy would never have come to the surface if he and Mary had not been chained by circumstances to their bare cabin and their pitiful new farm."[113] Quite the contrary, Mary comes to understand that Michael was wrong for her from the start; that their marriage was doomed before it was ever consecrated, before vows were even taken. Marriage's deeply ingrained tradition in Western culture contributes to Mary's confusion, thus prohibiting her from fully comprehending her situation. At the outset of the play Mary possessed everything society instructed her to want, yet "something" was "wrong." Now she no longer knows what to want. She only knows she must escape from what she has.

Like Othello, to whom many critics compared him, Michael's jealousy overwhelms him. After Mary exits, he continues to rage at Sverre. He even lashes out at Annie, insinuating her lack of sex appeal led Sverre to look elsewhere. He questions why Sverre should want "to come between Mary and me—or any woman I ever wanted?"[114] Herein lay the crux. Sverre has threatened Michael's masculinity and what he perceives as his rightful claim to ownership of a woman. It is not, therefore, the loss of Mary, specifically, that Michael bemoans. Rather he rages at the loss of his property to another man. Subsumed with jealousy, Michael grabs his rifle and, after struggling with Sverre, who tries to wrest the weapon from him, he shoots Mary, killing her.[115]

Conclusion

While *White Desert* was not, so far as we know, raided by authorities as some provocative plays were just four years later, it did produce quite a stir among some observers. Mary's Act III seduction, combined with the "strong language" in Act II, proved so offensive that one of *White Desert*'s producers "modestly withdrew his name from association with the play."[116] One critic cited *White Desert* among a host of

New York openings dealing with sexual matters as evidence that, "[t]he blush of shame has gone on strike."[117] Critic John Corbin conceded the play possessed "really admirable qualities," but that "its main theme" was not among them.[118] The opening line of another review ran thus: "Even if it was worth while (*sic*), it would be impossible to analyze or describe *White Desert* in any way that would be interesting or acceptable to decent readers."[119] This same critic further complained the play "bears every evidence of…bad taste" and that it "indulges in the crudest sort of vulgar sensationalism."[120] Paradoxically, this same reviewer also found the characters "objectionable, but well-drawn."[121] Such puritanical reviews were not, however, typical. Burns Mantle placed the blame for the production's brevity on the reactions of general theatre-goers, observing that Anderson's initial Broadway offering "was too heavy for popular consumption. The play won enthusiastic endorsement from many reviewers but not from the public."[122] George Abbott was most succinct in summing up the play's fate, calling *White Desert* "an artistic failure." "It raised Maxwell Anderson's standing as a writer," Abbott continued, "but it left him just as [financially] poor as before."[123]

However, not all theatre-goers and critics were turned off by the anti-puritanical themes, finding both the performances and the writing impactful and sympathetic. One member of the public, in a letter to the *New York Times*, praised *White Desert* as "a vivid play" and was especially laudatory of Abbott in the role of Sverre.[124] Anita Block also expressed admiration for Abbott, but reserved her highest praise for Beth Merrill in the role of Mary. Block credits Merrill with giving Anderson's heroine "an extraordinarily intelligent and simple interpretation."[125] Other critics, such as Arthur Pollock, hailed the playwright as "[a] new American dramatist of the first rank," speculating Anderson might someday ascend the same heights as Eugene O'Neill.[126] Pollock praised Anderson's characters as "sharper than O'Neill's" and singled out Mary Kane as "a first-rate achievement."[127] Moreover, Pollock asserts the play "tells a few facts about women that are seldom successfully disclosed in the theater." What, exactly, those few facts were he fails to elucidate. However, in surveying the play's action and the response of some reviewers, one can readily imagine what Pollock might have meant: Anderson's stark candor in representing female sexuality. Such representations in 1923 could not have done other than create controversy.

The moralistic and somewhat contradictory reaction from critics to *White Desert* reflects the uneasiness of the times toward issues of sexuality, gender roles, and marriage. The tactic, for example, of praising the play, but deploring the theme or certain aspects of the content express the reality of Americans struggling to come to grips with a radically evolving society. Anderson blends nineteenth century conceptions of womanhood with American frontier ideology to express how these ideologies conspire to suppress and destroy an individual within the institution of marriage. Anita Block embodied this idea in her glowing review of the play. Block describes Michael as having "possessive instincts" and representing a "primitive male whose property another has enjoyed." Michael resorts to violence "because he demands [Mary] shall have been a sexless angel until he aroused her and because he cannot endure the realization that she was a human being like himself, with the same erotic impulses and even experiences."[128] Percy Hammond echoed this sentiment, almost in the same words, observing that Michael "could not face the fact that she was human" despite the fact that they engaged in premarital sex with each other.[129] Michael's idealization of Victorian womanhood created an impossible standard for Mary to personify.

Mary's death at the end of the play is not the most provocative or revolutionary denouement Anderson could have chosen. In fact, such an ending places him in concert with the standard literary and dramatic treatments of strong-willed women at the time. From Madame Bovary to Hedda Gabler to Edna in Kate Chopin's *The Awakening* to Young Woman in Sophie Treadwell's *Machinal*, the idea of the woman meeting or choosing death in response to frustrated attempts at individual prerogative was quite common in the nineteenth and early twentieth centuries. Nora from Ibsen's *A Doll's House* stands out as a marked exception. However, Mary is more Desdemona than Nora, which would align with Anderson's lifelong devotion to Shakespeare and his averseness to modernism. However, this analogy is not entirely fair to Anderson either. Desdemona represents a "sexless angel" above all reproach who stood on her sacred feminine purity till the end. Mary, by contrast, arrives at a powerful realization of who she really is and comes to represent a stronger woman at the end than she was in the beginning. That her assertion of equality results in destruction is not a reflection of a fallen woman punished for infidelity. Indeed, most critics tended to view Michael less favorably than Mary, despite Mary's expressions of sexuality and independence. Rather, Mary serves more as a victim of the combined ideologies of Victorian womanhood and the American obsession with property. It is this combination, as codified and reinforced within the institution of marriage, that leads to Mary's demise. Furthermore, the physical isolation of the prairie permitted no practical escape. When Mary attempts to extricate herself in the final moments of the play, she walks off into the wintry landscape with no guide and no stated sense of direction. Even if Michael does not murder her, it is not entirely clear where she will go or if she will even survive the trek. Thus, once again, the land itself symbolizes the realities of marriage: cold, barren, unforgiving, and inescapable, particularly for women.

Given the rapid failure of *White Desert*, one might have anticipated a different tack from the playwright. Anderson, however, proved unflinching with regard to controversial representations of women and sex. Moreover, the controversy about marriage not only endured in the United States at the time, but seems to have accelerated. According to one observer, 1924 witnessed a 50% increase in divorces from the previous year.[130] Anderson's next playwriting endeavor centered on another doomed married couple set in nineteenth century America. Only this time he would focus his critique on the roles religious bigotry and superstition play in suppressing feminine sexual identity.

NOTES

1. Burns Mantle, *The Best Plays of 1923–1924* (Boston: Small, Maynard, 1924), 1.
2. Ibid.
3. Ibid., 4.
4. Box Office Statements for the Princess Theatre. Maxwell Anderson Papers. Harry Ransom Center. The University of Texas at Austin.
5. Alfred S. Shivers, *The Life of Maxwell Anderson* (New York: Stein & Day, 1983), 83.
6. Letter to Arthur Hobson Quinn, 4 May 1927 in *Dramatist in America*, 29.
7. Anderson Memoir in *Dramatist in America: The Letters of Maxwell Anderson, 1912–1958*, edited by Laurence G. Avery (Chapel Hill: University of North Carolina Press, 1977), 307.
8. Laurence G. Avery, *A Catalogue of the Maxwell Anderson Collection at the University of Texas* (Austin: University of Texas Press, 1968), 80.
9. Maxwell Anderson Papers, Works, *White Desert* by Alan Anderson. Harry Ransom Center. The University of Texas at Austin.
10. Avery, *Catalogue*, 80.

11. Shivers, *Life*, 81–82.
12. Act I contains 18 pages total, but pagination is off. There are pages numbering 1–10 in purple ink, then the page numbers run 7–14 in black ink. However, page "7" clearly picks up in mid-dialogue exactly where page 10 leaves off. The remaining pages follow in perfect continuity. Act II then picks up with page "15" and the play ends on page "51." Avery notes in the Catalogue a complete verse draft written in four acts with pages numbered 1–51. Avery appears to be referencing this draft, but failed to recognize the mistake in pagination. This draft, therefore, consists of 55 pages of unbroken continuity.
13. Mantle, *Best Plays 1923–1924*, 339.
14. Alan Anderson, "Introduction" to *White Desert*, Maxwell Anderson Papers, Harry Ransom Center, 1.
15. Ibid.
16. Letter to Lela Chambers in *Dramatist in America*, 277.
17. Burns Mantle, *American Playwrights of Today* (New York: Dodd, Mead, and Company, 1929), 70–71; Barrett H. Clark, *Maxwell Anderson: The Man and His Plays* (New York: Samuel French, 1933), 3–4.
18. Letter to Heywood Broun, *Dramatist in America*, 19.
19. Shivers, 81.
20. Ibid., 42.
21. K. Jack Bauer, *Zachary Taylor: Soldier, Planter, Statesman of the Old South* (Baton Rouge: Louisiana State University Press, 1985), 286.
22. John Locke, *Second Treatise on Government*.
23. Joseph J. Ellis, *American Sphinx: The Character of Thomas Jefferson* (New York: Alfred A. Knopf, 2002), 57.
24. Anders Stephanson, *Manifest Destiny: American Expansion and the Empire of Right* (New York: Hill and Wang, 1995), 32–33.
25. Frederick Jackson Turner, "The Significance of the Frontier in American History," in *The Frontier in American History* (New York: Holt, Rinehart, and Winston, 1962), 1–38.
26. Stephanie Coontz, *Marriage, a History* (New York: Viking, 2005), 7–8.
27. Groves, 47.
28. Maxwell Anderson, Page one of Prologue to Prose Typescript of *White Desert* as reconstructed by Alan Anderson. Works, Maxwell Anderson Papers. Harry Ransom Center. The University of Texas at Austin.
29. Ibid.
30. Ibid.
31. Ibid., 2.
32. Ibid.
33. Ibid.
34. Arthur Pollock, *Brooklyn Daily Eagle*, 19 October 1923.
35. Maxwell Anderson & Alan Anderson, Prologue, 2.

36. Emma Goldman, *Red Emma Speaks: An Emma Goldman Reader*, edited by Alix Kates Shulman (Amherst: Humanity Books, 1998), 57.
37. Maxwell Anderson & Alan Anderson, Prologue, 2.
38. Ibid., 3.
39. Goldman, 205.
40. Maxwell Anderson, Verse typescript of *White Desert*, Act I, page 1. Works, Maxwell Anderson Papers. Harry Ransom Center. The University of Texas at Austin.
41. Ibid.
42. Ibid., 3.
43. Ibid., 4.
44. Albert K. Weinberg, *Manifest Destiny: A Study of Nationalist Expansionism in American History* (Chicago: Quadrangle Books, 1963), 59–71.
45. Stephanson, 43–44.
46. Edna St. Vincent Millay, *The Harp-Weaver and Other Poems* (New York: Harper & Brothers Publishers, 1923), 66.
47. *White Desert*, Verse Typescript, Act I.
48. Ibid., 9.
49. Ibid., 8.
50. John Corbin, "The Play," *New York Times*, 19 October 1923.
51. *White Desert*, Verse Typescript, second page 10 (the typescript has handwritten numbers on each page, but Act I was missed paginated; it begins 1–10 and then number 7–14; this citation occurs on the second page numbered "10").
52. Ibid.
53. Ibid., 11.
54. Anita Block, *New York Leader*, 19 October 1923.
55. *White Desert*, Verse Typescript, 11.
56. Ibid., 11–12.
57. Ibid., 12.
58. Ibid.
59. Ibid., 13–14.
60. Ben B. Lindsey and Wainwright Evans, *The Companionate Marriage* (Garden City, NY: Garden City Publishing, 1927), 71–72.
61. Block.
62. Act II of the verse typescript corresponds almost identically to Alan's Act I, scene 2 in prose. The original verse has been relied upon.
63. *White Desert*, Verse Typescript, Act II. Works, Maxwell Anderson Papers. Harry Ransom Center. The University of Texas at Austin, 15.
64. Ibid., 16.
65. Ibid., 16.
66. Ibid., 18–19.

67. Block.
68. Percy Hammond, *New York Herald Tribune*, 19 October 1923.
69. *White Desert*, Verse Typescript, Act II, 19.
70. Ibid., 20–21.
71. Ibid., 22.
72. Ibid.
73. Ibid.
74. Ibid.
75. Ibid., 25.
76. Ibid.
77. Ibid., 26.
78. Ibid., 27.
79. Ann Douglas, *Terrible Honesty: Mongrel Manhattan in the 1920s* (New York: Farrar, Straus and Giroux, 1995), 158–159.
80. Abbott, 104.
81. *White Desert*, Verse Typescript, Act II, 27.
82. Ibid., 28.
83. Ibid.
84. Ibid., 29.
85. Lindsey and Evans, 165.
86. Act III of the verse typescript corresponds almost identically to Alan's Act II, scene 1 in prose. The original verse has been relied upon.
87. *White Desert*, Act III, Verse Typescript. Works, Maxwell Anderson Papers. Harry Ransom Center. The University of Texas at Austin, 30–32.
88. Ibid., 32.
89. Ibid., 33.
90. Coontz, 159.
91. Charlotte Perkins Gilman, "Toward Monogamy," *Nation* 118 (11 June 1924): 671.
92. *White Desert*, Act III, 38.
93. Ibid., 38–39.
94. Ibid., 39.
95. Ibid., 40.
96. Ibid., 41.
97. Ibid., 42.
98. Act IV, scene 1 represents the most difficult and speculative part of *White Desert* to assess. The end of the play appears to have undergone extensive revision. Of the verse typescript, Act IV numbers pages 43–51 and concludes the play. However, significant sections are crossed out and the draft is followed by an alternate Act IV, separated into two scenes. This draft, in turn, appears to have undergone significant revision and changed to prose. Alan's reconstruction does not completely correspond to either draft. Hence, for the sake of clarity, I have deferred to Alan's

Act II, scene 2, which picks up the action immediately following Act III in the verse transcript.
99. Maxwell Anderson and Alan Anderson, Act II, Scene 2, pgs. 1–2.
100. Ibid., 3–4.
101. Ibid., 7.
102. William Shakespeare, *Othello*, Act V, ii.
103. Maxwell Anderson and Alan Anderson, Act II, scene 2, page 8.
104. Ibid., 8–9.
105. Ibid., 11.
106. Ibid., 9.
107. Ibid., 14.
108. Ibid., 15.
109. Ibid., 17.
110. Alan's Act II, Scene 3 intersperse verse drafts of Act IV, scene 2 and "Act V." The play was apparently conceived as fives acts, then conflated to four (see Alan Anderson, "Introduction," 1). Once more, for the sake of clarity in citation, I have deferred to Alan's reconstruction.
111. Maxwell Anderson and Alan Anderson, Act II, scene 3, page 2.
112. Ibid., 4.
113. Barrett H. Clark, *Maxwell Anderson: The Man and His Plays* (New York: Samuel French, 1933), 10–11.
114. Maxwell Anderson and Alan Anderson, Act II, scene 3, page 5.
115. Ibid., 6–7.
116. Hammond, 19 October 1923.
117. Unsigned, *Wall Street Journal*, 20 October 1923.
118. *New York Times*, 19 October 1923.
119. C.P.S., "White Desert' an Unpleasant Play," *New York Evening Post*, 19 October 1923.
120. Ibid.
121. Ibid.
122. Mantle, *American Playwrights of Today*, 67.
123. George Abbott, *Mister Abbott* (New York: Random House, 1963), 104.
124. Knowles Entrikin, "Views from the Mailbag: Concerning George Abbott," *New York Times*, 28 October 1923.
125. Block
126. Arthur Pollock, *Brooklyn Daily Eagle*, 19 October 1923.
127. Ibid.
128. Block.
129. Hammond, 19 October 1923.
130. Ruth Scott Miller, "Masterless Wives and Divorce," *Ladies Home Journal* 42 (January 1925): 20.

CHAPTER 3

Sea-Wife: Marriage and Superstition

Of the four plays under consideration in this book, *Sea-Wife* may seem the most unusual for inclusion. Originally written in longhand in 1924, the script was revised within the following two years into a typescript dated 1926.[1] Unlike the other plays covered in this book, *Sea-Wife* was never produced on Broadway. Anderson confided to Barrett H. Clark that "others" found the play "a difficult subject for representation," but he fails to elaborate as to who those "others" were and why or in what manner the play was deemed too problematic for production.[2] In another letter to Clark, Anderson confessed his ambivalence to the play, which was connected to his general antipathy to revision: "My enthusiasm for my plays cools very shortly after they are written and I don't care now whether *Sea Wife* is produced or not."[3] Clark, however, expressed curiosity for *Sea-Wife* and Anderson acquiesced in sending him a copy in part because "it contains some fairly good poetry and you may like to read it."[4] Clark indeed admired the play, describing it as possessing "strange and peculiar beauty."[5] With Anderson's permission, Clark forwarded copies to "certain non-professional theatres," including Professor A. Dale Riley at the University of Minnesota where *Sea Wife* saw its premiere in 1932.[6] Whether the script circulated through Clark or some tertiary source, the play achieved at least two other productions in the 1930s, one in New Orleans in April 1936[7] and later that same year

© The Author(s), under exclusive license to Springer Nature Switzerland AG 2022
F. D. Geary II, *Maxwell Anderson and the Marriage Crisis*, https://doi.org/10.1007/978-3-031-13241-4_3

at Syracuse University.[8] These productions mark a rarity for Anderson who, as we have mentioned, tended to aim his plays for Broadway.

Though these three obscure productions occurred outside of New York and beyond the social climate of the Jazz Age, they nonetheless offer a window for gauging the impact of the play before an audience familiar with the culture of the 1920s. The meager evidence we have suggests *Sea-Wife* rendered a powerful impact on stage despite Anderson's misgivings. In response to the Minnesota production, one critic defined the play as "folk melodrama," another hint at the potential influence of Frederick Koch on Anderson's writing, and found the play possessed "an ephemeral kind of lyric beauty."[9] Another Minnesota critic went further, hailing *Sea-Wife* as "a dramatic fabrication of gripping intensity" and proclaiming it the best production from the University of Minnesota's theatre under Riley's tenure.[10] A critic of the New Orleans production was less effusive, but nonetheless found *Sea-Wife* "creditably staged and performed."[11] Likewise, Professor Sawyer Falk reported that his production at Syracuse was "exceptionally well received."[12]

In addition to critics of the 1930s this lyric drama has also garnered some scholarly attention. Decades after these productions, *Sea-Wife* was the only unpublished play to receive significant attention in Alfred S. Shivers' critical study of Anderson's work.[13] Shivers justified its inclusion with his estimation of the play as "much superior" to some of Anderson's Broadway productions and asserted the play bore "distinct literary merit."[14] Though Anderson's output from the 1920s includes other unpublished, non-Broadway plays, I include *Sea-Wife* as part of this study for two reasons. First, like the other three plays, *Sea-Wife was* produced, albeit mostly by non-professionals in the 1930s. Second, and most important, the themes surrounding gender roles, sexuality, and marriage match up well with the other three plays in terms of how the dramas reflect 1920s American culture. Anderson's other unpublished plays from this decade were not produced and did not address the marriage theme in a manner consonant with the other plays under consideration.

With its inclusion justified, the question shifts to which version of the play to focus upon. *Sea-Wife* centers on the mysterious reappearance of a woman, Margaret, who reports having been abducted by a magical merman. The merman forces her to live under the sea as his wife and Margaret bears two sea children by him. Longing to revisit her husband on land, the merman permits her a brief return. Once reunited with her earthly husband, Margaret hears the voices of the merman and her two sea children, tormenting her to come back to their underwater kingdom. Substantive differences exist between the 1924 manuscript and the 1926 typescript. The manuscript version makes plain, with the physical appearance of the merman, the veracity of Margaret's story. Confronted by her oceanic spouse expressing disapproval for her refusal to return to him, Margaret commits suicide.[15] However, the typescript version omits the merman's appearances altogether and presents Margaret's death as unexplained, not self-inflicted.[16] The audience, then, is left to wonder whether Margaret's fantastical story was a blatant lie, the product of some supernatural force, or the result of mental dysfunction. Clark, in sending out copies of the script, offers no clues as to which version he sent. However, reviews from the production at the University of Minnesota report characters in the typescript that are not present in the manuscript and their descriptions of the production, particularly the ending, indicate the typescript version.[17] Moreover, an article covering a staged reading of *Sea-Wife*, performed in 1985 at the behest of Anderson's widow, reports the play was written in 1926 and references the ambiguous conclusion.[18] Given this evidence it seems most likely it was, in fact, the typescript version that became the performance version. Thus, this analysis centers on the typescript as definitive.

Rationale

Whereas *White Desert* relies heavily upon frontier ideology, the presence of religion becomes a focal point in examining *Sea-Wife*. This distinction bears importance in that it demonstrates Anderson's sensitivity to how different facets of American life influence conceptions of marriage and gender roles. For while American marriages are licensed under the authority of individual states, religious ceremony is often viewed as an important legitimizing element. Critics of marriage in the 1920s often took aim at religion in their attacks. Bertrand Russell, for example, assailed religion as little more than superstition, asserted that adherence to religious law did nothing to guarantee morality, and criticized religious leaders for their condemnation of adulterous women, which he noted stood them in stark contrast to Christ's conduct toward such women in the Bible.[19] Judge Lindsey took a more practical point of view. Lindsey argued that marriage was little more than a "civil contract" into which Americans have applied a "pseudo-religious meaning." This meaning,

Lindsey asserts, represents "a thoroughly mythical conception, having no relation to the sociological reality" Americans face.[20] These criticisms correlate with a growing secularization of marriage noted by Robert and Helen Lynd, who reported a 22% drop in religious marriage ceremonies in Muncie, Indiana in 1923 compared to 1890.[21] Nevertheless, American culture remained largely Protestant in its religious temperament.

Sea-Wife represents one of Anderson's most innovative dramatic creations, combining elements of history, fantasy, and psychology. In contrast to *White Desert*, with its spartan five-person cast, *Sea-Wife* contains 16 characters despite its relative brevity. Shivers incorrectly identifies the play as a "one-acter."[22] Anderson divided the action into three acts. That the typescript consists only of thirty-one pages is deceptive in that the pages are double-columned.[23] Nevertheless, *Sea-Wife* is a short play despite its three acts structure. Anderson drew inspiration from Matthew Arnold's 1849 poem, *The Forsaken Merman*.[24] Arnold conveys his poem in the voice of a merman lamenting the loss of his love, the earth-born Margaret, whom he permitted to return to earth on Easter to observe her Christian religion. Once secure on land, Margaret ignores all pleas from the merman and her oceanic children to return to the sea, thus leaving them in anguish.[25] In *Sea-Wife*, however, Anderson inverts the plot, emphasizing the torment of the earthly woman over that of the otherworldly merman. The drama thus transforms Arnold's distinctly nineteenth century patriarchal theme into a story of feminine struggle reflective of the challenges faced by women of the early twentieth century.

Act I, Scene I: Damn the Women! They Drive You Mad!

While *White Desert* opened with the married couple contemplating their new life together, Anderson spends the entirety of the first scene in Act I establishing the atmosphere of the play and the back story of his protagonist. The action occurs on "an island off the coast of Maine" in the early 1800s.[26] As in *White Desert*, isolation becomes an important theme, though it comes with a twist. The sparse cast in *White Desert* coupled with the desolation of the prairie created a sense of Mary's prison as one of solitary confinement. In *Sea-Wife*, however, Margaret finds herself among the general population of an island crawling with people, most of whom are men. The opening scene establishes a host of secondary characters who gossip and speculate about Margaret before she ever appears.

Everyone seems preoccupied with sex and sexual propriety while also voicing convictions both religious and superstitious. The early part of the play echoes the reality of others, mostly men, judging and making decisions about women who are voiceless and unseen in society. It also begins to establish the oppressive impact religion can bear upon a woman's position in society.

The first woman we meet in the play symbolizes unabashed nonconformity to the island's social strictures. Biddy Stewart, described as "an earthy woman in homespun,"[27] represents a combination of superstition and worldly wisdom, an elderly woman who suffered branding as a witch decades earlier due to her promiscuous lifestyle. Having encountered two fishermen, Harry and Kenneth, at the start of the action, Biddy flirts with the former and antagonizes the latter with salacious gossip. "You're growing up handsome, Harry. I knew you would. Trust me to see it coming," she says before teasing him about having "to look out for the women from now on."[28] She then reveals Kenneth's affair with his own father's young wife, Hallie, before advising Harry to leave the island "and marry a clean, Christian girl with a sewing machine. It's a bad, evil island, and the women are sluts here, as treacherous as the water around it. A man's never any better than his woman, and he'll rise no higher."[29] Biddy establishes the island as a den of sexual iniquity and echoes religious ideals by contrasting the "clean" Christian girls of the mainland with the "sluts" on the island. Furthermore, she reflects the nineteenth century ideal of the woman as the moral center for man. Harry can never expect to rise to anything worthy in life if he fails to marry the right kind of woman. For his part, Harry reinforces the stultifying atmosphere of the environment: "If a fellow stayed away from girls and the sea he wouldn't find much to do on this island."[30] One critic called the play "neurotic and sex-haunted."[31] Anderson establishes those facets from the start. Far from a sacred act performed by two lovers in matrimony, *Sea-Wife* reduces sex to a mere biological pastime to kill boredom. In this respect, the play parallels Mary's assertion of the "natural law of sex" revealed in *White Desert*. The difference in *Sea-Wife*, as we shall see, derives from the impact of religion as a means of reining in this natural law.

Biddy also serves as an important female connection with Margaret. When Margaret's husband, Dan, enters we learn that Biddy nursed Margaret through the loss of an infant child.[32] Biddy reminds Dan that that event coincided with her first mention of the merman.[33] Whether the loss was a still birth or a death in infancy, the fact that Margaret lost a child establishes a profound sense of grief unique to women as childbearers. Furthermore, the death of her baby and Biddy's revelation about the merman brings into question Margaret's mental state. Did Margaret concoct her oceanic children as a means of replacing her dead child in her mind? Dan seems to take this attitude. He dismisses both Biddy's concerns and his wife's reaction to the loss, labelling Margaret as "out of her head" at the time,[34] thus echoing the common fact that women are not believed or taken seriously. Dan, however, was not present when the child died. Presumably he was out on a fishing venture. Thus, his knowledge of her state of mind comes after the fact rather than in the moment. His disconnection from his wife at a time of immense sorrow reinforces the idea of men and women existing in different worlds. Moreover, his questioning her mental stability places him in line with Michael in *White Desert*, who at times insinuated his wife was not mentally sharp. As Mary from *White Desert* was childless, Anderson emphasizes in *Sea-Wife* a different element to his female protagonist's struggle. Margaret would likely receive greater sympathy from an audience due to her maternal loss.

Anderson expands the maternal theme with the major subplot of the play, that of Kenneth's affair with his father's wife. Kenneth cryptically complains to Harry about finding himself "in a hell of a mess," which is "getting no better fast, but you can't do anything about it." When Harry inquires as to specifics, Kenneth remarks, "You're too young to know."[35] Though never stated outright, it seems likely the problem in question, which grows fast and permits no remedy, is pregnancy. Given the sensibilities of the time, it is unsurprising Anderson would avoid use of the word "pregnant." But from a playwright's point of view, if Kenneth has impregnated his father's wife, it would certainly intensify the dramatic stakes. Kenneth adds to the intrigue when he reveals that the only reason Hallie married his father to begin with was because "[s]he thought something was going to happen."[36] In other words, she incorrectly believed she was pregnant. In the previous moments of the play, Anderson depicts pregnancy as a source of despair through Margaret's loss. He follows that moment by representing pregnancy as a threat to both men and women. On the one hand, Kenneth's lust leads him to shaming his family through the appearance of a child. On the other hand, in believing she was pregnant, Hallie recognized marriage to Kenneth's father, MacQuarrie, as the only means of rescuing her from being ostracized or worse. Discovering she was not pregnant then left her legally committed to an older man she does not love. Such scenarios played a significant role in Lindsey's persistent advocacy of birth control in his companionate marriage model.

From matters of maternity the play next moves to enhance the superstitious theme. Hallie, along with her friends, Maisie and Nell, represent an independent attitude more in line with women of the 1920s than the 1800s. As she strides onstage with her cohorts, Hallie greets Kenneth and Harry with "Hello, boys,"[37] evoking the suggestiveness of Mae West more than the prudishness of a young nineteenth century woman. These three secondary women reveal Margaret's habit of walking along the beach late at night, presumably in search of the merman and her sea children.[38] Maisie adds that Biddy has corroborated Margaret's story, claiming to have seen both the merman and the two children walking near the water.[39] Everyone naturally considers Biddy a spurious source due to her previous branding as a witch. However, when Harry calls out excitedly that he sees a merman off in the distance, Maisie rushes to look and becomes indignant upon realizing Harry has pranked her. Anderson reinforces two impactful aspects of the play. First, the readiness of many people to believe even the most outlandish stories. Second, with the reference to Margaret walking the beach in search of the merman, Anderson further layers the questions surrounding her mental state and the veracity of her claims.

Having established the superstitious proclivities of the island populace, the play next evolves to the introduction of legitimate religion. Dr. Fallon enters with his friend, Corey, a visitor to the island. Fallon serves as minister at the island's only church and therefore represents religion as well as advanced formal education. Corey, hailing from the mainland and described as a "school-teacher,"[40] further symbolizes formal education with the added perspective of an outsider. Arriving on the heels of so much superstitious talk, these two men embody the only rational voices among the inhabitants. After brief pleasantries with the islanders, the two men talk among themselves regarding Margaret and the rumors swirling around the island. Corey expresses marked incredulity to the merman story with such interjections as "You can't be serious," "But really to believe an old wives' tale," and "It's an ancient belief, I suppose."[41] Fallon, on the other hand, takes a much more measured approach: "I can't make out whether they're serious about it or not…. In fact, it's only at certain times…when there's some excitement (sic) in the air, that any of them credit such ideas."[42] Rather than dismissing the beliefs out of hand, Fallon demonstrates his learning and reason by searching for an answer, perhaps mass hysteria. He also investigates the origins of the legend, noting that belief in mermen was common among other seafaring civilizations and seemed to be associated with fears of feminine promiscuity.[43] Fallon offers that certain behavior then reinforces the superstitious belief, noting the island's recent influx of promiscuity, even confessing having often heard, while walking along the beach at night, "muffled screams and prayers of the sort that bode ill to virginity."[44] Corey, the hardened skeptic, retorts: "These things happen on the mainland without the assistance of the gods of wind and water."[45]

The discourse between Fallon and Corey highlights the dissonance between America's enlightenment ideals versus its proclivity for vulgar, superstitious, and traditional ways. On a visit to Massachusetts in the 1840s, Charles Dickens complained, "Too much of the old Puritan spirit exists in these parts to the present hour."[46] Dickens further noted the incongruity of the "decorous and dignified" manner of the United States Senate juxtaposed with the presence of a spittoon for tobacco in the Senate chamber.[47] Historian Stacy Schiff notes an even starker example, pointing out that in July 1787, as the American founders in Philadelphia tussled over how to structure a reasoned government of the people, an elderly woman was killed in the street for the crime of witchcraft.[48] Anderson's juxtaposition of Fallon and Corey with the superstition of the islanders demonstrates a similar kind of incongruity. Anderson's use of isolation also becomes important when considering this theme of the play. Corey, coming from the mainland, embodies a different world whereas Fallon, though an islander, is shielded by his education. The islanders, however, represent Americans untamed by virtue of their separation from America's more enlightened values. Here we see a hint of Turner's frontierism present in *White Desert*. Turner famously argued that American character was shaped by a combination of its isolation from English refinement and its exposure to the wilderness. From the necessity of living on their own, Turner reasoned, Americans formed an identity grounded in an individual's will to derive order out of chaos. This order led, eventually, to the advent of the American Founders.[49] Fallon and Corey thus represent the civilized, enlightened character of America while those isolated on the island reflect a brand of anarchic self-determination elucidated by Turner.

Near the end of the first scene of Act I we have the character of MacQuarrie, who symbolizes what twenty-first century observers might describe as toxic masculinity. MacQuarrie enters with several other minor male characters all actively discussing what to do with adulterous women.[50] MacQuarrie establishes the tone of his character by making three things quite clear.

First, he hints at using physical force against his wife or daughter should he discover them guilty of promiscuity, proclaiming "there'd be Hell to pay" once he discovered the offense.[51] Second, he reinforces a long held double-standard in stating he would not punish a son for promiscuity because "I guess a boy's got to have it, sooner or later."[52] Finally, he unequivocally rejects the notion that his wife would cheat on him in the first place: "It hasn't happened to me yet, and, by God, it won't!".[53]

In MacQuarrie, Anderson effectively satirizes the nonsensical nature of the gender double-standard of promiscuity. MacQuarrie condemns loose sexual behavior among women while excusing it in men. He also takes special care to insist that his wife would never betray him. The audience, of course, already knows that Hallie is, in fact, engaging in an affair with one of MacQuarrie's own sons. MacQuarrie's reasoning would fault Hallie for her sin, but not Kenneth. Yet one imagines MacQuarrie would not dismiss his son's sexual indiscretions when those indiscretions happen with his wife. Indeed, MacQuarrie meets any suggestion of his wife's unfaithfulness or his own inadequacy as a man with intimidation. He even threatens an elderly man with physical violence when the man opens up about rumors of Hallie's infidelity and MacQuarrie's inability to perform sexually.[54] MacQuarrie's brutishness was evident in the Minnesota production with one critic summing up his character as "the town bully"[55] while another described him as "a sadistic hulk of a man."[56] With his first appearance in the play Anderson solidifies MacQuarrie as a man proactive in quelling resistance and accustomed to being obeyed.

The final major confrontation of scene one comes with MacQuarrie facing off against Dan over Margaret's honor. Through the course of the struggle, MacQuarrie reveals his obsession with Margaret. He plays to the superstitious culture of the island when he blames his recent poor luck in fishing (and Dan's recent good luck) on Margaret's promiscuity. Several times MacQuarrie rages with some variation of "damn the women"[57] as he fixates on Margaret's three-year absence from her husband, in effect globalizing Margaret's behavior as an individual to the behavior of all women as a whole. Dan rebuffs him at every turn and even knocks him to the ground when threatened. However, with the support of all the other fishermen, MacQuarrie resolves to force Dan and Margaret into a mock remarriage ceremony in order to revalidate their bond. To this threat, Dan remains as defiant as ever: "You can go to hell—and I'll see some of you there before you lay a hand on her or set foot in my place! My wife's my own! Yes, my house is my own!".[58]

Herein Anderson raises two significant points relevant to this analysis. First, the obsession with Margaret's alleged licentiousness speaks to the threat many men viewed in women's sexual liberation. Historian Lewis Erenberg has noted, speaking of the late nineteenth century, that women's sexuality was often thought of as "potentially anarchic and dangerous."[59] Writing of the 1920s, Lynn Dumenil observes that the New Woman was often blamed for the increased divorce rate and the decrease in religiously sanctioned marriage.[60] Groves hinted at this same point in 1928 when he asserted that the advent of birth control generated a "pleasure philosophy," causing marriage to devolve into "a sex union...devoid of social obligations."[61] Though Anderson set *Sea-Wife* in the early 1800s, the actual time period of the play seems irrelevant. As noted earlier, Hallie's entrance evokes more of a 1920s flapper. In fact, neither the play's language nor the behavior of the characters (especially the women) seems indicative of a drive toward historical accuracy. Anderson appears more interested in the events and culture of his own time than in an authentic representation of the early nineteenth century. The men perceive Margaret's alleged promiscuity as a threat, in part, because it might set other women to doing the same. Moreover, the men are single-mindedly obsessed with Margaret's sexual behavior. As one critic observed, "In the minds of the islanders' infidelity is the only possible explanation" for Margaret's three-year absence.[62]

The second major point Anderson emphasizes in this moment parallels the theme of marriage as akin to ownership so prominent in *White Desert*. Dan's defense of Margaret, though valiant, essentially equates his wife with home ownership. He will defend both because they belong to him. Dan seems reminiscent of Sverre from *White Desert*, who conquered Annie because of propinquity. Meanwhile, MacQuarrie's obsession with Margaret's behavior and his impenetrable resolve to root it out are reminiscent of Michael's need to punish Mary when he finds her less than the Victorian ideal of womanhood. The historical settings of both *Sea-Wife* and *White Desert* appear somewhat arbitrary for, apart from a belief in witchcraft, Anderson presents characters that could just as easily exist in the 1920s. In so doing, he effectively demonstrates that the strictures connected to marriage and gender roles and how those strictures oppress women are, unfortunately, timeless concepts within the culture of the United States.

ACT I, SCENE 2: IT'S SO BITTER A WORLD

Anderson contrasts the near frenetic pace of the first scene, wherein he introduces a barrage of characters, with a tone of tender intimacy at the outset of scene two. After so much said of her already, Margaret finally appears to give voice herself. Her voice, however, begins muted in domesticity. Her appearance, before she even speaks, reflects the painful isolation of a woman's silent suffering. Anderson pictures her in the cottage she shares with her husband. Her first action consists of setting the dinner table. Having completed this task, she looks out a window in expectation, then turns her attention to the fireplace. She watches the flames a moment, then kneels down and begins sweeping around the hearth. With her back to the door, Dan enters. The noise surprises her and she jumps to her feet. The stage directions thus paint a portrait of domestic drudgery; of a woman encapsulated by the duties of the home, devoted to a life of preparation for her husband's arrival.

Margaret's meekness further manifests when she speaks. In her first speech she criticizes herself as "a bad housewife," a critique Dan rejects.[63] She then describes losing track of time "between dreams and stopping to think… and I'll work and not think at all, and then I catch myself looking at my flowers or sitting by the hearth, and nothing done and you almost here."[64] Dan rejects Margaret's self-abasement, but he also further reveals the depth of her detachment: "You are always away somewhere/In your mind—and I don't mean much to you--/You don't care much for me—you don't even say no--/You've never told me you loved me."[65] While not explicit, one imagines Dan refers to Margaret's indifference to the couple's sex life. She does not refuse her husband's advances, but neither does she truly engage with him as a lover. Dan connects her emotional distance back to the loss of their child, labeling the islanders "evil" because "they don't understand you--/They don't know what it could mean to lose a child/And long for it--/."[66] Margaret stands in isolation not only due to the ignorance of the men, but of the women as well. The men pay no heed to her past emotional trauma because they feel threatened by her violation of norms. The young women fail to empathize due to their own preoccupation with sex and titillating stories about mermen. In fact, aside from Dan, Biddy is the only other person to empathize with Margaret on an emotional level. Even Dr. Fallon, despite his education and Christian morals, cannot grasp the emotional impact of losing a child. Biddy's presence with Margaret during her loss represents Margaret's strongest emotional bond, perhaps even stronger than that which she shares with her husband. Biddy's status as an outcast and her connection to Margaret further reinforces Margaret's position as pariah.

Margaret's detachment from Dan's reality emblematizes a woman's need to escape the mundanity of this world for something more fulfilling. This point was evident to one critic of the Minnesota production, who remarked of the play that "one may read the yearning of a woman to detach herself from the squalor and trials of [her] environment."[67] When Dan presses Margaret for more details regarding her disappearance, Margaret speaks to how separate gendered spheres suffocates feminine individuality: "Dear, you had your sea. You went to it every day--/But to be a wife here—to be a wife here alone--/Alone with pots and pans and a little house and the neighbors running in, and no more sea/...Making the bed and sweeping...it was more than I could bear."[68] Margaret confesses to sneaking out late at night to walk along the beach because the merman and her sea children called to her. However, the sea, though mystical and alluring, offers no freedom. Margaret complains the sea is "so bitter a world" surrounded by the "threat of death," but then later adds, "So is all this world,/Bitter and desperate and desolate/Save for the hearth-fires of one small earth here."[69] Margaret thus faces a catch-22. The merman beckons her return to a cold world where she would at least have her children while Dan's world offers the warmth of a love affair surrounded by the fiery hostility of religious bigotry. In 1920, poet Robert Frost pondered whether the world would perish by fire or ice.[70] Margaret, it seems, finds her world ensnared by both.

The coming of violence disrupts Margaret and Dan's sanctuary. Biddy arrives with news of MacQuarrie having literally taken the whip to Hallie upon discovering her infidelity (though he does not yet know the identity of her lover). Fueled by this humiliation, MacQuarrie resolves to give the same harsh treatment to Margaret, whom he believes the catalyst for all things ailing the island culture. He also demands Margaret and Dan renew their vows in the church. The couple, however, manages to slip out of the house just before MacQuarrie arrives, whip in hand, with a mob of other islanders, men and women.[71] Finding the home deserted, MacQuarrie remains undeterred. He dispenses the men to fan out across the island in search of Margaret. As they exit, Kenneth and Hallie stay behind along with Dr. Fallon and Corey. The fear engendered by MacQuarrie becomes even clearer. When Dr. Fallon inquires of Kenneth whether or not he intends to make a stand, Kenneth demurs. Corey suggests the pastor give in and officiate the mock marriage ceremony, to which Fallon agrees, thus exiting with Corey.[72]

Alone with Kenneth, Hallie reveals more of the true nature of MacQuarrie's brutality. She no longer embodies the carefree young woman she did in her first appearance. She now exudes a dark and bitter tone. Alluding to the whipping at the hands of her husband, Hallie challenges Kenneth, her lover, to protect her by escaping the island. Again, Kenneth demurs, which provokes Hallie to insult his masculinity, first dismissing him with "much good you are for a man," and then baiting him by asserting she would never abscond with only "half a man."[73] This last remark tips Kenneth's courage. He orders her to prepare herself and the children and meet him at his boat.[74] Here we learn another important fact about Hallie's marriage with MacQuarrie. When Kenneth tries to use her children as an excuse for not escaping, Hallie responds: "They're yours. I'm sure of that much about you."[75] This confirms earlier insinuations as to MacQuarrie's lack of virility. Thus, the figure in the play physically representing traditional masculine traits of strength and dominance, becomes symbolic of the patriarchy's ultimate barrenness. MacQuarrie lords over everyone with his self-righteous religious morality long after he has ceased producing anything meaningful himself. His "children" are, in fact, not his children. They are lies put forth to make him appear strong despite his sterility.

The final moments of Act I pose a faceoff between MacQuarrie and Dan in a battle over Margaret's fate. MacQuarrie and the others pour back into the cottage with Margaret and Dan in tow. MacQuarrie insists on holding a mock marriage to, in his mind at least, re-consecrate and re-legitimize Margaret and Dan's union. Dan, however, speaks right to the heart of this mock wedding:

> I can tell you why
> You hold my wife so hard. I've seen you look at her
> And lick your lips, and all the rest of you
> I've seen you look at her! The only use
> You have for beauty is to get your damned
> Claws on it, and tear it till you've dragged it down

> To your own level, and you can tramp on it
> And feel you've made it part of you!...
> You know it's the truth!
> You know what you want![76]

These fiery lines contrast the traditional sanctity of marriage with the raw power of physical lust. Beauty, purity, and virginity, concepts associated with womanhood and marriage, are here subsumed by the licking of lips and the tearing of claws. Sex becomes a primitive beast and women become objects for desecration and possession. Unlike in *White Desert*, wherein Anderson connects conquest with the mere circumstance of physical proximity, *Sea-Wife* poses men as hunters and independent-minded women as threats that must be torn down. The mock marriage MacQuarrie insists upon represents exactly that: a mockery. The men have no interest in forming a healthy, equitable partnership between a man and a woman. Rather, the men use marriage as a means of ensuring Margaret's submission to male dominance. Interestingly, MacQuarrie makes no reference to actual religious sanctity in marriage. Marriage in a church seems to represent little more than a talisman in his mind, as if the symbolic action of Margaret and Dan going through a ceremony will exorcise some evil infecting the island as a result of Margaret's errant behavior. Threatened with both whipping and branding with hot iron, Margaret still refuses to answer MacQuarrie's questions about the merman. Frustrated at her obstinance, Act I ends with the men hauling Margaret and Dan out of their home and toward the chapel.

Act II: They've Gone Forever!

In the opening of Act II, Anderson utilizes minor characters to achieve transition and further advance important themes of the play. Maisie and Nell arrive inside the chapel after hearing the bell ringing of the church sexton, an elderly man named Peter. When the young women discover Peter cannot hear their calls over the ringing, Nell dares Maisie to sneak up and kiss him on the cheek. She does so, much to his embarrassment, and the women enjoy a little light-hearted teasing of the old man. They learn from Peter than MacQuarrie will soon arrive for the mock marriage of Margaret and Dan. Peter returns to ringing the bell after which Nell makes a tawdry confession to Maisie, alluding to having recently engaged in an illicit sexual liaison. While this affair appears to represent a first for

Nell, Maisie makes it known, without a hint of shame, that she long since surrendered her virginity. Even though their discourse lacks explicitness, both women are titillated by speaking of sex in roundabout ways. This moment concludes with a lesson in how to gain a husband. Nell asserts that all men "want the bait without the hook"[77] and that permitting a man to "get away with the bait once or twice" lures him back again and again. Eventually the man grows "reckless," gets caught, and, as Maisie finishes it, "they lived happily ever after."[78]

As noted earlier, one of the key contrasts between *Sea-Wife* and *White Desert* lay in Anderson's exploring the complications children impose on sexual relationships and marriage. In the earlier play, children are never mentioned as Anderson focuses primarily on lustful desire, jealousy, and the notion of viewing spouses in terms of ownership. *Sea-Wife*, however, addresses the maternity theme in myriad ways and we see it here again. The idea of marriage resulting from conception rather than conception resulting from marriage is certainly not new. This point represents one that Judge Lindsey notes incessantly throughout *The Companionate Marriage*. For Lindsey, access to and education about birth control was crucial to remolding marriage to suit modern society. Earlier in the play we learn that Hallie married MacQuarrie only because she feared "something was going to happen," presumably pregnancy. This moment with Maisie and Nell takes the matter a step further. These young women are not discussing conception as an accident, but rather as a means to securing a man at the altar. In so doing, the playwright runs against certain notions of the status quo while simultaneously feeding others. On the one hand, Maisie and Nell represent young women of desire who possess both knowledge of and experience with sex. Such a portrayal flies in the face of the traditional ideal of women as inherently pure, sexless, and morally sound. On the other hand, however, the cunning demonstrated by the two women in weaponizing sex to trap men plays into the traditional notion of female sexuality as alluring and dangerous. That Anderson plays two sides of the coin here indicates the complexities of sexual behavior and marriage as they were understood (and misunderstood) in 1920s America. Moreover, Anderson's iconoclasm gains further accentuation by placing two women discussing lurid sexual relations in a church, thus emphasizing Christian hypocrisy.

The salaciousness exhibited by the women continues upon the arrival of three men with the discussion moving into anatomical references. One of the men, James, finds himself teased by Maisie about an ongoing affair with an unnamed female.[79] Embarrassed, James warns Maisie to "tend to your knitting," which spurs one of the most provocative exchanges in the play. Nell tries, ostensibly, to cool the tension with "Nothing torn that couldn't be mended," which Maisie follows with "No—I thought there was."[80] Clearly embarrassed, James warns the women to quiet down. Though again not explicit, Maisie seems to allude to the rupture of the hymen that sometimes occurs during a woman's initial bout of sexual intercourse. This conclusion is not farfetched considering the pervasiveness of sex throughout the play and James's embarrassed reaction to the comment. The women continue tantalizing the men by making subtle references to the church altar in terms of penis size. Ostensibly speaking of the altar, Nell says she wants "a bigger one put in." James replies uncertainly: "I don't know as you could get a bigger one in." Maisie, however, insists, "Oh, yes, any size." The stage directions indicate the women then look at each other and are unable to stifle their laughter.[81] Anderson pushes the envelope as far as discussions of anatomy and intercourse, but does so in a manner cloaked in creative allusion. Perhaps these provocative undercurrents represent part of the reason that, according to Anderson in his letter to Clark, some had found the play problematic for representation on the stage. In any case, Anderson intensifies his iconoclasm in relation to the Christian church, thus undermining the principal proponent of traditional marriage in the United States.

The play further emphasizes the tenuousness of religious influence with the arrival of Dr. Fallon. Fallon enters with Corey and the two share a brief moment of contemplation before the mob arrives. While Corey suggests Margaret invented the merman story to conceal an adulterous affair, Fallon argues Margaret's belief in her own story. In fact, Margaret's sincerity is so strong that both men confide that they almost believe her despite the tale's fantastical nature.[82] Whether *Sea-Wife* represents a true fantasy remains dubious, but the fact of the only rational men in the play lending credence to Margaret's claims suggests that she is not, in fact, conniving. In her own mind, Margaret believes she was abducted by a merman. Thus, if the play is not a true fantasy, then Margaret has clearly suffered some mental disturbance, possibly in reaction to the loss of her child. Furthermore, Fallon recognizes that the mock marriage merely serves to add a veneer of legitimacy to MacQuarrie's real purpose, which Fallon believes far more violent.[83] The Christian minister doubts his ability to sway the mob despite his spiritual authority. Fallon's doubt speaks to the power of sexual desire mixed with violence. The notion that an institution such as marriage could tame such passion, harness it, and civilize it appears little more than a fool's errand, particularly when society stifles education about sex.

Fallon's doubts are followed by the angry mob hauling Margaret into the church. Fallon seizes his opportunity as the officiant of the "marriage" to assail the proceeding. "This form means nothing," Fallon proclaims, "It may do no harm./It may do no good. It's a/kind of punishment--/A public shame you want them to bear to remind them/You don't tolerate unfaithfulness."[84] Though referencing a mock marriage, Fallon's words align with the sentiments of Judge Lindsey regarding actual marriage. Lindsey never tired of criticizing the strictures of traditional matrimony imposed by a hyper-moralistic church. The Christian church, Lindsey argued, rejected true religion in favor of spouting "superstitious poppycock."[85] While Fallon does not resort to such colloquialisms, he does reduce the ceremony to insignificance. Fallon next attempts to guilt the men by alluding to their own lascivious dreams, lustful desires, and illicit affairs thereby assuming a "judge not lest ye be judged" tack.[86] Thus, the play equalizes men and women insofar as expression of sexual hunger. To paraphrase Michael from *White Desert*, women are not different from men in the realm of lust. Both are equally capable of feeling and pursuing affairs. The difference lay in how these desires and affairs are viewed within society.

While Fallon's appeal fails to sway the mob from violence, he does extract one concession from the truculent MacQuarrie, who agrees to give Margaret a "trial" before condemning her. MacQuarrie installs himself as judge and inquires where she has travelled during her three-year absence. With the men threatening to lay a hot brand upon her breast, Margaret pleads that she could never explain her absence to their satisfaction. Significantly, though she admits terror at branding, she does not attempt to placate the men by telling them a story she thinks they want to hear. Rather, she asserts that "If you were to live/A hundred years and every year you came/To lay your brand on me you wouldn't change me."[87] Provoked, the men accuse her of witchcraft. Margaret rejects this assault: "No—NO! No witch but only/An unhappy woman, a woman unhappier/Than any you've ever known, broken and lost…I'll never know you and you'll never know me/And that is my only crime."[88] Margaret's poignant defense echoes the separation of men and women imposed by Protestant Victorian culture. While obviously not a witch, Margaret's position as a woman renders her something of an alien to the men.

The play demonstrates how the lack of exchange between genders stifles real understanding and empathy between the sexes. With power mainly residing on the male side of the equation, an unhappy woman has little hope of altering her condition.

Despite Margaret's appeal, the sanguinary appetite of the men takes hold. Finding themselves totally flummoxed by Margaret's response, the mob demands the branding iron, which leads Dan to vainly appeal to MacQuarrie's sense of reason. When this gambit inevitably fails, MacQuarrie presses Margaret again as to her whereabouts. This time, Margaret grows confused, stating she bears no memory of the event. MacQuarrie labels her a liar, dispenses with further questions, and calls for the iron as a means of forcing Margaret's memory. When Fallon objects, MacQuarrie sends his younger son, Harry, to bring Hallie, whom he believes has spoken with Margaret and will thus serve to offer testimony as to her guilt. MacQuarrie, however, does not wait for Hallie. He sets about with the branding iron, overruling Fallon's vehement opposition and even threatening the minister if he persists in objecting. Panicked under threat of the iron, Margaret begins recalling her experience as a dream: "I remember—It was a dream/It was a long dream—there were two children--/And they were beautiful...And I loved them."[89]

Here again we see the importance of children as Margaret's earlier loss of one child appears to result in her psychologically reimagining and idealizing two children. While focusing on maternity does not exactly set Anderson apart from his contemporaries, the manner in which he emphasizes it does insofar as it dramatizes a woman's suffering in isolation. Matthew Arnold's original nineteenth century poem centered on the merman as a jilted husband. Moreover, most plays written in the 1920s tended to view maternity in a strictly joyous light. In Frank Craven's *The First Year*, for example, the marriage becomes solidified in happiness with the advent of pregnancy.[90] By highlighting the grief in Margaret's maternity, Anderson emphasizes a struggle unique to women, foreign to men, and unusual for the stage at the time. As Margaret points out, the men cannot understand her. Her torture represents the sum of separate gendered spheres and communicates the abhorrent lack of civil discourse between genders. Anderson does not go as radical as Sophie Treadwell in *Machinal*, where the expectation of maternity in marriage leads Young Woman to bear a child she does not want or love.[91] However, Margaret's suffering, combined with her struggle over the impossibility of communicating that suffering to men who cannot or will not understand, underscores the rampant inequality American women faced in the 1920s.

A combination of chivalry, superstition, and jealousy ultimately save Margret from the branding iron. Just as one of the men is about to apply the brand to Margaret's breast, Dan breaks loose from his bonds and knocks the brand away. Just then a wind causes the bell to ring and the chapel door to swing open, thus giving pause to the men who suspect supernatural powers at work. Margaret plays into these fears by speaking toward the door, addressing the merman and her two sea children. MacQuarrie and his lot are genuinely frightened while Dan and Fallon work to convince Margaret that she is hallucinating. Finally, as MacQuarrie once again seeks to apply the iron, Biddy storms in and gleefully informs MacQuarrie that Hallie has escaped the island with Kenneth. MacQuarrie at first refuses to believe it, but Harry confirms Biddy's information moments later. Distracted by the trouble in his own house, MacQuarrie and his mob go out after Hallie.[92]

The end of Act II thus points up the power of primal thoughts such as superstition and jealousy. Dr. Fallon's rational appeals to the genuine Christian tenets of mercy, grace, and self-reflection bear no weight against MacQuarrie and his mob, but a blowing wind stemmed the tide of violence and the jealousy inspired by an absconding wife immediately redirected it. One critic rightly characterized Act II as "an inquisition."[93] A second critic took the matter even further, stating Margaret became "the target of merciless persecution by as foul a set of superstitious fishermen as ever were put on the stage."[94] The play's highlight of the ungovernable nature of human emotion echoes the problematic nature of many marriages. That is that people often enter into marriage to sate sexual passion. As that passion fades, so fades the principal bond that provoked the union. Jazz Age critics and moralists wrestled with the sex conundrum often in trying to reframe the marital institution one way or the other. Groves used this point in argument against the companionate model, stating that a marriage based solely on sex could not survive due to the couple's lacking other bases for connection.[95] Lindsey, on the other hand, often observed the dissipation of sexual passion as justification for the companionate model.[96] The play seems to suggest that if human beings are so ungovernable in their general relationships with each other, then the notion that society can govern something as intimate and unpredictable as sexual passion through traditional strictures of marriage represents pure folly.

Act III: Yes—One Can Believe in Death

The final act of the play opens with further emphasis on Margaret's isolation. The scene begins early the next morning back in her and Dan's cottage. Margaret enters and "walks blindly, as if asleep."[97] Moments later, Dan arrives thinking his wife is still in bed and startles to find her standing idly in the room. We learn that while Dan worked through the night to fix the sail in preparation for their escape, Margaret has walked the beach. She reports encountering the merman, who threatens to murder their two children if she refuses to return to the ocean with him. She doubts this threat, but as she pleads with him to allow her to remain on land, the merman killed first one child and then the other. It is important to emphasize that none of the action involving the merman appears on stage. The audience only learns of it through Margaret's report. Margaret characterizes this encounter as a "dream" and Dan reinforces her in this notion. However, she then insists that everything she reported about the murders seemed wholly true to her.[98] Dan struggles once again to convince Margaret that they must escape before MacQuarrie and his mob return to the island.

At this point, Harry, having slipped away from the mob, arrives bringing vital news. MacQuarrie and the rest of the men spent the entire night out at sea searching for Kenneth, Hallie, and Hallie's children. However, despite fervent efforts, they found not a trace of any of them. Harry informs the couple that the mob believes Kenneth and Hallie were lost at sea and, true to their superstitious natures, they blame Margaret for the tragedy. Harry warns Dan this fresh circumstance has rekindled sentiment against Margaret and that the mob intends to see its inquisition through. Finally, Harry confides that he, himself, saw two children lying dead on the beach. He was alone and by the time he returned with the other fishermen, the tide had taken the bodies away. Not having gained a close enough look, Harry suggests they were Hallie's children. Margaret, however, becomes convinced they were the bodies of her sea-children murdered by the merman.[99]

The play nears its conclusion with the reappearance of MacQuarrie and the mob. Margaret, now wracked with overwhelming grief, unbars the door, allowing the men access to the cottage, but the men halt in their tracks before speaking a word. Margaret, who once wavered at the threat of branding, stands defiant before them and demands they lay the hot iron "[h]ere on my breast and hold it till it burns/Into my heart."[100] She goads them to burn out her eyes and tongue as well. She blames herself for the loss of her sea children, whom, she says, died "[b]ecause I would not come."[101] As the men remain dumbstruck, Margaret lays forth perhaps the starkest, most heartfelt allusion to the radically different worlds of men and women: "You are afraid./For you there is no fire but fire, no sea/But sea. You will live long and never/Want to die. I would rather die in the sea."[102] In other words, once the men have done what they will with Margaret, they will all return to their normal lives. As a woman grieving the loss of children, however, Margaret can never exist in the world as she once did.

The final moment brings with it an air of mystery. Seeing the men paralyzed, Margaret draws a knife and threatens suicide. She prays "to a cold god—not yours—not mine" to strike her down. Dr. Fallon attempts to disarm her, but before he does Margaret simply drops the knife to the floor and proclaims, "He [presumably the aforementioned god] has looked at me, and I thank him!"[103] She falls forward and dies. One character notes the absence of blood and, upon examining the body, comments that Margaret bears no physical injury. Dr. Fallon then leans down to Margaret and confirms the observation. This observation is important in that it establishes a measure of clarity for the demise of Anderson's female protagonist. Margaret did not commit suicide. Suicide represents a common trope for sexually faithless women in nineteenth century and early twentieth century literature. Making plain that Margaret died mysteriously rather than by her own hand verifies her sexual innocence. In this respect, Anderson reinforces traditional expectations. However, in highlighting the suffering related to her maternity and the connection of that suffering to her death, the playwright focuses attention on an aspect of a woman's world grossly misunderstood and unappreciated by every man on the stage. Having confronted such a degree of superstition, Corey comments that "[t]his much one can believe in." Fallon then ends the drama: "In death? Yes—one can believe in death."[104] These final lines, uttered by the rationalists in the play, speak to the ultimate frailty of marriage and all earthly institutions created by human beings with the only certitude in life coming in the form of physical demise.

Conclusion: Of Strange and Peculiar Beauty

The few critics exposed to *Sea-Wife* tended to corroborate Barrett Clark's initial assessment of the drama as one of "strange and peculiar beauty." Critic of the Minnesota production, such as E. N. Pomeroy, labelled the play "an odd but interesting mixture of poetry and vividly incisive dialog; metaphysics and superstitious lore; realism, symbolism, and an ephemeral kind of lyric beauty."[105] Another Minnesota critic, John K. Sherman echoed these sentiments, finding the play "a strange and frequently strained amalgam of realism and tortured fantasy."[106] Yet another critical observer, Merle Potter remarked that the play "leaves the spectators groping about, blindly seeking an answer to many riddles."[107] A viewer for *Variety* commented on the stylistic marriage of fantasy and realism[108] while another reviewer noted this combination rendered the drama "frankly experimental" compared with Anderson's other work.[109] Likewise, a review of the New Orleans production in 1936 hinted at the challenges inherent in *Sea-Wife*, calling it "[a] difficult production for professionals to perform."[110] Covering the 1985 staged reading in Stamford, Connecticut, Alvin Klein characterized the play as "an unresolved mood piece rife with symbolism."[111]

In examining the critical response to *Sea-Wife*, one must not overlook the peculiar circumstances of said response. The reaction of critics of the 1930s was colored both by their perceptions of Anderson's previous work and by the change in social climate brought by the Depression. The critics tended to examine *Sea-Wife* with the hindsight of Anderson plays such as *What Price Glory* (famous for its gritty realism) and *Elizabeth the Queen* (noted for its florid historical verse).[112] These are the plays on which, by 1932, Anderson had built his fame. None of the critics mentioned Anderson's initial Broadway effort, *White Desert*. Indeed, given these critics hailed from Minnesota and Louisiana, it seems unlikely they would have seen *White Desert* or even possessed a great deal of knowledge about it. Furthermore, by the time these productions took place, the Great Depression was ravaging America, thus altering the cultural focus among the majority of the populace. With unemployment reaching 25% in 1932,[113] the economic crisis of the 1930s subsumed the marriage crisis of the previous decade. The Jazz Age must have seemed a distant memory to Americans struggling to survive.

However, when one examines *Sea-Wife* in relation to *White Desert* as well as with respect to the time in which it originated, stark parallels are evident. Stylistically there exists the potential influence of Professor Frederick Koch, under whom Anderson had studied at the University of North Dakota. As noted in Chapter 1, Koch emphasized folk drama centering on distinctly American themes as a means of propagating theatre throughout the country. As Anderson's biographer points out, both *White Desert* and *Sea-Wife* evince "a strong folk element."[114] Indeed, one critic categorized *Sea-Wife* as "folk melodrama."[115] It is difficult to fully assess the strength of a direct connection between Koch's teaching and Anderson's work. Nevertheless, there seems little question that in writing one play about life on the plains of North Dakota and another centering on the detriments of superstitious religion in New England, this nomadic son of a Protestant minister was writing about distinctly American subjects he knew well. One might deem these plays "experimental" in hindsight, but, at the time, Anderson's career as a playwright was, in itself, experimental.

Two particular critics of the Minnesota production offer potentially important insights into Anderson's conception of *Sea-Wife*. The critic for *Variety* (who signed only as "Rees") speculates that perhaps other reviewers extended symbolic readings of the play too far. Rees reports that Anderson "simply describes his drama as a 'social satire' which 'depicts the efforts of a woman trying to live without adhering to conventions.'"[116] Merle Potter echoed these sentiments in his review and did so with greater specificity. Potter acknowledges that reaching any consensus on the more profound meanings in the play proved elusive. However, he asserts, "The author's own explanation is that he has attempted to throw into sharp contrast the distrust of the ignorant for things they do not know and cannot comprehend, with ideas of spiritual significance."[117] This simple assessment is important for two reasons. First, it appears to germinate from direct quotes from or interactions with Anderson. But this assumption also generates an air of mystery as to how these Minnesota critics discerned their information. Potter indicates Anderson was present for the premiere, but Anderson himself reports to an acquaintance that he did not attend the Minnesota production.[118] Perhaps Anderson contributed a note to the production's program, but that seems unlikely given his distaste for being quoted.[119] Nevertheless, it seems unfathomable that two independent critics would quote a playwright without verifying the information came, indeed, from the playwright. Second, assuming this assessment did come from Anderson, it demonstrates how the play relates both to his previous effort, *White Desert*, as well as to the social climate of the 1920s. For both plays depict women trying to live outside the boundaries of convention, specifically outside the boundaries of matrimonial conventions and gender roles. In this sense, *Sea-Wife* stands very much in line with Anderson's Jazz Age drama. While both plays have historical settings and are written in often ornate language, those settings and language stylings are incidental to the primary aim, which is social commentary.

Most critics and scholars have commented on the fantasy elements of *Sea-Wife*, but this aspect also seems misunderstood. Granted, the 1924 manuscript places the merman on stage in front of Margaret and all the fishermen, rendering the verity of his existence within the world of the play unquestioned. The 1926 rewrite, however, which was the one produced, does not offer such on-the-nose fantastical elements. In fact, while inuendo and suggestion abound, there exists no physical evidence or indication within the world of the play that the merman actually lives anywhere other than in Margaret's mind. Such dramatic creativity may have resulted in unintended ambiguity for Anderson. Indeed, Potter reports a reception given following the play wherein a spirited discussion "developed as many theories as there were persons participating in the general discourse."[120] However, if one carefully evaluates the given circumstances within the world of the play, *Sea-Wife* appears less a fantasy and more a psychological drama with a satirical bent. While most commentators note Margaret's obsession with her sea-children, they offer little to no coverage of the loss of her earthly child. It appears most, if not all, of these critics were men, which may have disconnected them from the maternity angle. When one takes into account the severity of Margaret's delusions (assuming they are delusions as the script would indicate), the loss of her earthly child cannot be overstated. This interpretation, however, appears less than satisfying. Once again, Potter's incisive review offers keen insight. In his view, "Margaret...represents an aspiration for the higher things of which the merman is the symbol, while the unknowing mob speaks the language of bigotry." To turn Margaret over to "the eager attention of the psychologists" would be tantamount to obliterating Anderson's higher purpose.[121]

The depth and complexity of *Sea-Wife* as well as the vast array of characters place it in stark contrast to the spartan structure of *White Desert*. Despite Anderson's observation (and the observation of some critics) that *Sea-Wife* made for a difficult challenge to represent on stage, the play's complexity may have benefitted it in production. The benefits are most in evidence in Minnesota. One reviewer recorded that while observing the play "on the fourth night, with the temperature well below zero, the 600-seat theatre was nearly filled,"[122] which suggests word-of-mouth rendered the production a must-see for many despite the harsh weather. Moreover, Potter notes that while the audience was "confused and muddled," they were also "held fascinated by its power, its mysticism, and its poetic beauty."[123] It may be, perhaps, that *Sea-Wife* succeeded in Minnesota because, as some critics suggested, the production was given in an academic rather than a commercial setting.[124] But the framing of the message may have played a significant factor as well. Mary in *White Desert* represents an Ibsen-esque woman who learns exactly what she wants and actively seeks it out. Margaret in *Sea-Wife*, on the other hand, seems closer to a Strindbergian creation, a tortured woman who succumbs to human frailty. The pseudo-mysticism of *Sea-Wife* allowed Anderson to cloak his satire more effectively. Margaret acts less than she is acted upon and thus she never comes off as intentional in challenging social norms as does Mary in *White Desert*. This distinction may have rendered the former more sympathetic and therefore more palatable to a 1930s audience. However, Margaret is undeniably a victim of oppression at the hands of strict adherence to religious conventions propagated by patriarchal authority. Moreover, one could argue that her willfulness in facing down the mob and dying on her own terms represents a more powerful form of martyrdom than the case of *White Desert's* heroine, who is killed offstage while walking away.

A year after completing the rewrite of *Sea-Wife*, Anderson would achieve commercial and critical success with *Saturday's Children*. This prose play brings Anderson clearly into the realm of contemporary realism, thus severing himself stylistically from *White Desert* and *Sea-Wife*. But the theme of marital disharmony remains and, in fact, becomes even more pointed and openly provocative.

Notes

1. Manuscript located in the Maxwell Anderson Papers at the Harry Ransom Center. The University of Texas at Austin; Typescript located in the Billy Rose Theatre Collection of the New York Public Library.
2. Anderson to Clark in a letter dated 16 June 1930 in *Dramatist in America: The Letters of Maxwell Anderson, 1912–1958*, edited by Laurence G. Avery (Chapel Hill: University of North Carolina Press, 1977), 32.

3. Anderson to Clark in a letter dated 23 August 1930 in *Dramatist in America*, 35.
4. Ibid.
5. Barrett H. Clark, *Maxwell Anderson: The Man and His Plays* (New York: Samuel French, 1933), 30.
6. Ibid.
7. David Devall Mays, "The Group Theatre of New Orleans: A History," Master's Thesis, Tulane University, 1960, 38–39; A photograph of this production appears in *Theatre Arts Monthly* 21 (1937): 504.
8. Vedder M. Gilbert, "Maxwell Anderson: His Interpretation of Tragedy in Six Poetical Dramas," Master's Thesis, Cornell University, 1938, 19–20; also, a photograph from the production appears in *Theatre Arts Monthly* 20 (1936): 502.
9. E.N. Pomeroy, "Drama," *Minneapolis Tribune*, 7 December 1932.
10. John K. Sherman, "Sea-Wife Vividly Played by 'U' Actors in Premiere," *Minneapolis Star*, 7 December 1932.
11. *Times-Picayune* (New Orleans), 29 April 1936, quoted in "The Group Theatre of New Orleans: A History," David Devall Mays, Master's Thesis, 1960, Tulane University, 39.
12. Gilbert, 19–20.
13. Shivers, *Maxwell Anderson* (Boston: Twayne, 1976), 101–103.
14. Ibid., 101.
15. *Sea Wife* Manuscript. Maxwell Anderson Papers, Works. Harry Ransom Center. The University of Texas at Austin.
16. *Sea Wife*, Typescript. New York Public Library. Billy Rose Theatre Collection.
17. Pomeroy; Sherman.
18. Alvin Klein, "Anderson Play in Stamford Series," *New York Times*, 6 October 1985.
19. Bertrand Russell, "Styles in Ethics," *Nation* 118 (30 April 1924): 498.
20. Ben B. Lindsey and Wainwright Evans, *The Companionate Marriage* (Garden City, NY: Garden City Publishing, 1927), 192.
21. Robert S. Lynd and Helen Merrell Lynd, *Middletown: A Study in Modern American Culture* (New York: Harcourt Brace, 1929), 112.
22. Alfred S. Shivers, *The Life of Maxwell Anderson* (New York: Stein and Day, 1983), 6.
23. *Sea-Wife* Typescript.
24. Anderson to Clark, 16 June 1930, *Dramatist in America*, 32.
25. Matthew Arnold, *The Forsaken Merman*. Public Domain.
26. *Sea-Wife* Typescript, title page.
27. Ibid., Act I, 1.
28. Ibid.
29. Ibid.

30. Ibid.
31. Pomeroy.
32. *Sea-Wife* Typescript, Act I, 2.
33. Ibid.
34. Ibid.
35. Ibid.
36. Ibid.
37. Ibid., 2.
38. Ibid., 3.
39. Ibid.
40. Ibid.
41. Ibid.
42. Ibid.
43. Ibid., 3–4.
44. Ibid., 4.
45. Ibid.
46. Charles Dickens, *American Notes* (New York: Modern Library, 1996), 97.
47. Ibid., 161.
48. Stacy Schiff, *The Witches* (New York: Back Bay Books, 2015), 415.
49. Turner.
50. *Sea-Wife* Typescript, Act I, 4.
51. Ibid.
52. Ibid.
53. Ibid.
54. Ibid., 4–5.
55. Sherman.
56. Pomeroy.
57. *Sea-Wife*, Act I, 6.
58. Ibid.
59. Erenberg, 86.
60. Dumenil, 130.
61. Groves, 44–45.
62. Pomeroy.
63. *Sea-Wife* Typescript, Act I, 7.
64. Ibid.
65. Ibid., 8.
66. Ibid.
67. Pomeroy.
68. Ibid., Act I, 9.
69. Ibid.
70. Robert Frost, "Fire and Ice," Public Domain.
71. *Sea-Wife* Typescript, Act I, 10–11.

72. Ibid., 11.
73. Ibid.
74. Ibid., 11–12.
75. Ibid. 11.
76. Ibid., 12.
77. *Sea-Wife* Typescript, Act II, 1.
78. Ibid., 1–2.
79. Ibid., 2.
80. Ibid.
81. Ibid.
82. Ibid., 3.
83. Ibid.
84. Ibid., 4.
85. Lindsey and Evans, 232.
86. *Sea-Wife* Typescript, Act II, 4–5.
87. Ibid., 5.
88. Ibid.
89. Ibid., 6.
90. Craven.
91. Sophie Treadwell, *Machinal* in *Norton Anthology of Drama*, Vol. 2, 2nd edition, edited by J. Ellen Gainor, Stanton B. Garner Jr., & Martin Puchner (New York: W. W. Norton, 2014).
92. *Sea-Wife* Typescript, Act II, 7–9.
93. Pomeroy.
94. Sherman.
95. Groves, 65.
96. Lindsey and Evans, 265–267.
97. *Sea-Wife* Typescript, Act III, 1.
98. Ibid., 1–2.
99. Ibid., 3.
100. Ibid., 4.
101. Ibid.
102. Ibid.
103. Ibid.
104. Ibid.
105. Pomeroy.
106. Sherman.
107. Merle Potter, "Author Sees U. Premiere of His Play," *Minneapolis Journal*, 7 December 1932.
108. Rees, "Plays out of Town: Sea Wife," *Variety*, 20 December 1932, 46.
109. *Player's Magazine*, IX (March–April 1933): 14.
110. *Times Picayune* (New Orleans), 29 April 1936.
111. Klein.

112. Pomeroy; *Players*.
113. Terry A. Cooney, *Balancing Acts: American Thought and Culture in the 1930s* (New York: Twayne, 1995), 3.
114. Shivers, *Life*, 42.
115. Pomeroy.
116. Rees.
117. Potter.
118. See letter from Anderson to George Middleton dated 9 February 1934 in *Dramatist in America*, 44.
119. See letter from Anderson to George Middleton dated 1 February 1934 in *Dramatist in America*, 43–44.
120. Potter.
121. Ibid.
122. Rees.
123. Ibid.
124. Pomeroy; Sherman; Rees.

CHAPTER 4

Saturday's Children: Love Before Marriage

In Chapter 6 of *The Companionate Marriage*, entitled "The Chemistry of Love," Ben Lindsey leads with the true story of a young couple pseudonymously addressed as "Fred" and "Inez." The couple married at a tender age only to find that the ceremonial trappings of matrimony did nothing to sustain their love affair. Too young to file for divorce (both were under 21; old enough to marry in Colorado at the time, but not, apparently, to divorce) the pair sought out Judge Lindsey for an annulment. Once they believed the annulment complete, they promptly moved back in together and continued living as lovers. Lindsey, however, believing the marriage salvageable, held up the paperwork filing in case the young couple changed their minds. Inez became horrified upon discovery the annulment had not taken effect. She protested to Lindsey that while she and Fred could never survive matrimony, they were doing just fine as lovers. She demanded the annulment and if Lindsey refused, they would simply wait until they were of age and file for divorce. Lindsey counselled Inez that, from a practical point of view, the institution of marriage served only to protect the rights and welfare of any children resulting

---

An earlier version of this chapter appeared under the title "Love and ... Marriage? Maxwell Anderson's Advice to 'Saturday's Children' Regarding the Marriage Crisis in America," *New England Theatre Journal* 24 (2013): 13–31.

© The Author(s), under exclusive license to Springer Nature Switzerland AG 2022
F. D. Geary II, *Maxwell Anderson and the Marriage Crisis*, https://doi.org/10.1007/978-3-031-13241-4_4

from the union. She and Fred, therefore, could continue as lovers and hold up their marriage license to protect themselves from societal scorn. Lindsey reports, "Inez departed, quite happy over being able to eat her cake and have it too."[1] This arrangement represented, in essence, the crux of Lindsey's companionate model. It also reflected the social sanctimony connected with marriage that Lindsey so often derided. In 1927, Lindsey's real-life anecdote from Colorado might have been mistaken for the plot of a Maxwell Anderson comedy then playing in New York.

Rationale

For her 2005 book on the history of matrimony, historian Stephanie Coontz chose the apt subtitle of "How Love Conquered Marriage." Throughout the study, Coontz skillfully lays out the evolution of marriage with conciseness, demonstrating that the notion of marriage as a natural result of romantic love was not only rare prior to the nineteenth century, but almost unheard of. Marriage, Coontz points out, existed for myriad practical reasons, but love was rarely one of them. Rather, marriage as an outgrowth of love represents a distinctly modern invention born of the Victorian era and recognizing its full bloom with the progress of the twentieth century. Because marriage was not, contrary to popular belief, invented to consummate love, it often found itself in conflict with love relations.[2] In *Saturday's Children*, Maxwell Anderson directly confronts the dissonance between the expectations of institutional marriage and the reality of romantic desire.

Unlike *White Desert* and *Sea-Wife*, *Saturday's Children* achieved significant success in its time. The play's initial run went for 310 performances,[3] far exceeding most productions of that era. Though it failed to win the Pulitzer Prize, Pulitzer Board secretary John Hohenberg recalled the play as among "the wealth of glittering, professional material" on Broadway that season.[4] Anderson, of course, had achieved fame three years before in collaboration with Laurence Stallings on *What Price Glory*. His plays following that breakout hit, however, were largely unsuccessful by comparison. Each one of those plays (*First Flight*, 1925; *The Buccaneer*, 1925; and *Outside Looking In*, 1926) were either collaborative or adaptive and none of them focused on marital relations in the manner of *White Desert* and *Sea-Wife*. *Saturday's Children* thus represents the second major turning point in his theatre career, that being his first solo success. The play also re-centers Anderson back upon the conundrum of marriage, a subject he had clearly been preoccupied with just a few years before. In *Saturday's Children*, Anderson offers up a view of marriage, gender roles, and societal mores much more nuanced than his previous efforts.

ACT I: I WOULDN'T MARRY ANYBODY

The plot of *Saturday's Children* focuses on a young woman, Bobby Halevy, in love with a co-worker, Rims O'Neil. Bobby represents, in many respects, the challenges faced by the "new woman" of the 1920s: single, working, and independent minded, yet financially insecure. Similar to *Sea-Wife*, Anderson delays the entrance of the protagonist for dramatic effect, utilizing the first third of Act I laying the groundwork for her character and situation. Accordingly, the play opens with an extended interaction between Bobby's sister, Florrie, and her husband, Willy, with Mrs. Halevy, mother of the two sisters, occasionally interjecting. This approach permits Anderson to introduce the contentious nature of modern marriage marred by traditional strictures and foreshadows the coming conflict between Bobby and Rims.

Florrie represents something of a hybrid figure, embodying concepts of both Victorian and Jazz Age womanhood. The fact that she once held employment veers her toward New Womanhood. Many feminists in the 1920s viewed compensated employment as key to achieving equality with men.[5] Florrie held gainful employment as her future husband's stenographer before quitting her job and marrying at age 23. Soon after, she became a mother. The decision to cease employment following matrimony holds with societal conventions at the time, which allowed females to work in between high school and their inevitable marriage.[6] Employment statistics bear out this observation. In 1920 42.3% of women ages 18 and 19 were gainfully employed. That figure drops to 38.1% for women 20–24 and further plummets to 22.4% for women 25–44.[7] One historian observes that throughout the decade of the 1920s, only 10% of all married women worked outside the home.[8] Moreover, that Florrie found her husband in the workplace represents yet another way in which the culture of the 1920s was breaking away from that of the Victorian era. As historians John D'Emilio and Estelle Freedman explain:

The novelty of young women working outside the home threw men and women together in a variety of ways. On downtown sidewalks and streetcars, in offices, department stores, restaurants, and factories, and in parks at lunch hour, young men and women mingled easily, flirted with one another, made dates, and stole time together.[9]

Working women altered the dynamic of separate spheres. The concept of dating was born in the 1890s and solidified as the norm by the 1920s. Unlike a young man "calling" upon a young woman, the date offered meetings outside the home. This trend was spurred, in part, by the technological advent of the automobile, which increased mobility.[10] It was now not only possible, but socially acceptable for men and women to steal away in public without parental chaperoning. Thus, Anderson establishes Florrie very much as a woman of her time with regard to her work and marriage experience.

On the surface, the union between Florrie and Willy appears to manifest all the trappings of traditional Victorian marriage. The couple have a child together and Florrie devotes herself to the domestic sphere while Willy exists in the business world, functioning as sole breadwinner. By contrast with the Halevy marriage, however, Anderson presents a much more complex view of gender ideology and the strictures marriage imposes. When the play opens, Florrie stands in a seemingly submissive position, taking dictation as her husband rattles off advertisements from the newspaper. Florrie's first line and Willy's reaction to it, however, clues the audience to their antagonistic dynamic:

> FLORRIE: Wait a minute! Read slower!
> WILLY: Oh, all right.[11]

Willy does not assert himself, but rather acquiesces to his wife's demand. As the play progresses, we find Florrie mixing seduction and abuse, objectifying herself in third person, and then resorting to mild physical violence (pulling his hair) during an argument:

> FLORRIE: [*Loosening her hold*] And is it a good little secretary?
> WILLY: Sure thing.
> FLORRIE: The best in the world?
> WILLY: Best in the world.
> FLORRIE: Because it's very vain of its stenography, you see, and it thinks a perfectly good little secretary is being perfectly thrown away being wife and mother to such a horrid beast! It does think so.

WILLY: Don't I know it?
FLORRIE: Don't you know what?
WILLY: Don't I know it thinks so?
FLORRIE: [*With a ferocious yank*] And doesn't Willy think so?
WILLY: [*Climaxing with yell*] Sure I do. She's a love and a darling and hellcat and she can take two hundred to the minute and there ain't nobody like her! Now leggo.[12]

Though Willy seems cowed, Florrie's domestic tyranny does not endow her with any real power. Rather, she asserts herself more like a frustrated bully. This action illustrates Emma Goldman's contention that, as an institution of coercion, marriage creates an attitude of petty resistance in women:

Marriage guarantees woman a home only by the grace of her husband. There she moves about in *his* home…until her aspect of life… becomes as flat, narrow, and drab as her surroundings. Small wonder if she becomes a nag, petty, quarrelsome, gossipy, unbearable, thus driving the man from the house. She could not go, if she wanted to; there is no place to go.[13]

Florrie remains financially dependent upon Willy, which provokes a childish kind of rebellion in order to subdue him. In other words, her despotism stems more from fear than strength because if Willy ever took a mind to leave, she would be the one facing destitution. As one scholar observed, Florrie "represents marriage as a social requirement and a tyranny."[14] Florrie has accepted traditional marriage, but chafes under its bridle.

Mrs. Halevy reacts little in the play and when she does so, she serves as a representative of the old way of things. Silent for most of the repartee between Florrie and Willy, she finally interjects for the first time. The stage direction offers the adverb "vaguely" to describe her first line,[15] suggesting a disconnect between herself and the modern world around her. When Florrie jokes about running away with the ice man, Mrs. Halevy starts to admonish her daughter, but Florrie cuts her off and Mrs. Halevy does not speak again for three and a half more pages.[16] Mrs. Halevy's near silent, almost invisible, presence pervades until she exits later in Act I, never to return in the play. While her part may seem an underwritten throwaway character, she nevertheless serves a valuable purpose for Anderson's exposition. Mrs. Halevy personifies the traditional nineteenth century Victorian wife: submissive, ineffectual in matters of direct conflict, and wholly suborned within the domestic sphere. These qualities are reinforced later in the first act as we shall see.

Though they interact frequently in the early part of the play, Anderson depicts the relationship between Florrie and Willy as almost devoid of emotional love. We have already witnessed comic violence and antagonism from the beginning. Their further interactions in the first act reinforce the view of marriage as corrosive to passionate love:

> FLORRIE: Will he give his secretary a kiss?—Just like he used to when she really was his secretary and there weren't any babies or ice-men?
> WILLY: Come on, get it over with. [*He lets her kiss him.*][17]

This exchange suggests Willy displayed greater fervency in his courting of Florrie, but marriage finds him submitting to a kiss rather than seeking it. We see this same apathy moments later when Florrie again demands a kiss and the stage directions report "she kisses him," while offering no indication of his receptivity or reaction.[18] We have already witnessed Willy bullied into resignation and these displays of passionless affection serve to solidify his passivity.

For the first time, we hear mention of Bobby's arrival, which naturally segues into discussion of her situation. All three characters speculate as to Bobby's whereabouts, with Willy suggesting she may have sought dinner with her boss with aspirations of seducing him into marriage just as Florrie did with him.[19] This insinuation soon reveals Florrie's fixation with Bobby's love life. She openly worries Bobby may "drift into an affair" and confides she would "feel a lot safer about her if she was married."[20] The dialogue then turns to suitors, which leads to the first mention of Bobby's co-worker, Rims O'Neil. When Florrie discovers Rims will soon transfer to Argentina for his job, she laments Bobby's ill-luck, but takes solace in the fact that Rims could not afford to support a wife anyway. She changes tack, however, when Rims fortuitously telephones. Florrie seizes the opportunity and baits Rims into visiting Bobby that evening by falsely telling him that Bobby has a date with another man.[21] After the call ends, Florrie dismisses the inept protestations of her mother and husband: "I was just gambling. One last throw—Winner take all."[22] Florrie's likening Bobby's love life to a dice game, reminiscent of Mary's roulette reference from *White Desert*, symbolizes a woman's lack of control. Before Bobby even appears on the scene to exert her own will, others in her world have planned for her. In this way Bobby bears some resemblance to the heroines of *White Desert* and *Sea-Wife*, both of whom find themselves ensnared by circumstances.

Once Bobby arrives, we see evidence that she is, indeed, a new kind of female character unlike any Anderson had previously drawn. She confirms that she was, in fact, having dinner with her boss, Mr. Mengle. However, while Florrie probes to gauge the seriousness of this meal for Bobby's marital prospects, Bobby makes her distaste for Mengle plain:

> FLORRIE: Since when does Mr. Mengle take you to dinner?
> BOBBY: Ever since six o'clock and it's been a long time.
> FLORRIE: And his conversation was so charming you couldn't think of food?
> BOBBY: (*Vague and a little bored*) I hope he didn't lay himself out to be charming because I didn't hear a word he said.
> FLORRIE: Well, dearest, when you go to dinner with a man you ought to at least listen to him.
> BOBBY: I'll get him to say it over again sometime. He won't mind. If he does he can always fire me.[23]

Bobby evokes no romantic interest with her boss despite his apparent persistence, even if rebuffing him endangers her employment. A little later in the first act, Bobby alludes to Mengle making a "proposal," at which point Mrs. Halevy reveals that Mengle is already married. Bobby clarifies: "Oh, this wasn't a proposal of marriage. It was just a—proposal."[24] The obvious sexual implication and Bobby's stern rejection of it bolsters her standing as an independent agent. Bobby will not drift into a destructive sexual affair, as Florrie fears she might. Quite the contrary, Bobby emblematizes the bolder choices many American women were making in the 1920s. She works for her own money and resists sexually compromising herself to powerful, designing men. The staunchness of her attitude in this regard separates her from the protagonists of *White Desert* and *Sea-Wife* and firmly establishes *Saturday's Children* in the context of the cultural moment of the Jazz Age in 1927.

If the audience suspected that Bobby's fierce independence stemmed from sexual frigidity, she dispels that notion moments later. Florrie, with faux casualness, informs Bobby that Rims called while she was out. Bobby responds instantly at the mention of his name: "Rims? Rims telephoned?"[25] Her excitement turns to confusion when she learns Florrie misinformed Rims of her evening plans as a means of baiting him to visit.[26] She describes Florrie's pretense as "perfectly silly" and refuses to manipulate Rims or any other man: "If I cared enough about anybody to want to keep him—I'd care too much to want to keep him that way."[27] When Mrs. Halevy agrees, Florrie quickly shunts her aside, speaking to her almost as one would a child: "Mother, you never grew up a day after you were married."[28] Once again we see Mrs. Halevy's ineffectiveness at self-assertion. Bobby and Florrie espouse competing ideas regarding courtship and the battle clearly resides between the two Jazz Age sisters, not their Victorian mother.

Despite Bobby's initial rejection of Florrie's manipulation, she gives over her fate to a coin toss, which she loses, and agrees to change into a pink party dress as part of Florrie's design to woo Rims. This moment hearkens back to Florrie's reference to love as a dice game and women compelled to cede vital decisions to chance. Bobby's absence from the stage allows Florrie to expound upon her approach to courtship and marriage, speaking authoritatively to Mrs. Halevy, who concedes Bobby never accepts maternal advice:

> Use just the right touch and you can get her to do anything. You see, mother, she's just a child. There's a psychologist writing for the American that says people don't really begin to think until they're nearly thirty. They walk around and talk and they seem human, but they're really practically unconscious.... That's one reason why it's easy for a girl to get married young, and not so easy afterward. The idea is to catch your man while he's still unconscious. If he begins to think about it there really isn't any reason why he should get married at all. And so the psychologist says the only hope for a girl is to start thinking young and that's why girls have to be cleverer than men.[29]

The tonal shift from *White Desert* and *Sea-Wife* is palpable as Anderson exchanges the weight of historical verse for the bite of contemporary satire. Florrie's reliance on popular psychology from dubious sources renders her symbolic of Jazz Age culture. As one historian notes, the 1920s witnessed "a spectacular eruption of...efforts to popularize knowledge," most notably psychology.[30] Anderson uses this craze for popular knowledge to poke fun at the modern temper. However, Florrie's cast of young people as "unconscious" and her stress on the necessity of women requiring more cleverness also speaks to notions of gender inequality. That is, women need marriage and benefit from marital unions more so than men. Marriage represents, in Florrie's estimation, the only way in which women may procure financial security. Brooks Atkinson opined that Florrie "represents what is cynically known as the practical point of view."[31] Indeed, this dialogue, fairly early in the play, further separates Florrie from her seemingly helpless Victorian mother. Florrie understands marriage as a means to an end and utilizes popular psychology as the basis of and the justification for her motives.

The next action introduces arguably the most important character in the play other than Bobby and Rims: the father of Bobby and Florrie, Merlin Halevy. Anderson presages Mr. Halevy's appearance by the sound of the violent destruction of a radio offstage, which startles his wife and elicits her strongest protest in the play: "Good heavens! Merlin, what did you do to it?"[32] Mr. Halevy dismisses her concern: "Nothing." Florrie attempts to interject, but her father cuts her off, proclaiming he has demolished "the infernal machine that has wrecked our peace."[33] In annihilating the radio and dismissing the women's concerns, Mr. Halevy demonstrates patriarchal dominance and the animalistic fervor Victorians believed prevalent in the male. Mrs. Halevy, by contrast, manifests the civilized demeanor of the Victorian woman, metaphorically throwing up her hands: "I don't know what's come over you, Merlin. You're so sudden lately."[34] Mr. Halevy responds by once again asserting his masculine authority:

> Yeah! Toward the end of his life the human male, having learned there is nothing to be gained by gentleness and compromise begins to assert himself. You didn't want me to build a radio and I built it anyway. After I got it built I didn't like it so I smashed it. If you tell me to get another one I won't. If you tell me not to get another one I will.[35]

When Florrie suggests that, "It's best not to tell him anything," Mrs. Halevy again reinforces the stereotype of the passive woman: "Goodness knows I never tried to tell him anything."[36]

This moment concludes the single marital interaction between the Halevys. They remain in the room together for the next seven pages, but they never speak to each other again. Near the end of the first act, they exit separately and Mrs. Halevy never reappears. She receives only one other mention in the play. In the second act, when Mr. Halevy visits the newly married Bobby and Rims, he reports that his wife was too tired and stayed home to rest, thus reinforcing her frailty as well as her inextricable connection to the domestic sphere. Furthermore, at no point are we informed of Mrs. Halevy's first name, further subsuming her individual identity to her marital identity. In the Halevy marriage, Anderson dramatizes the emotional barrenness often associated with separate gendered spheres. The couple never exchange any terms of endearment nor does the script ever indicate that they kiss, hold hands, or even touch. With the Halevys, Anderson depicts a married couple barely communicative; the husband frustrated and the woman virtually anonymous.

Following Mr. Halevy's dramatic introduction, the plot returns to its main thread. Rims telephones and Florrie takes the call once again in order to continue her machinations. This time, however, Bobby is present. She rushes down, literally wrestles the phone out of her sister's grasp, and takes over the conversation on her own terms. Bobby informs Rims, without the slightest hedge, that she has no engagement for the evening, inferring Florrie, in effect, lied to him. She then assures Rims that she awaits his arrival, ends the conversation, and then turns on Florrie to reassert her own mind: "After this I'll answer the phone for myself, thanks."[37] Bobby vows not only to tell Rims the full truth when he arrives, but refuses to put on the pink dress. Tensions simmer even higher when Bobby learns that Florrie has arranged for the family (excepting Bobby) to attend a band concert, thereby insuring an empty house for Bobby and Rims. Bobby is indignant at her sister, but once again relents when Florrie reminds her of the coin toss.[38]

The dissonance between what Bobby says and what she actually does in the early part of the play cannot be denied in the early part of the play. Her vicissitudes might make her seem indecisive. However, her indecision is indicative not of weakness, but rather of both inner and societal conflict. First, Bobby's genuine desire for Rims as a lover provokes her need to snare him, even if her principles tell her otherwise. Second, as a woman trying to exercise self-determination in 1920s America, Bobby faces incessant pressure from all corners. The struggle no doubt becomes exhausting and, as we have seen, Florrie presents a strong, demanding character in her own right, though in a manner much different from her sister. Mrs. Halevy, of course, is too weak and absent to provide any firm motherly advice. Bobby, therefore, finds no feminine support in the room. The play shortly reveals, however, that she does possess the support of a man who proves her most powerful, if traditionally unlikely, ally: her father.

Mr. Halevy lingers on stage after the others exit for the concert, providing a moment wherein the audience sees from whom Bobby inherited (or learned) her independent mind. Having observed something amiss in her behavior, Mr. Halevy calls Bobby in and inquires after her well-being.[39] When Bobby offers a half-hearted response, he exhorts her: "Well, be yourself, girlie. Don't let anybody run over you."[40] He then advises her not to "do anything I wouldn't do." When Bobby says, "Tell me something you wouldn't do," he definitively replies, "Not a damn thing I didn't feel like doing."[41] Not only does Mr. Halevy affirm his rebellious nature seen earlier with the destruction of the radio, but he imparts that rebellious nature upon his youngest daughter. Interestingly, he never interacts in such a way with Florrie at any point in the play. In fact, he barely interacts with Florrie at all. Anderson thus aligns Bobby closer to the traditionally masculine temperament. Despite Mr. Halevy's usage of the demeaning term "girlie," he nevertheless imbues Bobby with an independence of mind, which we already see budding in the first act and which will flower to full bloom toward the end of the play.

Upon Mr. Halevy's exit, Florrie re-enters the scene to coach her sister on coaxing Rims into a marriage proposal. Bobby reveals for the first time that she is, in fact, in love with Rims, but believes his acceptance of a job in South America proves her love unrequited.[42] Bobby's confirmation of love, however, serves to fuel the game for Florrie. She insists Bobby could have Rims if only she was willing to "tease him—till he was wild."[43] Similar to Maisie and Nell from *Sea-Wife*, Florrie implies she would deploy sexual manipulation to entrap Rims, but Bobby flatly refuses to engage in any such dishonesty: "I like him too much to cheat him into anything."[44] Bobby's reasoning once more speaks to her sense of individual freedom. If Rims wants South America more than he wants her, then nothing should impede his choice. However, Florrie's devotion to the courtship and marriage game wins the moment. She feeds Bobby a set of lines to say when Rims arrives, even going so far as to write the script down in a notebook. Bobby finds the scenario, which requires her to cry at one point, ludicrous. For one thing, she insists that tears are not something she ever resorts to and, for another, she does not believe Rims would fall for such a foolish, obvious setup.[45]

Act I ends with the encounter between Bobby and Rims in what one could describe, given Florrie's efforts at direction and scriptwriting, as something of a play within a play. Anderson establishes this moment as akin to a fantasy with Bobby in her presumably sexy pink party dress awaiting the arrival of her gallant beau. The fantasy image receives reinforcement when Rims enters and finds himself struck by her appearance: "Flaming youth! Bobby, you're a dream in that! Stand still and let me gaze at you!"[46] Rims's use of the phrase "flaming youth" almost certainly refers to the popular and controversial 1923 film of the same name, which was noted for its racy portrayal of the flapper.[47] The use of that phrase combined with Rims' immediate command for Bobby to display herself serve to both sexualize and objectify her. Anderson's depiction of courtship as a fantasy presages romance's ultimate collapse under the reality of marriage. This moment also supports the traditional notion of men as consumers of sex while women use it as a commodity to gain male attention. Whatever plan Rims had before he arrived, Bobby's striking appearance immediately throws him off-balance, giving her the advantage in Florrie's constructed scenario.

Though Bobby takes a moment to indulge Rims, she soon discovers the pitfalls of mixing fantasy with reality. She confirms that, contrary to what Florrie said, she did not have a date that night, but Rims condescends her: "You're a poor liar, kid...."[48] She attempts to tell him the truth, but he reasons she would not have dressed up unless she intended to go out. Seeing the truth as helpless, Bobby decides to play along and baits Rims into thinking that not only did she have a date, but that she has not officially broken it off. As the scene proceeds, Bobby finds herself more and more carried away by the moment. She and Rims reminisce about all their dates around the city. The script never explicitly indicates any of these dates resulted in sexual encounters. However, one could certainly take the implication of a sexual affair. For example, Rims comments of their relationship "it was certainly a nice Spring while it lasted" to which Bobby replies, "The best I ever had, Rims."[49] Spring, of course, has long been associated with youth and sexual renewal. Moments later, Bobby says she will send Rims postcards "with an X to mark the spot" of their dates. Rims replies, "Which spot, though? The route's sprinkled with 'em."[50] This assertion implies the couple made their way around various parts of the city. Whether they were seeing the sights or engaging in sexual interludes is left to interpretation.

Despite all efforts at resistance, Bobby discovers she simply cannot resist the allure of a relationship with Rims. She finds herself falling into Florrie's script, surreptitiously reading the lines off the page. Moreover, Rims responds to each line in exactly the manner Florrie anticipated. The final straw lands when Bobby, following Florrie's script to the letter, tells Rims she plans to marry someone else because "a girl's got to get married sometime"[51] and "I don't want to go on working forever."[52] Rims is taken aback:

RIMS: I see. Yeah, I see. I didn't know you felt that way.
BOBBY: [Breaking away] Well, I don't, really. I was just—I was just joking. You'd better go, dear. I wouldn't marry anybody. I wouldn't marry—anybody.
   Not even you.
RIMS: You wouldn't?
BOBBY: No, I wouldn't!
RIMS: Oh, yes, you will. I mean—
BOBBY: Do you want me to?
RIMS: Sweetheart—I don't want anything else. [They kiss.]
BOBBY: [Breaking away and crying on his shoulder] But you're—you're going to South America—
RIMS: [Still holding her] South America can go to the devil—! Somebody else can go to South America![53]

Bobby recognizes, too late, the danger of what she has done and tries to backtrack. Even Rims, with his "I mean," hesitates right after he declares his intention of marriage. The physical attraction they feel for one another, however, proves too strong to deny in that moment. Rims forsakes his career advancement in South America and Bobby surrenders her independent spirit in order to legitimize their sexual hunger under an institutional umbrella. Bobby's attempted resistance only to succumb to Florrie's script is reminiscent of Mary in the prologue of *White Desert* openly remarking on the paradox of what marriage meant for women: the forfeiture of personal freedom that women somehow accept with enthusiasm. Yet enthusiasm is not really what either Bobby or Rims display. The hesitations Anderson injects in the dialogue bespeak to uncertainty and their actions are born more from impulsivity than ardor. Bobby finds herself swept away in the play Florrie stage managed, which represents a microcosm of how society constructs rules, scripts, and standards for engagement between men and women that rapidly move beyond an individual's control.

Act II: You Can Wash Your Own Dishes!

Helene Cixous has written in depth upon the tropes of classic fairy tales. The women of these stories are typically passive, awaiting in sleep the arrival of the male prince. "Then," Cixous writes, "he will kiss her. So that when she opens her eyes she will see only *him*; him in place of everything, all-him.... He leans over her...Cut. The tale is finished. Curtain."[54] Such fairy tale yarns as *Snow White* and *Sleeping Beauty* end in marriage with the assumption of "happily ever after." The day after the honeymoon and everything that follows is conveniently omitted. Cixous argues that once the awakening happens "the voluptuous simplicity of the preliminaries would no longer take place."[55] Anderson, in effect, gives the audience the morning after the fairy tale. Act I ends in the fulfillment of a fantasy with Bobby in a beautiful dress, caught in her lover's embrace after having secured him by acting out a generic, contrived script. Act II opens with reality cascading over the newlyweds in a deluge that starkly alters the mood. The title of the play presumably stems from an old nursery rhyme dating back to the nineteenth century, which assigns attributes to children based on the day of the week they were born. As the rhyme goes, "Saturday's child works hard for a living." Accordingly, in Act II, we see Bobby and Rims struggling to survive and that struggle erodes any semblance of marital bliss.

Anderson accentuates the loneliness of married women at the outset of the second act. Bobby stands by herself in the kitchen. Rims, offstage, bellows to her that he cannot find his pipe cleaners.[56] This image bears a marked contrast from the blissfulness concluding the first act. By placing Bobby in the kitchen, a traditional venue for women, physically separated from her husband and enduring his complaints, Anderson paints the picture of marriage as both enervating to passion and a prison for the woman. When Rims enters, the argument progresses from pipe cleaners to the absence of pipe tobacco and then to the paucity of cigarettes in the house.[57] Throughout these moments we see Bobby trying as best she can to placate her cranky husband. Petty arguments over nicotine represent the beginning of the domestic snowball growing throughout the act as Anderson builds to the dramatic climax of the play. Soon the argument graduates from cigarettes to what will prove a most significant marital strain: money.

The discussion of finances quickly reveals the responsible member of the marriage. Bobby cajoles Rims into sitting down for a fiscal review of their household income and expenses. A rift develops when Bobby learns Rims has been squandering money through gambling in card games. Rims demeans his wife, calling her "kiddie," and evades the realities with a flippant attitude, which infuriates Bobby. "Rims, you idiot! If you don't take me seriously I'll never—never—You can take care of your own dirty old money! I can earn some for myself!"[58] This threat puts Rims back on his heels and he immediately tries to smooth things over. As the argument progresses, Rims points out that Bobby has made a mistake in her figures. She erroneously figured he made $60 a week, which amounted to $240 a month. But in reality, he makes only $40 a week. This miscalculation brings the direness of their fiduciary circumstances into crystal clarity. Their monthly expenses amount to $174. Rims only making $140 per month renders the budget impossible.[59]

This section of the play reflects an authenticity contrary to the mythology surrounding the so-called "roaring twenties." Despite the decade's historical reputation for unprecedented economic prosperity, historian Richard H. Pells reports that ordinary Americans did well to survive in the late 1920s, with little money left after paying the bills.[60] The economic boom for which the decade is so famous centered on an explosion of corporate profits, which "were never adequately rechanneled into private investment, higher wages, or fuller employment" with the end result being that most Americans lacked "purchasing power."[61] Moreover, despite the advances of women by the 1920s, the traditional roles of male breadwinner and female domestic remained prevalent. In 1924, Elsie Crews Parsons noted that "where income permits, the wife continues to be the consumer, the husband the producer."[62] But while Parsons limits the traditional dynamic only to when "income permits," Anderson depicts its persistence whether income permitted or not.

With their fiscal inadequacy all too clear, the struggle segues into solution-seeking, which brings to fore yet another aspect of the societal pressures generated by marriage. Bobby suggests she return to work. Act I revealed that her salary was equal to his.[63] Doubling their household income would more than allow them to live comfortably. Rims, however, despite his frivolous gambling habits, despite the evident economic crisis they face, will not hear of his wife returning to the workforce.

BOBBY: .... I wish I hadn't quit my job.
RIMS: Well, we both couldn't work in the same office after we got married. It doesn't go somehow.
BOBBY: It would have been embarrassing, but—it wouldn't really matter.
RIMS: Well, I'd mind if you didn't. It would make it look as if I weren't man enough to—to support my wife.
BOBBY: How I hate that word.
RIMS: What word?
BOBBY: Wife! I won't be a *wife*! It sounds so fat and stupid! I wish we hadn't *got* married! I wish you'd gone to South America.[64]

While Rims may not appear sympathetic from Bobby's point of view, Anderson's critique reveals that he, too, finds his individuality suppressed by the prevailing culture. Societal pressure demands that he alone take on the financial responsibility for the household. Rims' plaintive line about married couples not working in the same office because "it doesn't go somehow" reflects the blind adherence to tradition. He never offers a practical reason why Bobby should not work. He only knows that such an arrangement is impossible "somehow."

In having Bobby reject the title of "wife," the play depicts a burgeoning revolutionary spirit in the young woman. For no matter what disadvantages Rims may endure under the title of "husband," Bobby suffers far more under the title of "wife." Moreover, Bobby's outright denunciation of "wife" clearly separates her from Anderson's previous heroines. Neither Mary from *White Desert* nor Margaret from *Sea-Wife* came close to leveling such a pointed assault on the institution of marriage. Furthermore, most female characters in mainstream Broadway successes of the 1920s, such as *Anna Christie*, *The First Year*, and *They Knew What They Wanted* tended to embrace marriage as a remedy for all their ills.

After this explosive moment, tempers cool as both recognize the strain placed upon them by their marital union. Whereas one might assume with the Halevys, and even with Florrie and Willy, that the emotional disconnect occurred gradually over the course of some years, Anderson renders the emotional gulf as evident almost from the words "I do." Once lovers, Bobby and Rims are now just regular married people:

BOBBY: [*Looking up at him*] Darling, you do love me, don't you?
RIMS: Honest, kid, nobody ever loved anybody the way I love you. I'm just silly about you. I think about you all day long. And then I come home at night and—[*He turns away*] we get into some goddam mess—and it just shoots the works—
BOBBY: I know. It's just the same with me. I think all day how marvelous it's going to be when you come home—and then you get here—and I don't know—it isn't marvelous at all—It's just a house and we're just married people—and sometimes I hate it—everything's getting spoiled—.[65]

The trouble, therefore, between Bobby and Rims lies not in a lack of feeling, but rather in the conventions they feel they must adhere to as a married couple. In one of his own critiques of marriage, Floyd

Dell argued that "conventions are...inevitably a shackle upon the free motions of the soul, being imposed by fear."[66] The attraction between Bobby and Rims has not abated, but rather stagnated under the weight of convention.

With the walls metaphorically closing around them, Bobby retreats into the only realm offering happiness: fantasy. She openly daydreams with Rims about being married to someone else so she could have Rims as a lover. Rims indulges her somewhat and begins enjoying the fantasy a little himself. Their momentary bliss evaporates, however, when they revert to arguing about money, which leads back to the sticky situation of Bobby regaining employment. Rims implies Mengle only wants to make sexual advances and fears Bobby might allow it. In his most authoritarian moment in the play, Rims forbids Bobby returning to work. Bobby, however, stands firm against him, stating frankly that she will act as she sees fit.[67] Knowing Mengle invited Bobby to dinner to discuss her return to the office, Rims orders her not to go, to which Bobby responds: "I didn't intend to go to dinner with him, but if you say you won't let me I certainly will."[68] Here Bobby summons the anarchistic spirit of her father, who earlier proclaimed he would behave opposite any directive from his wife regarding the destroyed radio. Anderson endows Bobby with qualities traditionally masculine in character. That Anderson spells Bobby's name with the traditionally masculine "y" rather than the usually feminine "ie" underscores this facet.

The argument reaches stalemate when Florrie and Willy arrive unannounced and Bobby, at her wits end, seeks advice from her sister. With the men out of the room, Florrie mentions overhearing the dispute between the newlyweds. Hungry for gossip, she presses her sister for details and Bobby confides both her fear of losing Rims and her refusal to stay with him just because marriage demands it.[69] Florrie then suggests her remedy: "I think it's time for you to begin having a baby."[70] This advice seems patently absurd, particularly given the couple's financial hardship. Moreover, Florrie blatantly states that women only have babies in order to make themselves important to men, once again mirroring Maisie and Nell from *Sea-Wife*. Bobby is appalled by this sentiment: "But that's terrible.... To keep a man that way."[71] Florrie continues pressing the point, even outlining, as she did with the proposal at the end of Act I, the scenario necessary to lure Rims into accepting a pregnancy. Florrie's advice only serves to make Bobby more miserable and her indecisiveness returns.[72]

The arrival of Mr. Halevy hastens Florrie's exit and from her father Bobby receives the most honest and radical counsel. Many critics in the 1920s upheld the Victorian standard of the patient, sexually innocent wife. Moreover, such observations were not limited to those of men. One female advice columnist warned that marriages often suffer because women mistakenly seek "perpetual lovers" as opposed to "husbands,"[73] a stance that echoes Groves's warning about society succumbing to a "pleasure philosophy," but that is antithetical to progressives such as Judge Lindsey. When Bobby confides her trouble to her father, Mr. Halevy challenges conservative attitudes by suggesting that "Don Juan and Casanova chose the better part."[74] Bobby retorts, "Yes, I suppose that's true if you're a man, but I'm not."[75] Mr. Halevy then offers perhaps the most radical observation in the play. In response to what fathers think about having daughters he asserts:

> MR. HALEVY: Well, they [fathers] think—when they think about it—here I have two good-looking virtuous girls, and I'm putting in my whole life raising them up, feeding them, sending them to school—and for what? All for the service and delight of two unknown and probably disagreeable young men. So I used to wish I had sons, because they could have a good time at any rate. And then it occurred to me there was no reason why girls shouldn't have a good time.
> BOBBY: How do you mean?
> MR. HALEVY: Fall in love—have your affair—and when it's over—get out!
> BOBBY: Oh![76]

This exchange may have been, in part, what drew the venom of some conservative critics. Euphemia Van Rensselaer Wyatt complained that Anderson treated marriage as nothing more than "the legalizing of youthful passion."[77] R. Dana Skinner may have had Mr. Halevy's advice in mind when he criticized the play for "moments of brutal and quite unnecessary frankness in the dialogue."[78] Critic David Carb seemed to take a more moderate tone. Carb reported enjoying the play on the whole, but specifically objected that Mr. Halevy's advice "belongs in a different kind of play, if anywhere."[79] Barrett H. Clark, on the other hand, refuted the conservative criticism by describing Mr. Halevy's "words of wisdom" as "both just and delightful," recognizing that they were "wholly subversive of public morality."[80] This sampling of the critical reaction reveals that *Saturday's Children* was, at least to some extent, recognized as flying in the face of propriety at the time it appeared. That Clark, a man, applauded a woman subverting sexual standards while Wyatt, a woman, condemned it, reflects the topsy-turvy nature of the cultural moment Anderson was observing. Then again, one could argue that Clark and Wyatt both support the status quo; Clark delights in the baser male instincts while Wyatt defends feminine purity. Such nuance and, in some cases, dissonance were part and parcel regarding marriage and gender identity in Jazz Age America.

Bobby's "Oh!" indicates she is clearly shocked by her father's discourse, but still she struggles with the incongruity of love affairs and marriage. When Bobby asks why someone cannot have a love affair within a marriage, Mr. Halevy reiterates his decidedly unsentimental view of the institution:

> Marriage is no love affair, my dear. It's little old last year's love affair. It's a house and bills and dishpans and family quarrels. That's the way the system beats you. They bait the wedding with the romance and they hang a three-hundred-pound landlord around your neck and drown you in grocery bills.[81]

Anderson portrays the "system" and "they" as an invisible, conspiratorial, and omniscient force that drives young couples into accepting prevailing cultural doctrines. His characterization of the system mirrors Henry David Thoreau's lament, "wherever a man goes, men will pursue and paw him with their dirty institutions, and, if they can, constrain him to belong to their desperate odd-fellow society."[82] Joseph Wood Krutch seemed to recognize this idea when he wrote that Anderson "has envisaged frankly the fact that marriage and children and the humdrum life of the family is not what most lovers want, and no mere facile sentiment is enough to reconcile them to the fact that the stability of society requires that is what they shall get."[83] In effect, Anderson identifies "the stability of society" as the problem.

Mr. Halevy's radicalism does not stop with sexual mores. He also takes his shot at gender inequality in the workforce. Finding his daughter in such economic distress, he challenges tradition by pointing out Bobby's pre-marriage salary: "Why should he support you? You're his economic equal.... Yes, and if you had gone on working and he didn't support you, why take his name and label yourself? I don't see it."[84] Born in the nineteenth century and reaching maturity under the auspices of solid

Victorianism, Mr. Halevy nevertheless speaks in favor of the rights of a young woman to seek financial independence rather than marriage. Such rhetoric from a middle-aged male character once again shows Anderson subverting convention. In 1925, for example, Ruth Miller was just one social critic who complained that American men were lost in the nineteenth century regarding their attitudes about marriage.[85] In a sense, Mr. Halevy represents both society in transition and the power the prevailing culture continues to wield. He chose the Victorian mode for himself, but, perhaps regretting that choice, he welcomes the radicalism of the early twentieth century.

When Bobby finds herself alone with Rims again at the end of Act II, she once more confronts him about their marital troubles. At first, the discovery that Rims recently won money gambling only to lose more than he won in a different gambling venture exacerbates the already fraught tension between them. Rims kept these transactions secret because, as he puts it, "I am not used to telling anybody everything."[86] He resents what he perceives as Bobby's intrusion: "You think you've got a mortgage on everything I get."[87] Bobby attempts to placate him and when he recognizes the impact of his outburst upon her, he softens: "You know, I haven't anything against you—only I'm just not used to it, that's all....I'm the earning end and you're the paying end and we've got to work together. Only it comes kind of hard...."[88] Bobby plaintively replies, "It surely comes hard to me, Rims."[89] Overwhelmed by their troubles, Bobby seeks comfort in his embrace. In this tender moment, Bobby, almost reflexively, resorts to Florrie's playbook. She gently suggests they have a baby. However, when she apprehends this manipulation working on him, she dramatically alters course. She confesses not only that the pregnancy suggestion was a ploy, but also that she finagled him into marriage in the first place.[90]

Bobby's admission spurs the dramatic climax of the play, thus producing, arguably, Anderson's strongest stand against institutional marriage. Inflamed by Bobby's revelation, Rims goes on the attack.

> RIMS: Listen, kid—I think we're going to have a showdown right here and now! A fellow gives up a lot when he gets married. As long as he's single, he owns the earth, but when he's married his money's not his own, his time's not his own, he's got to keep on working whether he wants to or not, and there's hell to pay if he spends an extra dime.

Whenever I tired of my job I used to quit—if I didn't like one town I tried another—and now I can't—
BOBBY: Why not?
RIMS: Because I've got a wife—because I've got a family?
BOBBY: Good God—Am I a family? I won't be a wife—I won't be a family! I'm just me!
RIMS: All right, be yourself!
BOBBY: All right, I'll be myself—and if you think a man gives up a lot when he gets married, a girl gives up something when she gets married, and don't you forget it! I spend the whole day here taking care of this damned house for you and cooking your meals and doing your dishes and never going anywhere because we can't afford it—and every time I get a dime for myself I have to ask for it! It's degrading!
RIMS: It's your own home.
BOBBY: It's not mine. It's all yours. You earn the money so it's all yours! I tell you it's despicable! Asking![91]

This argument hits firmly at the paradox of societal strictures regarding marriage. Although Rims resents having to support Bobby, he fails to challenge the system by letting Bobby return to work, even though doing so would earn enough for comfortable living. For her part, Bobby bristles under a system of humiliating dependency. This inequality was recognized even by conservative commentator William Johnston, who wrote of wives in general, "So long as the husband pays for food, clothing, and shelter for her, assumes payment of all the bills she contracts, she can go through all the years of her married life without getting a dollar in cash from him, and there is nothing legally to be done about it."[92] Furthermore, evidence suggests that Bobby's indignation at having to ask her husband for money was not uncommon at the time. Nancy Cott reports that even those women in the 1920s who preferred traditional marriage to an independent life outside the home still resented being "provided for."[93]

Anderson produces a near-Ibsen-esque conclusion to Act II. Bobby makes a defiant stand. In contrast to Mary in *White Desert*, who still washes dishes late into the play, Bobby screams at Rims: "You can wash your own dishes!...I'm running along! And I'm not coming back!"[94] Bobby exits through one door, while Rims storms out through another. However, Anderson misses his full-on Ibsen moment. Moments after exiting, Bobby re-enters looking for Rims and, not finding him, exits again. Then Rims re-enters looking for Bobby only to find the house empty and so he departs again.[95] Some may view this as wishy-washy, but Anderson holds a different purpose in mind from Ibsen. Unlike Nora and Helmer, Bobby and Rims are, in fact, in love with one another. Gender inequality is certainly an enemy in this play. However, Anderson aims more directly at the infringement of individual liberty, for both man and wife, that is a byproduct of marriage itself. Anderson is not looking for a door slam finale as did Ibsen. While this argument represents the climax of the play, it lacks full recognition for the protagonist. Bobby's most complete maturation as an independent-minded woman occurs in the denouement of Act III.

Act III: What We Wanted Was a Love Affair, Wasn't It?

While the fairy tale embrace concluding Act I gives way to domestic acrimony in Act II, the final act of *Saturday's Children* gives a picture of the consequences that society impels when rejecting traditional norms. Act III opens on a dingy tenement house run by the indomitable Mrs. Gorlik, a judgmental landlady suspicious of all single young women residing in her establishment. Her first lines fully establish the tenor of her character. She calls from outside Bobby's door asking if she is in. Hearing no response, Mrs. Gorlik enters and registers indignation at finding the room empty, the windows open, and Bobby's stockings hanging up to dry: "Never knew a girl wasn't a born fool.... T'ain't decent!"[96] Her moralizing is interrupted by the entrance of Mr. Halevy, whom she takes, despite his age, to be a gentleman caller for Bobby, a subject for which she demonstrates rabid obsession.[97] She even doubts Mr. Halevy when he identifies himself as Bobby's father, a suspicion against which he feels compelled to defend.

> MRS. GORLIK: Well, if you're her father—
> MR. HALEVY: I am.
> MRS. GORLIK: Then I should say it's a very good thing you came....
>   Because she needs looking after....
> MR. HALEVY: What makes you think so?
> MRS. GORLIK: I can tell. When they come here looking for rooms late at night and when they have middle-aged gentlemen to call like she done last night—and when they smoke cigarettes—well—I can tell.[98]

In the 1920s, many women viewed smoking cigarettes as symbolic of their equality with men.[99] Mrs. Gorlik's broad moral judgments based, in part, on the fact that Bobby is a smoker exemplifies her Victorian fastidiousness.

Shortly after Mr. Halevy enters, Rims arrives on the scene. Rims demands to see "Mrs. O'Neil,"[100] thus demonstrating he has not yet accepted the fact that Bobby has left him. Rims bullies his way into the room and, when Mrs. Gorlik recognizes that Rims and Mr. Halevy know each other, she exits the room, leaving the two men alone.[101] The interaction between Rims and Halevy reveals several key facts. First, we learn that Mengle, Bobby's boss, has been taking her to dinner and visiting her in her room. Second, Rims confesses his obsession with Bobby. He confides that he followed her home from work the previous night, noted her movements with Mengle, and clearly assumes a sexual affair between Bobby and the older man.[102] Third, we learn that Mengle had Bobby transported in a private car with a chauffeur, which threatens Rims' masculine pride: "I guess that's what she wants. I don't earn enough."[103] Thus, once again we see the focus on pecuniary circumstances. Mr. Halevy quickly dismisses such material superfluousness in Bobby, but Rims proves incorrigible.[104] This moment reaches crescendo when Mengle's chauffeur arrives with a package for Bobby. The chauffeur inquires after Ms. Halevy, which sets Rims off again to insisting upon "Mrs. O'Neil." Brimming with indignation, Rims storms off, running into Mrs. Gorlik on the way out, who re-enters to check in on the situation.[105]

When Bobby finally arrives on the scene, we see a woman reaching full recognition of her will to independence. Mr. Halevy offers to allow Bobby to return home and live as before, thus extracting her from the slovenly tenement house. Bobby, however, refuses: "It would be like going around in a circle. I'd be right back where I started."[106] Her father then tries to assume partial blame for his daughter's troubles, but Bobby insists on taking full responsibility for her situation. Finally, she defends her steadfast decision to avoid her husband. When her father asks, "What about poor Rims?," Bobby responds, "What about poor me?"[107] In considering her needs, wants, and desires first, Bobby has clearly grown into a stronger character at the end of the play than she was in the beginning.

After Bobby confirms her break with the parental home, Rims arrives and she now must complete the severing of ties to her marital home. Rims employs myriad tactics to convince Bobby to return to him in a traditional marriage. He confesses having followed her the previous evening as a means of showing how much he cares for her. He needles her with his suspicions about Mengle, suspicions augmented with the revelation that the package Mengle sent contains a deadbolt. Rims interprets the deadbolt as indicative of Bobby's supposed desire to have a sexual affair with her boss secure from the prying eyes of Mrs. Gorlik. However, despite all inuendo around her employer throughout the play, Bobby makes clear, in no uncertain terms, that she is not romantically interested in, nor sexually involved with, Mengle. In fact, Bobby takes offense when she assumes Rims was driven by jealousy alone rather than a desire to see her.[108] Rims's obsession with Bobby's sexual behavior mirrors the attitude of Michael in *White Desert* as well as the townsfolk in *Sea-Wife*. Though not as overt as Michael, Rims subconsciously views Bobby as something to possess. The principal difference between the two men lies in the fact that Rims, while sometimes talking tough, is not given to Michael's brand of violence. However, Bobby's strength has grown beyond the power of societal strictures:

> BOBBY: No.... You see—Oh, I wonder if I can tell you—What we wanted was a love affair, wasn't it? Just to be together and let the rest go hang—and what we got was a house and bills and general hell. Do you know what I think a love affair is, Rims? It's when the whole world is trying to keep two people apart and they insist on being together. And when they get married the whole world pushes them together so they just naturally fly apart. I want my love affair back. I want hurried kisses and clandestine meetings, and a secret lover. I don't want a house. I don't want a husband. I want a lover.
> RIMS: So that let's [*sic*] me out.
> BOBBY: Does it, dear?[109]

Anderson could not have made Bobby's desire for sexual independence clearer in 1927. Moreover, she implicitly attempts to win Rims over into rejecting marriage and simply engage in the sexual affair that they both want.

Throughout the final moments of the play, Anderson rachets up the pressure on Bobby to accept convention, which renders her final rejection of marriage (though not of Rims) all the more powerful. Bobby has rebuffed the advances of her employer, turned down her father's offer to return home, and defied all attempts by her husband to resume married life. The repudiation of these three men (employer, father, husband), all of whom bear traditional positions of male power over women, represent symbolic victories as well as literal ones. As the play ends, Anderson drives the final nail into the coffin of convention. Bobby finds herself alone on her bed after Mrs. Gorlik forces Rims out and Rims makes no obvious move to accept Bobby's overtures of an affair. Bobby sets about preparing for bed, but becomes overwhelmed by the loss of her lover. She sinks down onto the bed in tears. Unseen by her, Rims sneaks in through the window, goes to the door, and begins installing the deadbolt. He accidentally makes a noise and Bobby startles, fearing an unwelcome intruder. Her spirit lifts when she sees her lover. Rims asks for a screwdriver to continue working on the deadbolt. She delivers the tool and cautions him to work quietly as the play ends with the clear implication that the sexual relationship will continue, but the marriage will not.[110]

Conclusion

The conclusion to *Saturday's Children* elicited some sharp criticism. Euphemia Van Rensselaer Wyatt, writing with indignation throughout her review, represented the conservative moralist perspective. Wyatt argued that the play should not be listed as a comedy because she found it "full of tragic implications." She complains that the audience responded to the ending with "delighted applause" despite it being "perhaps the saddest moment…for it summarizes the petty materialism that seems typical" of New Yorkers. Wyatt even went so far as to say that what Bobby really needed was a "spanking," but instead received "underserved sympathy." Furthermore, she bemoans how Bobby has taken advantage of Rims and expresses hope "for our young men's sake that most of them escape and make their careers before they meet with" such women as Bobby Halevy.[111] While Wyatt's reaction seems overripe, her sentiments are not unlike those of other conservative observers of the Jazz Age. Wyatt infantilizes Bobby, upholds tradition, and gives no heed or legitimation to Bobby's rights as an individual.

On the flip side, other critics recognized not only the legitimation of Bobby's autonomy, but also the dramaturgical uniqueness of the play itself. Barrett Clark praised Anderson for avoiding traditional romantic tropes so common on the 1920s stage.[112] Joseph Wood Krutch acknowledges the plethora of marriage plays witnessed in the 1920s, but opines that though the subject is "familiar…never has the theme been treated or the scenes represented with a more absolutely convincing fidelity."[113]

George Jean Nathan recognized the similarity to Craven's *The First Year*, but asserted that Anderson's play was "more honest and better written."[114] Finally, Robert Benchley declared that if the conclusion was intended to portend an ongoing affair outside of matrimony, then *Saturday's Children* represented "an almost startlingly new story."[115] There seems little question, therefore, that many critics recognized, to varying degrees, the potential subversive elements of Anderson's 1927 hit.

Saturday's Children's success was all the more remarkable when one considers the precise time of its premiere, which occurred during the height of moral policing in Broadway houses. The year 1927 was, after all, the season of police raids upon such scandalous productions as *The Captive*, *The Virgin Man*, and *Sex*. In fact, Barrett Clark channeled these controversies in sardonically suggesting *Saturday's Children* be shut down by "our guardians of other people's morals."[116] Meanwhile, George Jean Nathan said of Mr. Halevy's advice to Bobby about indulging in a sexual affair: "I detect Anderson necking Mae West."[117] Nathan's penchant for contemporary references sometimes obscure the meaning of his reviews for twenty-first century readers, but he appears to allude to West's arrest over the play, *Sex*. *Saturday's Children*, however, not only failed to engender public ire (notwithstanding indignant assessments from Skinner, who bemoaned Mr. Halevy's advice to his daughter, and Wyatt), but achieved popular success. This fact leaves us with the question of how Anderson was able to put this play over without finding himself victim to a moral witch hunt.

The answer to that question may lie in Anderson's masterful execution of threading the needle between challenging societal strictures while still upholding tradition just enough to generate ambiguity. For all its social critiques, *Saturday's Children* reinforces Victorian traditions in at least one important facet. Bobby, in a manner of speaking, maintains her sexual virtue. As aforementioned, insinuations are made throughout the play regarding a sexual affair between Bobby and Mengle. This inuendo emanates from Florrie, Willy, Mrs. Gorlik, and, of course, Rims. However, Mengle never appears in the play and Bobby remains steadfast that she has never slept with him and has no intentions of ever doing so. The audience may presume she is lying, but that does not seem to be Anderson's intention. In an early, unpublished draft of the play, Mengle makes a perfunctory appearance in Act III for the express purpose of confirming for Rims that he has never once had sex with Bobby. Anderson, however, must have felt this point was already clear and thus omitted Mengle's appearance from the final version.[118] Furthermore, no indication exists that Bobby engages in sexual activity with any other men. As one scholar observes, while Bobby's arrangement with Rims at the end of the play "is unorthodox, it is strictly moral."[119] Bobby remains faithful to Rims romantically, if not domestically, which, in its own way, adheres to traditional sexual morality. Her monogamy may well have lulled the audience into a sense that what was happening was not really so bad.

Saturday's Children seems to have benefitted a great deal from the dynamic performance of Ruth Gordon in the leading role. Gordon credits the production with catapulting her career, later recounting Bobby Halevy as "the first real acting I ever did. Acting in the deep sense."[120] Director Guthrie McClintic, whose prolific achievements on Broadway spanned six decades, counted his work with Gordon on *Saturday's Children* as among the highlights of his career.[121] These assessments gain support from a survey of critical reviews. Atkinson praised Gordon for her "subtle penetration."[122] David Carb echoed Atkinson in describing Gordon's portrayal as "a gentle, appealing, touching impersonation" and proclaimed Gordon delivered "the best performance of her career."[123] Even critics taking issue with the play's moral stance tended to praise Gordon's performance. Skinner, who confessed disappointment in the play's "mixed values," nevertheless felt Gordon "never appeared more convincingly a human being, and surely never so fine an artist."[124] Meanwhile, Wyatt, who complained of the audience's "undeserved sympathy" for Bobby, actually blamed Gordon for playing Bobby "so delicately" as to pull the audience in her favor.[125]

Anderson's own conservative view of women, however, nearly sabotaged Gordon and, by extension, the play's success. By Gordon's account, Anderson was reticent about casting her in the role of Bobby. When McClintic broached the idea, the playwright responded frankly, "I'd rather not have [the play] done."[126] The reasons? Gordon was simply not, in Anderson's estimation, physically attractive enough for the part and, besides that, Anderson believed her range limited to comedy.[127] A meeting with Gordon, engineered by McClintic, who was not inclined to back down, did nothing to alter Anderson's disposition. Gordon was charming, yes, but in the end the dramatist declared, "If you do [the play] with her, it'll fail."[128] The value Anderson placed on feminine beauty, that physical attractiveness was so important he would rather decline to produce the play, reveals his own proclivity for idealizing women. However, despite his misgivings, he yielded to McClintic's persuasion.

Furthermore, to Anderson's credit, he remained silent and unobtrusive during rehearsals.[129] Gordon notes she did, in fact, struggle with the comedic aspect, reporting that tryout audiences twice laughed in inappropriate moments. She persevered, however, with the aid of McClintic's incessant coaching, adjusting herself to the challenge and, ultimately, making the show a hit.[130] Whether or not Anderson offered any amends, Gordon does not record, but Gordon's reflections on her experience reveal the significant impact a performer can have on a production.

Saturday's Children stands apart from many of the successful dramas of the era, such as *The First Year*, as well as more radical efforts such as *Sex*, because it challenges the status quo while avoiding drastic offense to sensibilities. This distinction is key. Judge Lindsey, regarded as a radical by many at the time, expressed his utter disdain upon seeing a play he described as "crude melodrama" with "a raw title" and "raw sex situations" that a "'play jury'" later "threatened to discipline."[131] Lindsey criticized the unnamed play as "bad taste passing for 'truth'" and for being "at the absolute zero of vapidity."[132] Now Judge Lindsey was no theatre critic, of course, and although he withholds the play's title, given the time frame of which he speaks and his description of the play itself, he almost certainly witnessed one of the three plays shut down in 1927. That a supposed radical like Lindsey could suffer such offense at the theatre speaks to the difficulty playwrights faced in treating the subject of sex and marriage with any modicum of verisimilitude. With *Saturday's Children*, Anderson offers sharp, reasoned commentary about the evolution of marriage in America. The audience discovers the tradition marriage came out of with the Halevys; a depiction of how marriage often existed during the 1920s in Florrie and Willy; and the movement toward a modern, less institutionalized form of monogamy in Bobby and Rims. We do not know if Judge Lindsey ever saw the play, but *Saturday's Children* comes closest to championing his ideal of the companionate model.

Two years later, Anderson would challenge sexual mores and gender roles in much more overtly provocative ways. This effort proved futile, however, and the play, *Gypsy*, closed after a brief run. But like *White Desert* before it, *Gypsy*, though a commercial failure, would earn adherents among some critics. Moreover, *Gypsy* represents, perhaps, Anderson's most subversive treatment of marriage and gender roles in the United States.

Notes

1. Ben B. Lindsey and Wainwright Evans, *The Companionate Marriage* (Garden City, NY: Garden City Publishing, 1927), 142–147.
2. Stephanie Coontz, *Marriage, a History* (New York: Viking, 2005).
3. Burns Mantle, *The Best Plays of 1927–28* (New York: Dodd, Mead, and Company, 1928), 562.
4. John Hohenberg, *The Pulitzer Prizes* (New York: Columbia University Press, 1974), 100.
5. Christine Stansell, *American Moderns: Bohemian New York and the Creation of a New Century* (Princeton, NJ: Princeton University Press, 2000), 244.
6. Elizabeth Ammons, "The New Woman as Cultural Symbol and Social Reality," in *1915, The Cultural Moment*, edited by Adele Heller and Lois Rudnick (New Brunswick: Rutgers University Press, 1991), 83.
7. *Statistical Abstracts of the United States* (Washington: Government Printing Office, 1931), 51.
8. Lynn Dumenil, *Modern Temper: American Culture and Society in the 1920s* (New York: Hill and Wang, 1995), 113.
9. John D'Emilio and Estelle Freedman, *Intimate Matters: A History of Sexuality in America* (New York: Harper & Row, 1988), 194.
10. Coontz, 199–200.
11. Maxwell Anderson, *Saturday's Children* (New York: Longmans, Green, 1927), 3–4.
12. Ibid., 8–9.
13. Emma Goldman, *Red Emma Speaks: An Emma Goldman Reader*, edited by Alix Kates Shulman (Amherst: Humanity Books, 1998), 209.
14. Perry Luckett, "The Mind and Matter of Maxwell Anderson." Ph.D. Dissertation (University of North Carolina, 1979), 204.
15. Anderson, *Saturday's Children*, 6.
16. Ibid., 6–10.
17. Ibid., 9.
18. Ibid., 10.
19. Ibid.
20. Ibid., 13.
21. Ibid., 14–17.
22. Ibid., 18.
23. Ibid., 23.
24. Ibid., 28.
25. Ibid., 24.
26. Ibid., 24–26.
27. Ibid., 26.
28. Ibid., 27.

29. Ibid., 30–31.
30. Warren I. Susman, *Culture as History: The Transformation of American Society in the Twentieth Century* (Washington: Smithsonian Institution Press, 2003), 108.
31. Brooks Atkinson, *New York Times*, 27 January 1927.
32. Anderson, *Saturday's Children*, 31.
33. Ibid.
34. Ibid., 32.
35. Ibid., 32–33.
36. Ibid., 33.
37. Ibid., 35.
38. Ibid., 36–37.
39. Ibid., 40–41.
40. Ibid., 41.
41. Ibid.
42. Ibid., 42–44.
43. Ibid., 45.
44. Ibid., 46.
45. Ibid., 46–50.
46. Ibid., 52.
47. "Marble Hearts and Halls," *New York Times*, 26 November 1923.
48. Anderson, *Saturday's Children*, 53.
49. Ibid., 58.
50. Ibid.
51. Ibid., 64.
52. Ibid., 65.
53. Ibid., 65–66.
54. Helene Cixous, *Performance Analysis: An Introductory Coursebook*, edited by Colin Counsell and Laurie Wolf (New York: Routledge, 2001), 69.
55. Ibid.
56. Anderson, *Saturday's Children*, 67.
57. Ibid., 68–69.
58. Ibid., 70–72.
59. Ibid., 73–76.
60. Richard H. Pells, *Radical Visions and American Dreams: Culture and Social Thought in the Depression Years* (New York: Harper and Row, 1973), 12.
61. Ibid., 20.
62. Elsie Clews Parsons, "Changes in Sex Relations," *Nation* 118 (14 May 1924): 552.
63. Anderson, *Saturday's Children*, 15.
64. Ibid., 77.

65. Ibid., 78–79.
66. Floyd Dell, "Can Men and Women be Friends?" *Nation* 118 (28 May 1924): 605.
67. Anderson, *Saturday's Children*, 80–86.
68. Ibid., 86.
69. Ibid., 89–95.
70. Ibid., 95.
71. Ibid., 96.
72. Ibid., 97–100.
73. Clara Savage Littledale, "So This Is Marriage!" *Good Housekeeping* 80 (January 1925): 115.
74. Anderson, *Saturday's Children*, 105.
75. Ibid.
76. Ibid., 106–108.
77. Euphemia Van Rensselaer Wyatt, *Catholic World* 125 (1927): 94.
78. R. Dana Skinner, *Commonweal* 5 (1927): 382.
79. David Carb, *Vogue* 69 (1927): 132.
80. Clark, "Police Censors," 200.
81. Anderson, *Saturday's Children*, 107–108.
82. Henry David Thoreau, *Walden and Civil Disobedience* (New York: Barnes & Noble Classics, 2003), 137.
83. Joseph Wood Krutch, "Drama: Contemporaneity," *Nation* 124 (1927): 194.
84. Anderson, *Saturday's Children*, 108–109.
85. Ruth Scott Miller, "Masterless Wives and Divorce," *Ladies Home Journal* 42 (January 1925): 20.
86. Anderson, *Saturday's Children*, 117.
87. Ibid.
88. Ibid., 117–118.
89. Ibid., 118.
90. Ibid., 118–124.
91. Ibid., 124–125.
92. William Johnston, "Should Wives be Paid Wages?" *Good Housekeeping* 80 (March 1925): 30.
93. Nancy F. Cott, *The Grounding of Modern Feminism* (New Haven: Yale University Press, 1987), 188–189.
94. Anderson, *Saturday's Children*, 127.
95. Ibid., 128.
96. Ibid., 129.
97. Ibid., 130–131.
98. Ibid., 132–133.
99. John Modell, *Into One's Own: From Youth to Adulthood in the United States 1920–1975* (Berkeley: University of California Press, 1989), 98.

100. Anderson, *Saturday's Children*, 133–134.
101. Ibid., 134.
102. Ibid., 134–137.
103. Ibid., 137.
104. Ibid.
105. Ibid., 139–141.
106. Ibid., 145.
107. Ibid.
108. Ibid., 146–148.
109. Ibid., 158–159.
110. Ibid., 159–166.
111. Wyatt, 93–94.
112. Barrett H. Clark, "Some New York Plays Not Yet Stopped by the Police Censors," *Drama* 17 (1927): 200.
113. Joseph Wood Krutch, *Nation* 124 (1927): 194.
114. George Jean Nathan, "The Theatre," *American Mercury* 10 (1927): 503.
115. Robert Benchley, "Drama," *Life*, 17 February 1927, 19.
116. Clark, "Police Censors," 200.
117. Nathan, *American Mercury*, 503.
118. Maxwell Anderson, Manuscript of "Saturday's Children," *Maxwell Anderson Papers*, Works, Harry Ransom Center, UT-Austin, 97.
119. Arthur T. Tees, "Maxwell Anderson: An Attitude Toward Man." Ph.D. Dissertation (University of Kansas, 1967), 175.
120. Ruth Gordon, *My Side: The Autobiography of Ruth Gordon* (New York: Harper & Row, 1976), 150.
121. Guthrie McClintic, *Me and Kit* (Boston: Little, Brown, and Company, 1955), 310.
122. Atkinson.
123. Carb.
124. Skinner.
125. Wyatt.
126. Gordon, 149.
127. Ibid., 149, 155.
128. Ibid., 149–150.
129. Ibid., 150.
130. Ibid., 151–156.
131. Lindsey and Evans, 3.
132. Ibid.

CHAPTER 5

Gypsy: Love After Marriage

Whereas Anderson paired satirical comedy with an ambiguous conclusion to mitigate the social message in *Saturday's Children*, with *Gypsy* the playwright seems to have pushed the moral boundaries beyond tolerance for the time. Concerns about "indecency" on the stage persisted during the 1928–1929 Broadway season. Mae West, fresh off her arrest in connection with the production of *Sex*, returned to Broadway in October 1928 in yet another provocative play, this one entitled *Pleasure Man*. The police shut down the production after only two performances.[1] The authorities spared *Gypsy* from closure, but the public did not. The production managed only a brief run of 64 performances,[2] placing it far below the success of *Saturday's Children*. However, despite its commercial failure, Burns Mantle included *Gypsy* among his ten best plays of the season. In justifying its inclusion, Mantle takes on a cautious, almost cryptic tone. He states the protagonist represents "those aspects of the newer feminine psychology" that "are none too flattering" to women.[3] He then attributes the production's failure to the fact that 1920s theatregoers were "notoriously shy of unconventional heroines, particularly when they are not sympathetic."[4] In summation of his defense, Mantle alludes to the cultural climate during the Jazz Age in recognizing *Gypsy* as "an honestly written drama inspired by changing social standards and values, a play of purpose, the artistic integrity of which cannot be questioned whatever the reaction may be to its characters and its story."[5]

© The Author(s), under exclusive license to Springer Nature
Switzerland AG 2022
F. D. Geary II, *Maxwell Anderson and the Marriage Crisis*,
https://doi.org/10.1007/978-3-031-13241-4_5

Rationale

Gypsy stands as perhaps the most obscure work among the plays under consideration. A number of factors play into its consignment to near oblivion following the production's closure. As was the case for other plays in this study, Anderson himself appeared indifferent as to the play's fate and uninterested in its publication. A few years before his death, when reflecting on his life for Columbia University's oral history project, the playwright mentioned the play once in passing, counting it among his "failures."[6] Anderson's apathy might have poisoned the scholarly well. The few book-length studies concentrated on Anderson's life and work barely even acknowledge *Gypsy* let alone treat it with any serious consideration.[7] The lack of a published script no doubt hampered meaningful scholarly inquiry, but the play's timing combined with its lack of success may have contributed to its decay. While *White Desert* also suffers from obscurity it at least held the advantage of being Anderson's first produced play and therefore always demanded some attention from scholars, however scant. *Sea-Wife* happened to elicit interest from an important critic, which led to its production on smaller stages during the 1930s, a decade in which Anderson achieved his most prodigious levels of success and popularity. *Saturday's Children* was, of course, a big enough hit to merit publication despite the playwright's apathy for the script. *Gypsy* bears the further disadvantage of being Anderson's final play of the 1920s, a decade containing work typically overlooked in favor of his Depression-era verse dramas. Were it not for Mantle's courageous recognition of the play and the fact that one typescript remains intact in the archives of the New York Public Library, *Gypsy* might have lost all chance for re-evaluation.

The merits of re-evaluating *Gypsy* lay principally in the stark boldness of the play's protagonist, Ellen Hastings. It would not take an audience familiar with Anderson's work long to discern that the playwright cut Ellen from a radically different cloth than he did Mary Kane, Margaret, or even Bobby Halevy. A married woman, Ellen enjoyed numerous lovers in her past and has already engaged in at least one extramarital affair. She manifests little serious regard for marriage as an institution, chafes at ever having married in the first place, and when she becomes pregnant, she solicits an abortion without a second thought. When Mantle labelled her "unconventional" and "not sympathetic" to a 1920s audience, he was being tactful to say the least. Anderson compounds her struggle by weaving in tacit theories of modern psychology and heredity to help explain her behavior. As in *Saturday's Children*, Anderson offers various takes on marriage from the supporting characters, but Ellen brings a boldness to the stage unmatched by the playwright's previous heroines. *Gypsy* places Maxwell Anderson ahead of his time with a radical depiction of feminine equality more at home in the twenty-first century than the Jazz Age.

ACT I: I'M WILLING TO BE FAITHFUL, BUT I HAVEN'T REALLY ANY INSTINCT ABOUT IT

The opening moments of *Gypsy* subtly establish the fact that Ellen Hastings exists in a world in which she does not fully belong. The play begins in interruption with Ellen and her male companion, Cleve, standing "a little distance apart, looking at each other as if something disquieting has occurred."[8] Having the first line in the play, Ellen tries to recall her train of thought, "Well, where were we? ... When I was interrupted." She and Cleve were discussing the confessions of either St. Augustine or Rousseau, but neither can remember which.[9] Anderson's juxtaposition of the religious doctrinaire with the revolutionary apostate immediately establishes a stark dichotomy, teasing the audience to wonder into which camp Ellen will land. A clue emerges when Ellen suggests that what she really needs is "a book on etiquette. The one that shows the picture of the girl...picking up the wrong fork."[10] If the audience had any doubts as to Ellen's meaning regarding proper use of silverware, she makes her intentions blunter with her next line: "What I want to know is, what the married woman will do when the well dressed man kisses her—I find I never know—."[11] In these early moments we see that Ellen does not conform to societal standards. Cleve is not Ellen's husband, but rather a potential lover with whom she enjoys flirtation. This opening action separates *Gypsy* from the previous plays. *White Desert*, in particular, represents a stark contrast in its beginning, with Mary newly married, standing with her husband, and enthralled by romanticism. *Sea-Wife* and *Saturday's Children* both work to construct the character of the heroine offstage, but make plain the fact that these are faithful, devoted women in their own idiosyncratic ways. With Ellen, however, the audience sees her as a woman under temptation and not entirely reluctant about it.

Ellen does not, however, lack some measure of compunction regarding sexual affairs. While she concedes to finding Cleve's advances "flattering" and that she wanted him to kiss her, she also cautions him not to fall in love with her.[12] Cleve, a novelist, poet, and intellectual (attributes similar to those of Anderson himself), burns with romanticism, exemplified by his characterization of Ellen's kiss as "when the pyramids catch fire and the mountains slip into the sea."[13] Ellen worries over this magnitude of passion, fearing Cleve may become carried away. In contrast to her potential lover, Ellen prefers a degree of distance: "I don't fall in love very easily—nor very suddenly—" and paints a picture of herself as emotionally cold.[14] She enjoys flirtation for amusement because "it doesn't affect me much."[15] However, she fears the point when flirtation becomes "serious."[16] Despite her admonitions, Cleve pursues his rapturous advance and Ellen does not object. They embrace for another kiss to which she confesses, "the mountains do begin to slip into the sea."[17] The doorbell breaks the embrace and thus ends the first dramatic beat.

Ellen stands in contrast to Anderson's previous heroines. She lacks the romantic idealism of Mary in *White Desert* as well as the religiously induced guilt of Margaret from *Sea-Wife*. Her behavior seems somewhat closer to Bobby's indecisiveness, but Bobby also displays a warmth and fidelity absent from Ellen in these early moments. Moreover, whereas Bobby desires romantic love, Ellen appears to prefer sexual affairs devoid of such fervent attachments. In this respect, the playwright seemingly inverts traditional gender roles as the trope of seeking sexual pleasure without emotional commitment typically manifests in male characters. Just minutes into the play one can already sense the controversy, hinted at by Burns Mantle, that *Gypsy* elicited for a 1920s American audience.

Though the couple fear the doorbell precipitates the entrance of Ellen's husband, David, they receive a reprieve. The janitor enters inquiring about a requested repair. He acknowledges Cleve before Ellen directs him to the kitchen to inspect a broken heater. Moments later, the janitor returns to inform Ellen he cannot make the repair today and will have to return tomorrow. With that statement, the janitor departs.[18] This seemingly superfluous character at first appears little more than a dramatic device to give the lovers a scare before David actually arrives. However, as we shall see, Anderson utilizes this moment as a setup for the climactic confrontation between husband and wife later in the play.

Alone with Ellen once more, Cleve renews his pursuit. He invites Ellen to the theatre, suggesting that it will provide a legitimate reason for them to appear in public together. Ellen balks and once more suggests they should end their affair now "while there's time."[19] Cleve refuses to relent and in the process, we learn a little more regarding Ellen's past:

CLEVE: Don't you want to see me?
ELLEN: Yes.
CLEVE: Then you certainly will.
ELLEN: And we'll go to the theatre?
CLEVE: Must we go to the theatre?
ELLEN: I think we'd better.
CLEVE: And dance afterward.
ELLEN: No, please.
CLEVE: Yes, please. Don't you want to dance with me again?
ELLEN: Yes, but—
CLEVE: Then, of course you will—Darling, there were a lot of things we were going to do together. Didn't you promise to come and see my place sometime, and wear that red dress for me, the one I saw you in first—
ELLEN: Perhaps I'd better not wear that red dress again. I wasn't very sane in that dress, was I?
CLEVE: I love you insane, and you love being insane, and you know you do!
ELLEN: You know very well I shouldn't go to your place—
CLEVE: And what better reason is there for going?
ELLEN: No, no, please—
CLEVE: Darling, darling—
ELLEN: I'll have to tell you something, Cleve.—I've had more experience with myself than you have. I am in love with David, and I think I'd always have been faithful to him if I hadn't been married to him. You see faith and trust can be a sort of tyranny. Anyway I thought so. I didn't really want to be married and I got tired of it and wanted to be free—and—there was somebody else—I had a lover—
CLEVE: When was this?
ELLEN: About a year ago. But it was horrible for David when I told him, because I was pretty mad about Jerry.—That's all, I guess, only I came back to David—and fell in love with him all over again—.[20]

This exchange highlights how Anderson constructed Ellen as a character as well as how her behavior was perceived by audiences in 1929.

For the most part, critics tended to lay the onus of sexual impropriety squarely upon Ellen. Brooks Atkinson, for example, echoed the classical concept of the tragic flaw when he noted that Ellen's positive qualities as a woman ("intellectually honest, independent, and self-reliant"), were negated by the fact that "she woefully lacks the instinct for monogamy."[21] Another critic described her as having "the fatal gift for infidelity."[22] Still another observer dismissed Ellen as one who "cannot be taken seriously."[23] Cleve certainly fails to take Ellen seriously when she protests his invitations. Furthermore, Ellen demonstrates marked self-awareness indicative of Atkinson's positive attributes. She does not evoke a sexually voracious vamp, but rather an intellectually astute young woman with sophisticated culture; one who enjoys theatre and reads titles such as *Confessions*, be they Augustine or Rousseau. Cleve, on the other hand, shows little restraint when it comes to amorous designs. That critics expected Ellen to resist incessant temptation illuminates once again the expected attitudes women were supposed to take in regard to sex.

Toward the end of this exchange, we see Ellen's attitudes about marriage seeping into the drama. She likens "faith and trust" as "a sort of tyranny." Faith and trust are, of course, hallmark expectations of traditional marriage. Ellen seems to advocate that such expectations are the principal reasons for acrimony in relationships. Similar to Bobby from *Saturday's Children*, Ellen muses she might have remained happy with David had she not married him and, presumably, remained his lover. When Ellen confides to David about her extramarital affair with Jerry she cites a longing for freedom as the motivation behind seeking the affair, which connects back to her notion of faith and trust as brands of oppression. Anderson thus depicts freedom as diametrically opposed to faith and trust, which underscores the notion of marriage as a blight upon individual autonomy. This uneasy juxtaposition of freedom versus faith and trust foreshadows much of the drama to come.

The contrast between the two men currently in Ellen's life becomes clear when the doorbell rings a second time and David enters. He greets his wife with "Hello, Gypsy,"[24] thus connecting the title of the play to a nickname for Ellen herself. As the scene progresses, David and Cleve expound upon their personal disappointments in life. Cleve has dreams of attaining the literary heights of Joseph Conrad, but compromises by publishing inartistic short stories in a local magazine instead. David, a violinist, came to New York with aspirations of becoming a musician, but circumstances compelled him to join a movie house orchestra playing accompaniment for silent films.[25] Ellen, it seems, gravitates to men with high cultural aspirations; aspirations that appear to reflect her own intellectual interests. So again, in Ellen's choice of husband and lover, we find evidence of the intellectual woman that Atkinson observed in his review.

Anderson next contrasts Ellen's intellectual attitude with her skills as a housewife. She brags to Cleve about darning socks, sewing buttons, cooking meals, and cleaning house. David, however, downplays the significance of her work and offers her not a hint of praise. Ellen appears almost desperate to prove herself. When David balks at confirming that she darns his socks "sometimes," she clarifies, "I said sometimes."[26] Still, David shows no affection to Ellen in this moment and Cleve only expresses his incredulity that anyone actually darns socks.[27] The indifference of the men toward Ellen's domestic efforts reflects the traditional separate gendered spheres of work, emphasizing the low value placed upon tasks typically relegated to women.

Receiving no plaudits for her domesticity, Ellen shifts to matters of culture. Implicitly defending her marital fidelity, she boasts of spending her evenings alone reading books to "improve my mind."[28] David does confirm this fact, citing her recent completion of Gibbon's *Decline and Fall of the Roman Empire*. That Ellen would undertake such a titanic read speaks to the fervency of her intellectual pursuits. However, David dismisses this achievement as well. When Ellen asks, "isn't my mind improved?" he responds, "I haven't noticed it." He then follows up with, "And by the way, try to keep the Roman Emperors out of the conversation this evening. They depress me."[29] In other words, not only does Ellen possess an avid appetite for reading, but also a hunger for sharing what she reads with others. This characteristic serves as more evidence of her febrile intellectual depth. But her husband rejects her efforts and her lover, once again, speaks nothing of consequence either way. As aforementioned, one critic labelled Ellen as a woman no one could take seriously. However, these interactions with the dominant men in her life reveal that no one *would* take her seriously. No matter what Ellen attempts, domestic or intellectual, she is essentially minimized or ignored. The only area in which she does not find herself minimized or ignored is when she turns on her sexual charms.

Anderson soon introduces a new dynamic to the marriage debate in this play in the form of Mac and Sylvia. Friends of Ellen and David, Mac is a struggling Broadway actor and Sylvia his love interest. Thus, among the men, Anderson establishes something of a triumvirate of broken artistic dreams with a writer, musician, and actor. That none of the men are successful in their chosen artistic aspirations eliminates pecuniary ambition among the women. Anderson thereby maintains dramatic focus upon the issue of marriage and relationships without the potential dilution posed by materialism. Indeed, once Mac and Sylvia arrive, the conflict returns to the issue of marriage. Mac announces to the room that he and Sylvia are engaged, a revelation that stuns Ellen. In response, Mac garrulously reports, "You and David did this to us. We've been ringside spectators long enough."[30] Ellen's retort stretches far from congratulatory: "We did it? I wouldn't do that to anybody. Didn't I tell you our marriage was an accident—all on account of a stubborn hotel clerk?"[31] David clarifies: "Seven stubborn hotel clerks."[32] We learn later in Act I that Ellen met David in St. Louis while working as an actress for a travelling theatre company. David enticed her to stay with him at a hotel, which caused them to run afoul of moralistic hotel clerks.[33] In essence, Ellen and David only married to legitimize their sexual affair. Such a scenario would have sounded familiar to Judge Lindsey, who often cited similar incidents as means of justifying his push for companionate marriage. Ellen's candor here is also quite remarkable. She pulls no punches and minces no words about what she thinks of Mac and Sylvia's decision. Moreover, when David inquires as to whether she likes being married, Ellen only replies, "One gets used to it."[34] From David's dismissiveness of Ellen's intellect and domestic efforts to Ellen's frankness about the truth of their union, Anderson paints a bleak picture of married life in the early stages of the play.

The temperature of the brewing conflict between husband and wife rises ever so slightly when the discourse returns to the issue of marital fidelity. Once again, Mac and Sylvia's relationship serves as the catalyst for an argument really centered on Ellen and David.

> MAC: Ours is to be a peasant or bourgeois marriage. Lifetime lovers—faithful till death.
> CLEVE: Faithful?
> MAC: That's what marriage is all about.
> DAVID: Hold that thought.
> MAC: Well, maybe not absolutely.
> SYLVIA: Well, if faithful doesn't mean absolutely, what does it mean? Don't you think I'm right, Ellen?
> ELLEN: Just another example of how the ideals of feudalism still permeate modern society.

SYLVIA: Yes?
DAVID: Ellen's quoting Roman history again.
MAC: Speak, oh, Sibyl, do you or do you not believe that husbands and wives ought to be faithful?
ELLEN: Why be so personal?
DAVID: Well, Gypsy, I never noticed you side-stepping before.
ELLEN: I suppose when things happen, one might as well admit them. I never had much use for faithfulness anyway, and less use for telling lies about it.
SYLVIA: But there's something in it, my dear, there's really something in it—two people sort of bending together against the world. It's pretty lonely unless you can trust someone.
ELLEN: But is that the only thing worth trusting people about? I'd much rather be trusted for telling the truth. That, at least, doesn't rob you of your independence.[35]

Rampant undercurrents rage in this dialogue. For one thing, Mac and Sylvia are aware of Ellen's previous affair with Jerry.[36] So when David tells Mac to "hold that thought," Mac qualifies his statement on faithfulness in response, presumably recognizing he had broached a touchy subject. Sylvia, however, tries to draw Ellen in on the side of fidelity, perhaps offering an out for Ellen to preserve her dignity. But Ellen responds with a defiant statement connecting the marriage institution to feudalism, which results in her once again suffering dismissal and mockery for her intellect. Finally, Ellen's questioning as to why "faithfulness" must always and only refer to sexual relations in marriage speaks to the crux of many arguments rendered by critics of marriage in the 1920s. Floyd Dell, for one, once mused whether "romance" was little more than "friendship mistaking itself for something else."[37] Sex, Dell opines, may serve to maintain a friendship, but sex alone "may prove unequal to the requirements of a more serious and intimate relationship."[38] For Ellen, it seems, sex represents little more than pleasure whereas truth and honesty stand much higher in her estimation.

Ellen's devotion to truth leads her to challenge the integrity of the men. Cleve criticizes people who use the truth "like the confessional" in order to justify any action. Ellen pounces: "That sounds like pure theory. Am I the only person present who has ever had to save his soul by confessing? Are you all pure as the driven snow?"[39] Cleve and Mac respond in the negative, but when David does not, Ellen pursues her attack: "As for David, he never really wanted to be bad. I don't think it's any special virtue in him. He just isn't tempted."[40] Most critics noted Ellen's alleged moral deficiencies. Few, however, pointed out the incongruity of David's rectitude. C.S. Lewis once observed that the modern world gains no moral foothold over medieval Europe in not executing witches because modernists have ceased believing in witches. Real moral superiority, Lewis argues, comes when one believes in witches and chooses not to execute them.[41] As David never encounters sexual temptation in the play there exists no virtue in his remaining faithful to her. Furthermore, the one time we know David faced libidinous impulses in the past (when he met Ellen) he surrendered to a sexual affair outside of marriage. In contrast, we saw Ellen at the opening of the play wrestling with temptation while Cleve broke down her defenses. Yet the men, both the characters in the play and the critics in the audience, saddle her with sexual waywardness. Ellen, however, rebels against the status quo, speaking for what Charlotte Perkins Gilman labelled the "reversed theory" of the Jazz Age wherein society rejected the "worship of virginity" and women began recognizing that the immensity of their sexual instincts is "just the same as men, if not more so."[42]

David summarizes his devotion to Ellen as well as his overarching need for faithfulness later in Act I. Finding himself alone with his wife for the first time in the play, David speaks less confrontationally. He confides to Ellen that "I get to feeling sort of far away from you some time, and some times (*sic*) it seems to me as if you wanted it that way" and confesses he doubts he can forgive Ellen for a second love affair.[43] He persists not only in re-hashing Ellen's relationship with Jerry, but presses her about the nature of her relationship with Cleve. Similar to Michael in *White Desert*, David seems almost masochistic in wanting details about her other intimacies. His perseverance echoes the idea of wives as proprietary to husbands. Unlike Michael, David possesses the advantage of modern thinking and a cultured awareness of evolving opinion. Nevertheless, despite his more cultivated intellect, David finds himself in the same trap as Michael. He confesses to Ellen, "I'm so terribly in love with you and I'm tortured some times because I look at you and it seems to me that you don't quite belong to me, or anybody—and you never will."[44] David is too reasoned, too sophisticated, and too in control of his own impulses to commit murder as does Michael. However, the tortured psychology, the obsession with fidelity, and the masochistic drive to discover the full extent of how their wives have wronged them are all evident and parallel in both characters.

A major difference between *Gypsy* and the other plays under consideration rests with the former's emphasis upon psychology and heredity. Anderson hints at Ellen's psychological development through revelations about her past. Heredity comes to the forefront with the appearance of Ellen's mother, Marilyn. Ellen makes her negative opinion of her mother evident when Marilyn unexpectedly calls and invites herself over: "Tell her the next time she comes to town, I wish she'd let me know in advance."[45] Ellen describes her mother as "a terrible liar" who neglects her husband (who is not Ellen's father) and enjoys tipping porters because it makes her feel "grown-up."[46] Moreover, when Cleve inquires as to Marilyn's "line" of business, David replies, "It's not a line—it's a string. Men mostly."[47] Anderson establishes Marilyn, at least from the perspectives of other characters, as a frivolous, sexually indulgent woman before she ever arrives on stage.

Marilyn's entrance confirms the negative perceptions. She bursts onto the scene with a flurry of physical affection, kissing first Ellen and then David, prompting Ellen to quip, "Oh, kiss everybody, Mother! Here's another man. Meet Cleve."[48] The stage directions do not indicate Marilyn follows through on the kiss, but Ellen's "here's another man" insinuates promiscuity. Furthermore, we soon learn that Ellen's stepfather is Marilyn's third husband. Marilyn confides that Ellen's former lover, Jerry, has visited her in Boston. In fact, Marilyn reports she "saw a lot of him for about a week" and when Ellen expresses disgust, Marilyn counters: "Well he was a friend of yours—so I was nice to him."[49] Anderson's intention seems cryptic as to whether Marilyn's comments connote a sexual affair. The hyphen indicating a pause in Marilyn's line, along with Ellen's obvious revulsion at this revelation, could certainly imply such a thing. Moreover, Anderson's setup of Marilyn's character as promiscuous might lead the audience down that path. In any case, the tension between mother and daughter is palpable, thus solidifying Anderson's like mother, like daughter theme.

The conclusion of Act I brings us another point of contention between Ellen and David. The conflict centers on David's probing as to whether she and Cleve intend to see each other again. Ellen confides to David that she and Cleve agreed to cease their friendship because she feared Cleve was enamored with her. When David presses, she finally confesses that she permitted Cleve to kiss her. David, heartsick again, wonders if Ellen really loves him as her husband. Ellen confirms her love, but qualifies her response: "Oh, I do love you, David. But it seems unreasonable to me to rule out the whole world just because you've chosen one person to live with. I'm willing to be faithful, but I really haven't any instinct about it."[50] The term "instinct" reinforces Anderson's hereditary theme. Ellen cannot help being what she is because her natural temperament will not permit her to adhere to societal norms. David, however, does not react as one might expect a husband would. Rather than flying into a jealous rage, as would Michael from *White Desert* or, to a less homicidal extent, Rims from *Saturday's Children*, David encourages Ellen to continue seeing Cleve. He reasons that any attempt to prevent Ellen from fulfilling her desires would only serve to generate resentment in their marriage.[51] "I don't want to be one of those watching husbands," David says, "asking questions and making rules."[52] Trust becomes paramount for David. If he cannot trust Ellen, then better to let her go.[53] In so doing, David presents himself open to the alternative marriage ideas propagated in the 1920s. Interestingly, having already severed her ties with Cleve, Ellen appears hesitant to reengage. David, however, does not merely suggest that Ellen go to the theatre with Cleve, he insists upon it:

> DAVID: Oh, darling—do you have to go?
> ELLEN: No, dear.
> DAVID: Of course you do. Or I'd be wishing you had.[54]

Ellen, cajoled by her lover into indiscretion at the beginning of the act, finds herself pressured by her husband to reengage with temptation at the end. She succumbs in both instances, but not before putting up resistance. Cleve and David are not as aggressive as Michael or even Rims, but they both represent the impact of male power. That the mostly male critics identified Ellen as the problem while ignoring the influence of the male characters upon her behavior further reinforces the patriarchal attitude.

Act II: And that Was Why I Couldn't Take the Money

Act II opens four months later on a scene of Ellen convalescing in the wake of a medical procedure. Jazz Age sensibilities no doubt led Anderson to avoid use of specific terms, but the dialogue leaves little question that Ellen has endured an abortion. The conversation begins after breakfast with David insisting Ellen restrain herself from dishes and housework. He also confesses he did not want her to have the abortion for fear it would endanger her life. Ellen, however, pushes back, "I'm perfectly all right. I've been all right all the time."[55] The conflict then escalates in two directions. First, we see a dispute over the financial arrangements, which reveals varying personal attitudes about the abortion itself. Ellen paid for the operation with her own money, but David wants to reimburse her and surreptitiously slips money into her purse. Ellen rejects the offer: "But I want to pay for it! I won't take it, David.... It seems to me having a baby is a woman's business—no reason for dragging you into it. And if I decide not to have it, that's my business too."[56] David retorts, "A baby looks to me like a purely cooperative affair," prompting Ellen to respond, "Well, I just don't feel that way."[57] Ellen ultimately wins the argument as David relents regarding payment.[58] The second escalation occurs when Ellen receives a visit from Marilyn and Sylvia. Anderson accentuates the mother/daughter tension when Marilyn complains of only learning of the abortion by chance. When Sylvia also objects to being left out of the loop, Ellen informs her, "I didn't want to argue about it. I knew what you'd say." Not only did Ellen keep the matter private, but she also returned to work the day after the surgery.[59]

These initial moments of Act II emphasize the ferocity of Ellen's independence more so than any other aspect of the play. Abortion, then and now, stirs febrile controversy among many people. Ellen pays for the procedure with her own money, rejects her husband's efforts to reimburse the cost, returns to work the next day, and works fervently to keep the procedure a secret from both her mother and her female best friend. Finally, Ellen questions, "What does one have babies for?" The responses from Sylvia and David are revelatory. Sylvia replies, "To make life worth living." David answers, "To perpetuate the ego."[60] These dichotomous responses encapsulate separate spheres in traditional Victorian thinking. Women were supposed to want children as a means of fulfilling their lives. Men, on the other hand, in their animalistic egocentricity, sought children as a way of extending their own image in the world. Ellen's questioning of maternity and her logical justifications for asserting her rights as an individual was uncommon for a female character in 1920s drama. The script offers a surprisingly modern statement in support of a woman's bodily autonomy, a statement one might expect more from a playwright of the 1960s or 1970s. This facet of *Gypsy* has long been overlooked by critics and scholars. In fact, few, if any, critics in 1929 addressed this part of the play, which seems strange given the moral climate of the time. It is difficult to believe critics were oblivious to the subject being discussed. As aforementioned, though Anderson never employs the term "abortion," the fact is unmistakable. It seems more likely that journalistic proprieties at the time prohibited addressing such a sensitive matter in print.

Ellen's justification for terminating her pregnancy, however, somewhat weakens the strength of her declaration of autonomy. For in Ellen's reasoning, Anderson tries to extend his theme of psychology and heredity. Ellen rationalizes the necessity for abortion with a question: "Suppose it [the baby] was a girl and she turned out like me?"[61] What follows is a host of self-deprecatory remarks from Ellen emphasizing her lack of self-worth. She muses about never being born, describes herself as "thoroughly useless," characterizes death as "the only escape" from a weary life, and laments, "There isn't anything to believe in when you don't believe in yourself."[62] Ellen's shift to rabid pessimism after rendering such strong avowals of independence seems a little heavy-handed, tempting one to speculate Anderson was trying too hard to graft his psychological theme onto the play. However, Ellen's rapid mood shifts are consistent with people suffering certain types of mental disorder. Moreover, as we have seen, Ellen is a well-read (if not formally educated) young woman with a propensity toward living life on her own terms. Her personality and temperament rub against the grain of the dominant culture under which she was born. It therefore seems reasonable to suggest that any mental ailments from which Ellen suffers might well be provoked by the suffocating societal strictures to which she, as a woman, would be expected to adhere. Again, one imagines Ellen's personality right at home in the radical feminism occurring later in the twentieth century. In the Jazz Age, however, Ellen is a fish out of water; a woman ahead of her time.

Shortly after her interaction with the women regarding the abortion, we learn of one person, besides David, that Ellen did inform about the procedure: her lover, Cleve. Ellen's reaction to inquiries about Cleve stand in marked contrast to her interactions with others in Act II:

DAVID: Is Cleve staying to dinner?
ELLEN: No.
DAVID: Isn't that unusual[?].
ELLEN: He didn't want me to bother this time.
DAVID: Did he know about—?
ELLEN: Oh, yes.
DAVID: Was that necessary?
ELLEN: Well—no—but—There's no great secret about it—is there?[63]

Ellen earlier indicates there was, in fact, great secrecy surrounding her abortion. However, she flippantly answers in the affirmative when asked if Cleve knows, as if his knowledge would be taken for granted. She then, as indicated by the hyphenation, balks when David asks why Cleve would possess that information. The play teases the implication that it was not David, but Cleve who bears responsibility for Ellen's pregnancy. Such an explanation would illumine why Ellen imparts Cleve with knowledge of such a sensitive medical condition. If one assumes Cleve's responsibility for the conception, this aspect would further accentuate the growing divide Ellen feels between her husband and lover. We learn at the start of Act II that David has lost his job at the movie house. By contrast, Cleve not only published his novel, but achieved the bestseller list. David feels his own inadequacy: "It's a wonder you don't fall in love with [Cleve].... Everything he does turns out well, and I'm a failure."[64] David's lament echoes that of Rims, who places a premium on societal expectations of male breadwinners despite his failure to fulfill that role. David's failure to conceive a child with Ellen would further degrade his masculine status as it was understood and valued in traditional society.

Ellen reasserts her feminist stand when the conflict shifts away from abortion and into the realm of labels. David, speaking of himself in third person, suggests Ellen have dinner with "your husband" rather than Cleve. Similar to Bobby Halevy firing back at Rims upon his use of the term "wife," Ellen rebels at David's use of the word "husband." When Marilyn tries to placate her, Ellen attacks:

ELLEN: He shouldn't have reminded me that he's my husband. I don't like the idea of anybody having marital rights over me—and he knows that.
DAVID: Oh, grow up, child. Be your age. Why take offense at a word?
ELLEN: It isn't the word. You meant it.
DAVID: You have some ancient infantile fixation on feminine independence—
ELLEN: It's not very ancient and it's not very infantile and I certainly have it—so you might as well accept it—.[65]

In his review for the *New York Herald Tribune*, Arthur Ruhl characterized *Gypsy* as containing "slightly feminist outbursts," but opined the plot was not "a case of a woman 'daring to live her own life'" because Ellen does not have a job.[66] We know, of course, that Ellen does have a job as she returned to work a day after the abortion. Furthermore, one wonders what, exactly, Ruhl thought Ellen was trying to do if not live her own life. She attempts throughout the play to oversee her affairs, but faces incessant pressure from the other characters, both male and female. She asserts and articulates empowerment over her own body by choosing to terminate her pregnancy and paying for the expense herself. And here she stands up to David's assuming rights over her as her husband and then infantilizing her behavior when she becomes angry. These actions clearly constitute something greater than "slightly feministic outbursts." Ellen demonstrates a keen desire for control over her life. David, on the other hand, having seen his status diminished through his loss of employment while his rival's star rises, attempts to reassert his traditional manly authority by referencing his rights as a husband. David's manliness receives a further blow when the janitor reappears and mistakes Cleve for Ellen's husband. David quickly responds and Ellen disabuses the janitor of his error, which causes the janitor some embarrassment.[67] This moment, occurring when it does in a state of high tension, augments the cessation of David's traditional masculine role in the marriage.

Ellen's psychological turmoil comes to the forefront once again when she finds herself alone with Cleve. Having just witnessed the row between her and David, Cleve apologizes for visiting. Ellen dismisses his concern by diminishing herself: "Nobody ever ought to pay any attention to me—when I get streaks like this.... I seem to go steely all over.... It's nobody's fault. It's the way I am. I'm a terrible sort of person."[68] Moments later, both she and Cleve share their mutual self-disgust at trying to maintain friendly relations with David when "he doesn't know."[69] This reference could naturally allude to David's lack of knowledge about their sexual affair. However, another more tantalizing possibly exists. As aforementioned, the action suggests Ellen's pregnancy may have resulted from her affair with Cleve rather than her husband. Ellen's darkening mood throughout Act II and her keeping the pregnancy secret from everyone except Cleve suggests something deeper than a sexual affair. Moreover, David already possessed awareness of her attraction to Cleve by the end of Act I and almost encourages an affair by suggesting she go on dates with him. It seems unlikely, then, that David would feel shocked or even surprised by an affair. A pregnancy, however, complicates matters. David clearly believed he caused the pregnancy and did not want Ellen to have an abortion, even though he acceded to her doing so. Anderson never provides an explicit answer to this question in the script, but the dramatic implications are compelling and would certainly serve to raise the stakes of Ellen's predicament.

By this point in the play Ellen has become more emotionally entrenched with Cleve, but her self-loathing restrains her. Cleve's ardent passion for her, however, has not slackened. He floats the idea of quitting his job and absconding with Ellen, arguing the financial success of his novel renders such a plan feasible.[70] Rather than jumping at the chance, Ellen dithers. She frets that his fame will lead him to rejecting her, expresses jealousy toward the possibility of another woman in his life, and despairs when he has to leave for a meeting related to his writing career.[71] Just as he prepares to depart, she baits him with a statement that no doubt embodied the frustrations of many women of the 1920s: "Go and have your career, dearest, and leave me to my dishes."[72] Cleve takes the bait. Like Rims, who boldly proclaimed his job advancement in South America could "go to the devil" if it meant securing Bobby as his bride, Cleve boasts: "To hell with my career."[73] Despite his protestation, however, Cleve ultimately leaves for his appointment, demonstrating the hollowness of male bravado.

Shortly after Cleve's exit, Ellen receives another visit from Sylvia and Mac, who come on a mission to confront Ellen regarding her behavior toward men. Mac takes it upon himself to admonish Ellen against "getting spoiled as the devil" with all the men she attracts and exhorts her to recognize the good fortune of being married to a man as virtuous as David.[74] Ellen, Mac advises, needs to "quit playing around."[75] Not surprisingly, Ellen takes umbrage with his presumption. When Sylvia comes to Mac's defense, Ellen delivers a lacerating rebuke:

SYLVIA: You've got to [gr]ow up, Ellen. A grown woman simply doesn't flirt with everybody.
ELLEN: I don't.
SYLVIA: But you do, dear. You may not know you're doing it, but you do. I could name a dozen—without stopping, really. You actually flirted with Mac—
ELLEN: Oh, did I?
SYLVIA: Didn't you even know it?
ELLEN: I think perhaps Mac had something to do with that.
SYLVIA: Ellen!
ELLEN: And I didn't ask for it, either! It looked quite the other way to me!

MAC: Well, maybe it was.[76]

Ellen's rebuttals speak to the inherent bias American society often bears toward women who seek sexual independence. First, there often exists the implication that such women flirt without provocation. Second, because this alleged flirtation happens uninvited, these women clearly seek reciprocation from men. We see this very bias in many of the critics, who tended to place the onus for Ellen's suffering on Ellen herself due to her supposed inability to remain faithful. As we saw in Act I, however, the action of the play represents something quite different from this biased implication. Ellen resists Cleve's advances, but cannot overcome his persistence. Similarly, Ellen is either ignored or denigrated by men for seeking to improve her mind and education. Her sense of self-worth is fixed on her sexuality as much by the society that surrounds her as by any action she takes of her own volition. She does, however, vigorously defend herself in challenging her friends' attitudes, thus further demonstrating a level of independence uncommon for female stage characters in the 1920s.

Marilyn's arrival prompts the departure of Mac and Sylvia and thus sets up Ellen's final confrontation with her mother. Anderson works hardest in this scene to solidify his psychological/hereditary theme. Marilyn reminds Ellen that they did have a good relationship when she was a child and implores her to reveal the source of her current disdain. Ellen balks at first, then relents. She recalls an incident that happened at the age of ten when she and Marilyn were visiting relatives and crowded conditions compelled them to share a bed. "And there was a man there I didn't like," Ellen says, "but you seemed to like him for some reason.... I don't know his name—I just remember there was an odor about him I didn't like—and one night I woke up shuddering—and that odor was in the room."[77] When Marilyn denies the accusation, Ellen only ratchets up the pressure. She begins to tell of another incident from her childhood, but cannot go on. Then she calls her mother a liar for her denials and excoriates her even further: "I know what you are, and I wouldn't like to tell you! I haven't begun to tell you what I know about you."[78] The implication that Marilyn engaged in sexual intercourse with a stranger while her ten-year-old daughter lay next to them in the bed evokes a horrifying scene of abuse. Some critics, while understandably avoiding specifics, commented on the particular intensity of this moment. David Carb, for example, though he disliked the play in general, conceded that the confrontation between Ellen and Marilyn "throbs with drama."[79] Another critic cited the mother/daughter confrontation as "[t]he most successful scene" in the play.[80] The scene ends with both women condemning each other, thus manifesting a likeness in viciousness Anderson no doubt expected would enhance his hereditary/psychological theme.

Not everyone was sold on the hereditary theme, however. A review of both critical and scholarly responses to the play demonstrates Anderson may have clouded his plot by his apparent reliance on heredity to sell it. R. Dana Skinner found Anderson straining credulity in emphasizing heredity. Skinner concedes, "The situation might happen," but concludes "it is a more universal human experience that each new generation has new life forces with which to battle against inheritance."[81] Skinner opined the play would work much better had Anderson simply written Ellen as psychologically afflicted rather than a victim of genetics.[82] In a retrospective analysis for his 1955 study, *Freud on Broadway*, W. David Sievers also took issue with the hereditary emphasis. Sievers labels *Gypsy* as "Anderson's most Freudian play," arguing Ellen suffers from "Electra jealousies."[83] Sievers contends, however, that in giving such emphasis to inherited traits, Anderson fails to grasp the full impact Ellen's "mother-rivalry" imposed on her psychological makeup.[84]

Anderson's effort at pressing heredity over sociocultural implications undermines Ellen's independence and, by extension, upholds the status quo. If Ellen's promiscuous behavior exists as a consequence of heredity from the mother, then the onus becomes one of poisoned female genes rather than restrictive cultural norms. Thus, the play perpetuates the idea that some women simply lack virtue and cannot help but prey upon unsuspecting, vulnerable men. We see this attitude evident in the response of several critics. George Jean Nathan described Ellen as having "inherited footslipping (*sic*) instincts"[85] while Atkinson found her possessing "a trace of madness"[86] in her blood. Another critic identified her as having "alley-cat (*sic*) instincts"[87] while still another dismissed her as "a girl with the fatal gift for infidelity."[88] Likewise, critics referred to Marilyn as having "tainted blood"[89] and being "slightly man-crazy."[90] Few reviewers, on the other hand, manifested any sympathy toward either woman or recognized the hardships Marilyn herself may have endured as a woman trying to survive in a man's world in the early twentieth century. Eleanor Flexner took particular umbrage with Anderson's overuse of genetics. In drawing Ellen as a woman who "cannot help herself" regarding sex, Flexner argues Anderson strips her of self-will. Flexner saw the problem as much simpler, noting "there is nothing obscure about Ellen's plight; it overtook a good many members of her generation, and had less to do with what kind of women their mothers were, and more with a profound sociological change which was taking place in morals and mores in the nineteen-twenties." Flexner concludes that "the pages of Judge Ben Lindsey's writings are full" of women like Ellen.[91] While Flexner's assertions certainly have merit, it seems overly simplistic to argue Anderson deprived Ellen of a will of her own. We have seen her throughout the play attempt self-assertion. She rebuffs Cleve, challenges her husband's authority, confronts her friends about their biased beliefs, and seeks and follows-through on an abortion which she pays for with her own earnings. Ellen is decidedly not a woman lacking personal will or conviction. Her weakness lies in her inability to resist the immense pressure outside forces place upon her. As Flexner alludes, that pressure would exist heredity or no. Anderson may well have muddied the waters by forcing heredity into the play, but whether the playwright intended it or not, Ellen's actions ultimately read more like those of an independent agent than a result of compulsion due to hereditary inevitability.

The second act concludes with Ellen reaching a climactic point of decision. The row with her mother spurs Ellen to finally break from David. She calls Cleve and arranges to meet him at his house where she intends to remain. She even assures him that he need not meet her there immediately because she possesses "the key,"[92] indicating the openness of their affair. As she prepares to exit, David enters for a last confrontation. He attempts to persuade her to remain in their marriage. Undaunted, Ellen makes her confession and, once again, references the abortion:

> ELLEN: I've lied to you.
> DAVID: When?
> ELLEN: All along—ever since I've known Cleve, almost.
> DAVID: I've known you were in love with him.
> ELLEN: It's more than that. Much more.
> DAVID: I thought you couldn't—couldn't lie. Not to me.
> ELLEN: I couldn't, not without damning myself utterly—and I've done it—so—and I've been so untrue you'd never believe me again—and it isn't over, with Cleve. And that was why I couldn't take the money.
> DAVID: You'd better go.[93]

The dialogue once again exudes that tantalizing, cryptic quality we saw earlier in discussion about the abortion. First, Ellen states that her entanglement with Cleve represents "much more" than simply falling in love. Second, she confesses her unfaithfulness reaches heights David would "never believe." Third, she identifies her guilt as the principal reason she could not accept repayment for the abortion. These statements seem to point to Cleve's responsibility for Ellen's pregnancy. Moreover, David's rejection may point to recognition of this fact on his part. Regardless, this moment signifies an irreparable break in the marriage.

ACT III: I KNEW HE WAS GOING TO KISS ME

One could sum up the final act of *Gypsy* as the fruition of the old adage that too much closeness breeds contempt. The act opens with Cleve alone in Ellen's apartment working over his next novel. Ellen calls and when Cleve answers the phone the tone of the conversation clearly indicates the withering of his romantic ardor. He informs Ellen he had no trouble gaining access to the apartment using the key she gave him, then teases that the reason she wanted him to have a key was "[s]o you wouldn't need to be on time meeting me."[94] Moments later, Cleve quips, "I'm pretending I live here and you support me."[95] Gone are Cleve's rapturous endearments, which were so prevalent in the first two acts. Though unmarried, the fact that Ellen and Cleve can have free rein in their affair instantly renders the affair less desirable. The dulling of passion is reminiscent of Bobby's revelation to Rims about wanting "hurried kisses and clandestine meetings."

Ellen's arrival further illumines the dissipation of the romance. She interrogates Cleve regarding his progress on the novel. Cleve initially limits himself to evasive monosyllables, prompting Ellen to inquire, "But, Cleve, what did you do all day?"[96] Cleve's dilatoriness and Ellen's apparent frustration inverts the traditional gender roles in that here the woman represents the worker outside the home, in effect supporting her homebound lover. The couple soon begin quibbling over their plans for the evening. Irked by his own inactivity, Cleve tries to persuade Ellen to go out so he can finish his work. Ellen resists, insisting going out to dinner or to the theatre "wouldn't be much fun without you."[97] The conflict intensifies with two new aspects injected. First, Ellen mentions a coworker, Wells, who wanted to take her out to the theatre and for a drive that evening. Second, Ellen receives a letter from her previous lover, Jerry, revealing that Marilyn has left her husband and absconded to Canada with another man.[98] These two factors provoke doubt in Cleve's mind about the stability of his relationship with Ellen. Ellen's protestations are then interrupted by the arrival of Sylvia, who, after trying to convince Ellen to return to David, brings word that Marilyn has committed suicide.[99]

News of her mother's demise strikes a crushing blow to Ellen's psyche. She begins doubting the veracity of Cleve's devotion as well as her own. In so doing, she condemns the falsity so often played out in courting: "I hate women who play the game with men and lead them on when it doesn't mean anything and play one man off against another! I hate it and loathe them and I'm always doing it. Oh, without intending to at all."[100] We see here in Ellen something of an amalgamation of Bobby and Florrie. On the one hand, she despises the machinations involved in manipulating men for romantic ends. On the other hand, she proves herself masterful in playing at such manipulations. Cleve tries to comfort her: "Isn't that perfectly natural?... Dearest, women have been that way since the world began!"[101] Cleve's cynicism does little to abrogate her negative feelings and reflects presumptions about women many men held and accepted as fact. Ellen, it seems, wants to rebel against societal norms of courtship, but feels powerless to do so. Rather than fight against cultural restrictions, she internalizes the fault within herself.

Stirred yet again with self-loathing, Ellen confesses a romantic encounter at her workplace. She tells Cleve: "Wells came in to-night when I was alone in the office, and had this long story to tell me about his new project, and I knew that wasn't what he was thinking about, and I knew that he was going to kiss me and I didn't want him to—and still when he did, I didn't do anything about it."[102] As we saw in Act I, Ellen resists the advances of a man only to find herself forced upon. Jazz Age sensibilities did not reckon victimization in remotely the same way as do many people in the twenty-first century. Cleve's response reflects this fact: "You let him kiss you?"[103] In using the term "let," Cleve, in effect, places the blame for the encounter on Ellen without so much as considering Wells's responsibility. Overwhelmed with guilt and shaken by her mother's suicide, Ellen rejects Cleve despite his efforts to remain with her. She convinces him to leave and the play ends with Ellen turning on the gas, seemingly fulfilling the hereditary cycle Anderson grafted into the play by committing suicide as did her mother.[104]

Conclusion

Or does she? The conclusion of *Gypsy* elicits a curious question in terms of cultural analysis. The resolution of suicide was not Anderson's original plan. On opening night, a phone call from Wells negates Ellen's self-destructive intent. Hearing Wells's voice buoys Ellen's spirit. She switches off the gas, throws open the windows to let in the fresh air, and soon departs for a date with her new lover. In his abridgement published in the *Best Plays* series, Burns Mantle notes that the suicide ending was the one most often played, but he elected to publish the version representing Anderson's original intent.[105]

Several critics commented on the two endings and there appears little consensus as to which was most pleasing or effective. One such critic suggested the play should have ended at the end of Act II, opining that "the rest of Ellen's days [after leaving David for Cleve] might better have been left to one's imagination."[106] Atkinson surmised that Ellen turning on the gas only to find redemption in the call of another lover "must have sounded false" to opening night audiences because of the play's dearth of "irony and cynicism."[107] The suicide ending, however, bore its own share of critical assault. One reviewer charged that Anderson's suicide angle was "a little harsh," astutely arguing that Ellen's unfaithfulness only shows she "acts as most men do" and therefore does not merit such condemnation.[108] Joseph Wood Krutch accused Anderson of propagating "cheaply moral fiction," arguing that Ellen's nature would prohibit suicide.[109] Arthur Pollock seemed to presage these reactions when, in response to a preview of *Gypsy* just prior to opening, he noted the weakness of the third act in comparison to the first two.[110] R. Dana Skinner seemed particularly vexed when he remarked that Anderson's indecisiveness about the ending "makes an intelligent review a somewhat baffling task."[111] Likewise, Arthur Ruhl, while not specifying which conclusion he witnessed, appears to sum up the overall critical reaction: "Just what was Mr. Anderson driving at?".[112]

Deciphering what Anderson was "driving at" poses a rather difficult challenge. *Gypsy*'s commercial failure (closing after 64 performances),[113] the fact that Anderson never codified his preferred version through publication of the play, the relative indifference of Anderson scholars toward it,[114] and Anderson's own lack of interest in it[115] conspire to obfuscate attempts at clearer understanding. As mentioned earlier in this chapter, one could argue *Gypsy* stands as, perhaps, Anderson's most provocative drama of the Jazz Age due to its depiction of abortion and Ellen's general sense of independence. None of Anderson's other plays, either in the 1920s or beyond, attempt to depict a woman's choice to terminate a pregnancy. Thus, this element goes a long way toward separating *Gypsy* from the previous three plays under consideration. Neither children nor pregnancy play any factor in *White Desert*. One could argue, perhaps, that *Sea-Wife* treats abortion in a symbolic, metaphorical sense, but Margaret's oceanic children lack the certitude of reality that Ellen's pregnancy possesses. Furthermore, Margaret was powerless in the termination of her progeny as her earthly child was either miscarried or stillborn and her oceanic children were murdered by the merman. As far as *Saturday's Children*, while Florrie presents the idea of Bobby trapping Rims with a pregnancy, Bobby ultimately rejects the idea and nothing more comes of it. However, curiously, few if any critics of *Gypsy* made any mention of the abortion. Though the word "abortion" never appears in the script, the conversation between Ellen and David seems clear enough. The idea that every critic either missed or misunderstood the reference is unconscionable. Perhaps it boiled down to a matter of propriety. Critics must have felt compelled to avoid such controversial subject matter in theatrical reviews. After all, as we have seen, the 1920s was rife with public efforts made to shut down plays exhibiting what many deemed objectionable material. It may well be that the critics avoided the topic of Ellen's abortion so as not to throw gasoline onto the fire.

Ellen's decision to terminate her pregnancy invites comparison of *Gypsy* to a much better-known work of the era, that of Sophie Treadwell's *Machinal*. Coincidentally, Treadwell's play appeared on Broadway in September 1928,[116] just a few months prior to *Gypsy*. While *Machinal* does not portray an abortion, it does include a scene wherein the protagonist finds herself faced with a newborn infant she did not want and for which she bears no maternal affection. Unlike Ellen, Treadwell's heroine demonstrates little knowledge of sex prior to her marriage and finds herself overwhelmed and despairing at the sudden onset of motherhood. Throughout the scene in the maternity ward, Young Woman never speaks when confronted with the child. She rejects all congratulatory overtures from the doctor, the nurse, and her husband. She finally voices her thoughts once she finds herself alone. Her first words reflect the starkness of her anguish: "Let me alone—let me alone—let me alone—I've submitted to enough—I won't submit to anymore."[117] One can imagine Ellen speaking these lines. Young Woman represents an attitude of greater innocence and less worldliness, but the result stands similar to Ellen. Disconnected from motherhood, Young Woman takes a lover who brings excitement into her life in ways her husband and child never could. The strain becomes too much and Young Woman murders her husband. In the end, both Young Woman and Ellen suffer death, one by execution and the other by suicide, as a result of their inability to reconcile themselves to societal mores. Atkinson characterized *Machinal* as "a tragedy of submission.... Events, people, circumstances stream by her, glib and optimistic, but they never relieve her loneliness."[118] Anderson's original ending for *Gypsy* permitted Ellen to reclaim a modicum of happiness. This result, however, was apparently so unpalatable to the opening night audience that the playwright took the unusual step of revising once again after opening.

Anderson's apparent preference for the non-suicide ending on opening night further undermines the hereditary theme or, perhaps, places a different spin upon it. If Ellen rejects suicide in favor of another romantic affair, then she ultimately rejects her mother's fatalism. Furthermore, Ellen demonstrates other important deviations from Marilyn's behavior. First, Ellen's penchant for forthrightness with David in her marriage and with Cleve at the end of the play contrasts with her mother's habit of obscuring the truth. Second, Ellen's independent stand against maternity demonstrates a desire to break the cycle of abuse Marilyn inflicted upon her. Third, Ellen manifests an intellectual curiosity and innate intelligence we never see from her mother. Ellen makes conscious efforts to improve her mind through reading; she seeks cultural outlets such as the theatre to broaden her horizons; and she maintains a work life in order to insure her own financial independence. Thus, despite all the talk of heredity in the play and by the critics, Ellen is, in many ways, not her mother.

If one agrees with Atkinson that *Machinal* represents a tragic case of feminine submission, then *Gypsy* may well stand as a tragic case of feminine rebellion. Contrary to those critics who viewed Ellen as a superficial woman incapable of faithfulness, Ellen fights for herself throughout the course of the play. She repeatedly resists unwanted advances, but most of the men she encounters are resolute in their pursuit of her. She frequently challenges patriarchal authority, gender roles, and the standard institutional conventions of marriage, only to have her opinions belittled, ignored, or minimized. Moreover, Ellen maintains her sense of agency to the end regardless of which conclusion you take. The suicide seems less satisfying as it plays into the traditional trope of the "fallen woman" suffering death as a result of her supposed malignant character. However, suicide endows Ellen with a sense of control over her fate. Unlike Mary in *White Desert*, Ellen does not endure destruction from a man. Likewise, Margaret in *Sea-Wife* seems helpless to stem the tide of masculine aggression swirling around her. Ellen, by contrast, seizes the moment and rather takes the matter into her own hands. Whether she runs off with another lover or commits suicide, Ellen goes out on her own terms.

NOTES

1. Burns Mantle, *The Best Plays of 1928–1929* (New York: Dodd, Mead, 1929), 385–386.
2. Ibid., 455.
3. Ibid., 283.
4. Ibid.
5. Ibid.
6. *Dramatist in America: The Letters of Maxwell Anderson, 1912–1958*, edited by Laurence G. Avery (Chapel Hill: University of North Carolina Press, 1977), 311.
7. See Mabel Driscoll Bailey, *The Playwright as Prophet* (1957); Alfred S. Shivers, *Maxwell Anderson* (1976) and *The Life of Maxwell Anderson* (1983); *Dramatist in America* edited by Laurence G. Avery (1977); and *Maxwell Anderson and the New York Stage*, edited by Nancy J. Doran Hazelton and Kenneth Krauss (1991).
8. Maxwell Anderson, *Gypsy*, Billy Rose Theatre Collection, New York Public Library, Act I, 1.
9. Ibid.
10. Ibid., Act I, 2.
11. Ibid.
12. Ibid., 2–3.
13. Ibid., 2.
14. Ibid., 3.
15. Ibid.
16. Ibid.
17. Ibid., 4.
18. Ibid., Act I, 5.
19. Ibid., 6.
20. Ibid., 6–8.
21. Brooks Atkinson, *New York Times*, 27 January 1929.
22. Robert Littell, "Brighter Lights," *Theatre Arts Monthly* 13 (March 1929): 170.

23. George Halasz, *Brooklyn Daily Eagle*, 27 January 1929.
24. *Gypsy*, Act I, 9.
25. Ibid., 10–11.
26. Ibid., 13.
27. Ibid., 12–13.
28. Ibid., 13.
29. Ibid.
30. Ibid., 16.
31. Ibid., 17.
32. Ibid.
33. Ibid., 37–39.
34. Ibid., 17.
35. Ibid., 18–19.
36. Ibid., 21.
37. Floyd Dell, "Can Men and Women be Friends?" *Nation* 118 (28 May 1924): 606.
38. Ibid.
39. Anderson, *Gypsy*, Act I, 20.
40. Ibid.
41. C. S. Lewis, *Mere Christianity* (New York: Macmillan, 1953), 12.
42. Charlotte Perkins Gilman, "Toward Monogamy," *Nation* 118 (11 June 1924): 671.
43. *Gypsy*, Act I, 30.
44. Ibid., 31.
45. Ibid., 24.
46. Ibid., 25–26.
47. Ibid., 34.
48. Ibid., 39–40.
49. Ibid., 41.
50. Ibid., 45–46.
51. Ibid., 47.
52. Ibid., 45.
53. Ibid., 45–47.
54. Ibid., 47.
55. *Gypsy*, Act II, 1.
56. Ibid., 2.
57. Ibid.
58. Ibid., 3.
59. Ibid., 6.
60. Ibid.
61. Ibid., 7.
62. Ibid., 7–8.
63. Ibid., 11.

64. Ibid., 4.
65. Ibid., 18.
66. Arthur Ruhl, "Second Nights," *New York Herald Tribune*, 3 February 1929.
67. *Gypsy*, Act II, 18–19.
68. Ibid., 21–22.
69. Ibid., 22.
70. Ibid.
71. Ibid., 25–26.
72. Ibid., 26.
73. Ibid.
74. Ibid., 28.
75. Ibid.
76. Ibid., 28–29.
77. Ibid., 31–32.
78. Ibid., 33.
79. David Carb, *Vogue*, 2 March 1929.
80. Charles Brackett, *New Yorker* 4 (26 January 1929): 25.
81. R. Dana Skinner, *Commonweal* 9 (6 February 1929): 406.
82. Ibid.
83. W. David Sievers, *Freud on Broadway* (New York: Hermitage House, 1955): 173.
84. Ibid., 173–174.
85. George Jean Nathan, *Judge* 96 (2 February 1929): 18.
86. Brooks Atkinson, *New York Times*, 27 January 1929.
87. Brackett.
88. Littell, 170.
89. *New York Times*, 15 January 1929.
90. Arthur Ruhl, *New York Herald Tribune*, 3 February 1929.
91. Eleanor Flexner, *American Playwrights, 1918–1938* (New York: Simon and Schuster, 1938), 84.
92. Anderson, *Gypsy*, Act II, 35–36.
93. Ibid., 36–37.
94. Ibid., Act III, 1.
95. Ibid.
96. Ibid., 4.
97. Ibid., 5.
98. Ibid., 6–7.
99. Ibid., 8–12.
100. Ibid., 14.
101. Ibid.
102. Ibid., 15.
103. Ibid.

104. Ibid., 16–19.
105. Mantle, *Best Plays of 1928–1929*, 315.
106. Brackett.
107. Atkinson, 27 January 1929.
108. Francis R. Bellamy, *Outlook*, 30 January 1929.
109. Joseph Wood Krutch, *Nation* 128 (6 February 1929): 168.
110. Arthur Pollock, *Brooklyn Daily Eagle*, 6 January 1929.
111. Skinner, 6 February 1929.
112. Ruhl, 3 February 1929.
113. Mantle, *Best Plays of 1928–1929*, 455.
114. The three main scholars to publish book-length studies focused on Anderson (Mabel Driscoll Bailey, Laurence G. Avery, and Alfred S. Shivers) offer little to no attention to *Gypsy*.
115. Anderson renders one reference to *Gypsy* in his autobiographical interview for Columbia University's Oral History Project, his only comment being only an acknowledgment of its failure. *Dramatist in America*, 311.
116. Mantle, *Best Plays of 1928–1929*.
117. Sophie Treadwell, *Machinal* in *Norton Anthology of Drama*, 2nd edition, Vol. 2 (New York: Norton, 2014), 597–599.
118. Brooks Atkinson, *New York Times*, 8 September 1928.

CHAPTER 6

Maxwell Anderson Reassessed

This chapter attempts to apply the implications of Anderson's dramas more broadly. The first section briefly revisits Jesse Lynch Williams's *Why Marry?* Though outside the parameters of the Jazz Age, Williams's play serves both as an important antecedent to the marriage plays to follow and a striking contrast between the 1910s and the 1920s. The succeeding two sections examine two theatrical extremes of the Jazz Age more in depth: Frank Craven's 1920 comedy, *The First Year*, followed by Mae West's controversial 1926 play, *Sex*. Given the preponderance of marriage plays produced in the 1920s, one is left with no shortage of choices. However, there are multiple reasons why I chose to isolate upon these two as consummate examples of Jazz Age matrimonial drama. First, both plays were major commercial successes, meaning they managed to reach a large number of people. Second, their success was achieved, in part, by indulging radical extremes of the social spectrum. Craven's play blatantly reinforced the status quo while West's play flew straight in its face. Third, there is the matter of each play's placement in time. That Craven's play occurred at the start of the decade while West's play arrived nearer its end offers instruction into the vicissitudes of marriage plays throughout the 1920s. Following discussions of *The First Year* and *Sex*, the next section will offer a brief examination of the potential impact of Anderson's life

© The Author(s), under exclusive license to Springer Nature
Switzerland AG 2022
F. D. Geary II, *Maxwell Anderson and the Marriage Crisis*,
https://doi.org/10.1007/978-3-031-13241-4_6

upon the output of his Jazz Age drama, an aspect of his plays previous scholarship has largely neglected to plumb. The final section will offer a summation regarding the importance of Anderson's legacy in American theatre.

THE PLAY WOULD GAIN GREATLY BY JUDICIOUS CUTTING: *WHY MARRY?* REVISITED

One might sum up Jesse Lynch Williams's contribution to the vogue of marriage dramas with the phrase "on the nose." As referenced in Chapter 1, Williams baldly stated his intention with the play: to depict "the truth about marriage." His truth, however, relies on grotesque stereotypes with the ultimate end of upholding convention and he sets upon this goal with all the subtlety of a sledgehammer. Early in Act I, John's wife, Lucy, who represents the voice of conservative females, complains that, "New Women" have achieved nothing aside from "destroying chivalry."[1] She goes on to paint herself as "just an old-fashioned wife" and insists, "Woman's sphere is the home. My husband says so."[2] Lucy diminishes Helen as "a sexless freak with a scientific degree" that no man would deign marry.[3] Helen, for her part, flaunts her "new woman" status throughout the play. She openly challenges her sister-in-law's Victorian mores: "Lucy, dear, do you always find your true happiness in duty?"[4] She needles John with statistics about the rising divorce rate and mocks conventional notions about how a woman should think.[5] When John leans on his male authority as he brother in ordering her not to travel with Ernest to Paris, she responds with marked defiance: "[You are] not my owner! You know, all women used to be owned by men. Formerly they ruled us by physical force—now by financial force.... But alas they are to lose even *that* hold upon us—poor dears!" (Ellipses and emphasis in original).[6]

Such discussions and confrontations pervade the play *ad nauseum*. The published version came in at over 240 script pages and this bloated length did not go unnoticed by some observers. Though generally positive in their critique, the critic for the *Brooklyn Daily Eagle* noted that Williams was "inclined to be carried away by his own loquacity" and suggested this verboseness was exacerbated by the playwright's singularity of purpose. Unlike Shaw, the critic opined, who aimed his satires at multiple facets of human life, Williams rather pounds away at the same problem for the entirety of three acts. "The play," this critic observed, "would gain greatly by judicious cutting. The repetition, particularly in the last act, adds no force to the argument and merely becomes tedious."[7] The critic for the *New York Times* did not go as far as labelling the play "tedious," but did concede, "There is, perhaps, a tendency at times to hammer away at current standards in conduct and to underline ideas."[8] Moreover, while most critics hailed the play a success and predicted a long stay on Broadway, the production's run of 120 performances, though solidly respectable, did not exactly connote a rousing smash. In fact, the 1917–1918 Broadway season saw over 140 productions and of those, no fewer than 26 achieved longer runs than *Why Marry?*[9] This suggests, perhaps, that audiences, over time, grew weary of the play's obvious message. Furthermore, that the play won the first Pulitzer Prize does not do as much to recommend it as one might expect. The Pulitzer jury manifested little enthusiasm for the play, but they had not given any prize in 1917 (the actual inaugural of the Pulitzers) and thus seemed compelled to pick one. *Why Marry?*, it appears, was simply the most agreeable of a mediocre lot.[10]

Anderson's four marriage plays of the Jazz Age are somewhat difficult to place alongside *Why Marry?* For one, three of Anderson's plays reach for serious, if not outright tragic, results. Of the four Anderson plays, *Saturday's Children* stands closest in context and style to *Why Marry?* But *Saturday's Children*'s denouement seems bittersweet by comparison to Williams's flimsy, convention-affirming happy ending. *Why Marry?* does offer some dramatic elements in common with Anderson's 1927 hit. Williams's Judge Everett bears some similarity to Mr. Halevy in that both are iconoclasts when it comes to tradition yet remain ensconced in marriage all the same. However, whereas Mr. Halevy becomes a conduit for Bobby's rebellion, Judge Everett ultimately facilitates Helen's entrapment into the supposed safety of matrimony. Both plays lay out the basic attitudes of women who seek marriage, such as Lucy and Florrie, versus women who eschew it, such as Helen and Bobby. However, Anderson does not satisfy himself with superficial social politics as does Williams. Bobby's character evolves over the course of the play into an assertive, independent woman. Helen, on the other hand, begins as lioness, but goes out like a lamb. When she finds herself humbugged in the end, this fiercely independent new woman offers not a single word of protest. One cannot imagine Bobby doing the same, for Anderson's purpose seems more profound and Bobby seems a much more dynamic, three-dimensional character. *Why Marry?* seeks to provoke laughter at the women of the Progressive Era. *Saturday's Children* searches to parse out the conflicting nuances for women of the Jazz Age who are struggling to locate and assert their individual identities.

Simple, Human and Joyous: Frank Craven's *The First Year*

With *The First Year*, Frank Craven scored one of the biggest commercial hits of the 1920s. By the end of the 1921–1922 season, Craven's light comedy, running for 760 performances over a near two year run, had become the third longest running production in Broadway history.[11] As the title implies, the plot centers on a young couple struggling through their initial year of matrimony. The young couple in question, Grace and Tommy, are naïve and unworldly. Early in the first act Grace declares no desire to work for her own living: "I want to be supported, and I want to be a help to the man that supports me, and I want to have children, and plan futures and arrange marriages for them."[12] In other words, Grace's ambitions have not grown past those of a nineteenth century aspiring Victorian matriarch. Tommy represents the prototypical "nice boy." He does everything he can to avoid offending anyone all the while feebly trying to draw Grace's attention away from a more physically attractive, athletic, and self-assured suitor.[13] The young couple receives guidance from Grace's bachelor uncle whose higher education (he is a medical doctor) and lack of marital attachment endows him with a more objective point of view on marriage. Grace's alternate suitor complicates things by stating that if she refuses his marital overtures, she will never have another chance to marry again. Enraged at this presumption, Grace responds by impetuously prodding Tommy into a marriage proposal, which she accepts with alacrity.[14]

Grace meets her first major domestic challenge at the start of Act II, but a challenge markedly different from anything in the Anderson plays. Grace must find a way to serve dinner to two important business guests in the absence of her African American servant. She settles on placing the servant's daughter, Hattie, in her place. Hattie represents little more than a minstrel-esque racist comic device; childish and ignorant, even the simplest tasks have to be clearly explained and defined for her. Dinner goes predictably awry due to Hattie's incompetence. Further tension derives from the appearance of Grace's former suitor, who conveniently arrives unannounced, purporting information that turns Tommy's business deal sour. Grace and Tommy have a bitter fight over their poor economic circumstances, which leads Grace to storm out of their flat and escape on the next train to her parents' house. Act II ends with the discovery that the former suitor was lying and that Tommy will be able to close his business deal as planned, making him exceptionally wealthy.[15]

A brief third act draws the comedy to a contrived conclusion. Grace frets over never seeing Tommy again. Once word reaches her of her husband's successful business deal, she determines she cannot return to him now that he is rich after running out on him when he was poor. Soon, Grace's uncle arrives to put matters square. Before he can, however, the former suitor and Tommy accidentally meet again and wind up in a fistfight. Matters come to a head when, after the dust settles, both Tommy and Grace vow never to return to married life. The uncle, refusing to accept that result, orders them to resume the marriage. Both, however, remain obstinate. In a *deus ex machina* moment reminiscent of *Why Marry?*, their attitudes instantly change when the uncle reveals that Grace is pregnant. Similar to Helen in Williams's comedy, Grace never speaks a word at the end of the play. When Tommy presses for confirmation of the pregnancy, she lowers her head. He promptly asks forgiveness and she promptly affirms said forgiveness by embracing him. Tommy then expresses his hope, on the last line of the play, that "he" (i.e., the baby) will like them,[16] thus assuming the child a boy.

The critics of 1920 were nearly universal in their praise of *The First Year*, catapulting the production to instant prosperity. The *New York Times* hailed the play as "[s]imple, human and joyous"[17] while the *Brooklyn Daily Eagle* proclaimed it "much the finest comedy of the season."[18] Still another critic praised Craven's skill for writing "freshly" and "entertainingly" on such a well-travelled dramatic subject as marriage.[19] Alexander Woollcott prognosticated not only a long Broadway run, but immense popularity among stock companies throughout the country.[20] Key to Woollcott's prediction was, in his opinion, the play's universality. *The First Year* was a play that everyone, regardless of their background or social status, would enjoy.[21] Other critics agreed in stressing the play's broad appeal with one observing, "It is a play about you and your wife, or about the grownup boy and girl in love around the corner."[22] It seems evident, given the high praise received and the production's protracted run, that critics and New York audiences alike recognized much of themselves at which to laugh in Craven's lighthearted play. Moreover, unlike Williams in *Why Marry?*, Craven does not indulge in pointed social philosophy or new woman politics. He keeps his plot straightforward and his characters vapid. Craven's drama did not trouble its audience with serious questions. Several critics noted the inoffensiveness Woollcott, who enjoyed the play, conceded that Craven made his point "[w]ith no great searching of hearts, with no unusual penetration."[23] At least three critics labelled the play "simple"[24] despite lauding its pleasurable elements. The *Brooklyn Daily Eagle* added that the play was "devoid of plot"[25] while the *New York Times* observed it as "undramatic."[26] Again, these foibles did not seem to interfere with the jovial attitude engendered by Craven's work.

At least one erudite observer, however, found Craven's play less than appealing or, at least, not outstanding enough to merit serious recognition. When the jury for the Pulitzer Prize for Drama met in 1921, they settled on debating two choices: *The First Year* and Zona Gale's *Miss Lulu Bett*. Two of the three jury members favored Craven, but William Lyon Phelps made a bold insurgency on behalf of Gale. It seems Phelps may have been motivated more by his admiration for Gale's work rather than an aversion to Craven's. In any case, Phelps launched a strident appeal in favor of *Miss Lulu Bett* despite its lukewarm reception from critics, its modest Broadway run, and the reticence of his two fellow jurors. When his colleagues tried to persuade him to award the prize to Craven, Phelps simply refused to countenance the award going to anyone other than Gale. There was even talk of a compromise choice, wherein neither of the two main selections would receive the prize. Finally, the three men agreed it would represent a watershed moment if the prize were awarded to a woman for the first time and it was primarily upon this basis that the decision was made to award *Miss Lulu Bett* the Pulitzer for 1921.[27]

Miss Lulu Bett reflects an uneasiness with independent women similar, in at least one respect, to Anderson's *Gypsy*. Gale's titular heroine is a young woman neglected by her family, but kept around the house to fulfill the domestic work her mother and sister refuse to do. Essentially, Lulu is an uncompensated servant trapped in the dependency of living on her sister's and brother-in-law's charity. Moreover, she marries a man who later remembers he was married to someone else, which scandalizes Lulu and the family. In the original ending, Lulu recognizes the drudgery of her plight and plots an escape on the train. Her family pleads for her to return to the home because no one else proves capable of running the household as effectively.[28] Lulu, however, resolves to abscond. When her mother demands to know where, Lulu responds: "Away. I thought

I wanted somebody of my own. Well, maybe I just wanted myself."[29] When another man makes overtures of marriage, she refuses: "Sometime, maybe. I don't know. But first I want to see out of my own eyes. For the first time in my life."[30] Like *Gypsy*, however, Gale alters the ending after opening night. In the revised version of Act III, Lulu's lover returns. His first wife turns out to have conveniently died and he apologizes to Lulu, thus bringing down the curtain with presumed wedded bliss to follow.[31] *Miss Lulu Bett* had a solid run in New York, but nothing close to the monstrous run of *The First Year*.

The phenomenal commercial success of *The First Year* coupled with the contentious deliberations of the Pulitzer jury are symbolic of the uneasy tension regarding marriage and gender roles during the Jazz Age. Though praised for its familiarity, supposedly a play to which everyone could relate, *The First Year* offers little, if anything, in the way of thoughtful, nuanced critique. It does not challenge an audience's perception of married life nor does it wrestle with the implications of patriarchy. Moreover, it relies on a blatantly racist representation of an African American servant to help sell its comic wares. *The First Year* was, in short, comfortable for a 1920 New York audience. By contrast, *Miss Lulu Bett* may not have been a great play (the Pulitzer jury actually acknowledged this precise sentiment in their recommendation),[32] but it certainly treated the sociopolitical predicament of women in marriage with more realism and sensitivity. Furthermore, Gale's achievement of the Pulitzer Prize just one year after the ratification of the 19th Amendment, granting American women the right to vote, stands as a signifier of the changing times. That American theatre could have a hit as vapid and condescending as *The First Year* while awarding a major prize to a woman for a play like *Miss Lulu Bett* emblematizes, in a microcosm, the dissonance of Jazz Age culture about marriage.

In examining Craven's play alongside the four Anderson plays under consideration one finds little substantive merit in the former. Unlike Anderson's heroines, Grace maintains stolid conventional attitudes about marriage. Her outright denial of any desire to work for her own money most closely aligns her with Bobby's sister, Florrie, from *Saturday's Children* and certainly lacks any of the intellectual probing of Mary Kane, the soul-searching of Margaret, or the independent streaks of both Bobby and Ellen. Moreover, Grace's immediate submission upon the revelation of her pregnancy, a pregnancy announced by her uncle and never verbally acknowledged by her, cements her embodiment of the patriarchal ideal of conventional womanhood. Unlike Ellen, one cannot fathom Grace considering termination of her pregnancy. Moreover, the fact of her pregnancy would render it all the more difficult for her not to return to her husband, despite her protestations. In effect, Grace acquiesces to marriage out of maternal duty rather than marital love.

Furthermore, what passes for domestic drudgery in *The First Year* does little to raise the dramatic stakes. *White Desert* relied on isolation and the brutal climate of the North Dakota prairie; *Sea-Wife* offered the isolation of an island coupled with nineteenth century religious zealotry and superstition; *Saturday's Children* emphasized the economic struggles of two people living on a single, insufficient salary; and *Gypsy* depicted condescending males who minimized and ridiculed Ellen's efforts at keeping a house and home. The worst thing that Grace faces in *The First Year* are the frustrations associated with explaining to a servant how to serve dinner and, later, complaining about the fact that Tommy makes too little money for her to purchase new clothes.[33] Such dramatic stakes are paltry when compared to that which Anderson's women must contend. One might argue Anderson bore different intentions in terms of genre as three of his four plays are serious dramas. However, *Saturday's Children* functions as a comedy and one could say *Gypsy* has its comedic moments. It is noteworthy that a few critics commented upon the similarities between *Saturday's Children* and *The First Year* and all stated or implied that Anderson's play was more thoughtful, honest, and effectively written.[34] By contrast, even critics who lauded *The First Year* all seemed in agreement that Craven's play hardly stood as meaningful dramatic art.

A Monstrosity Plucked from Garbage Can to Sewer: Mae West's *Sex*

Opposite *The First Year* on Broadway's 1920s moral spectrum stood Mae West's 1926 play, *Sex*, the controversy upon which we have previously touched. Set in the red-light district of Montreal, the play opens on a shabby apartment that the central character, Margy LaMont, shares with a petty criminal and pimp named Rocky. Margy, herself a prostitute, represents the streetwise, no nonsense, independent woman insouciant to societal mores. She serves as a mentor to young Agnes, another prostitute, but one who turned to sex work out of necessity to help support her family in the United States. Agnes wants to return home, but Margy counsels her against such a move because her parents will inevitably find out she succumbed to prostitution and, once the truth is out, she will never recover her reputation. Later, Rocky brings Clara, a wealthy socialite out for adventure, into the apartment. He drugs her and robs her of her jewels, then leaves her languishing in the bedroom. Margy discovers Clara near death from the overdose and revives her. The police are called and Clara, in order to avoid a scandalous disgrace for her wealthy husband, lies about how she came to the seedy apartment. She bribes the police officer to avoid arrest and accuses Margy of stealing the jewels. Aghast, Margy vows vengeance on Clara and thus ends Act I.[35]

Act II opens on a boat in Trinidad with Margy having absconded with one of her suitors for a holiday to escape the scandal that ended the previous act. Margy inspires the amorous affections of a wealthy young man, Jimmy, who pursues her charms with ideas of marriage. Significantly, Jimmy does not know Margy's profession. His affection also fosters jealousy in Margy's suitor, Gregg. In a flimsy dramatic coincidence, Margy is surprised to encounter Agnes on the same boat. Agnes confides that she had attempted to return home, but that Margy was correct in assuming her parents would not accept her. The action transitions to a conversation between Margy and Gregg wherein Gregg offers to run away with her to Australia where their anonymity would afford them the opportunity to begin life afresh. Margy rejects this offer, preferring instead to accept Jimmy's marriage proposal. Act II ends when they hear a splash and Margy discovers that Agnes has committed suicide by throwing herself off the boat.[36]

The final act in West's play completes the cycle of convenient contrivances. Jimmy brings Margy to his New England home to meet his parents. Margy, of course, worries over securing the approval of her future in-laws and she tries to avoid provoking any suspicion of her past life. Margy's efforts are compromised when Jimmy's mother turns out to be Clara, the rich socialite who suffered the attack in Act I. Clara resolves to tell her son the truth about Margy's identity. Margy responds in kind, threatening to pull the veil off of Clara's secret excursion to Montreal. These postures ultimately come to nothing when Rocky suddenly appears to blackmail Clara. Margy takes Clara's side, conniving with her to turn the tables on Rocky and have him arrested and hauled away without either Jimmy or Clara's husband ever knowing he was there. Margy then recognizes her position as untenable given her past history and determines she does not want to end up with the same fate as Agnes. She reveals the truth of her identity to Jimmy and accepts Gregg's offer to decamp to Australia to start life anew.[37]

The critics were virtually unanimous in excoriating *Sex*. Reviews were often brief and, one might say, to the point. The *New York Times* led off its observations thus: "A crude, inept play, cheaply produced and poorly acted."[38] The *New York Evening Post* echoed this sentiment, lambasting the play as "crudely vulgar and utterly without merit in text or performance."[39] The *Brooklyn Daily Eagle* also declined to mince words, calling it "a terrible play" as well as "vulgar and disgusting." This same review concluded: "*Sex* is just the type of play that makes one want a stage censor. Not because of its smut, but because it is vulgar, tiresome and not worth being seen." This critic, however, anticipated a long run for the play and took pains to minimize its potential commercial success by impugning the morals of New Yorkers, predicting that *Sex* "will probably do good business, as there always is an audience for vulgar pieces."[40] *Time* likewise declared it "[a] cheap and sleazy work" and "perhaps the dirtiest and the dullest play of the season."[41] Finally, the *Daily Mirror* reached for a more poetic condemnation, calling the play "[a] monstrosity plucked from Garbage Can to [the] Sewer."[42]

The vitriolic critical response to *Sex* reveals the moral stridency of the Jazz Age. The faults of the play in terms of its structure, characterization, and contrivances are numerous. However, the rancorous, sententious attitude expressed by reviewers speaks less to an inartistic work of drama and more to a marked discomfort with sexual subject matter so baldly presented on stage. Mae West was no Frank Craven. And *Sex* was certainly not *The First Year*. West's depiction of the seedier aspects of sex and gender roles presented a direct confrontation to conventional values. As one scholar has noted, West's placement of the brothel in Montreal rather than Trinidad served to make "sin a domestic product."[43] Likewise, Jimmy's status as the scion of a wealthy New England family brought the immorality even closer to home.[44] American audiences could not distance themselves from the vulgar tenets of the play through geography. Whereas *The First Year* was praised for its "familiarity," *Sex* presented audiences with a level of closeness that bred an immense degree of contempt. Nevertheless, the critic for the *Brooklyn Daily Eagle* proved correct in prognosticating a long run. *Sex* racked up 375 performances, its commercial success halted only because the production was shut down in 1927.[45]

When considering Mae West's play juxtaposed with Anderson's dramas, we find a marked contrast in the opposite direction from *The First Year*. Anderson was not nearly as conventional or conservative as Craven; nor was he anywhere near as bold or revolutionary as West. While *White Desert*, *Saturday's Children*, and *Gypsy* all garnered some measure of moral criticism from Broadway reviewers for their explicit content, Anderson did not draw near the ire that West did. Gender dynamics no doubt played a role, for the critics did not content themselves with merely assailing West's play, but insinuated ill-repute, or at least rank amateurism, upon West herself. One critic, for example, belittled West as nothing more than "a vaudeville actress."[46] A second critic refused even to dignify her with the term "actress," instead labelling her "a singer out of the two-a-day."[47] Anderson, a white, middle-aged, college-educated man who worked steadily as a journalist prior to achieving theatrical fame, was, by default, simply less offensive in personage to 1920s Americans. This social masking perhaps shielded Anderson from the harshest of criticisms as long as his critiques did not venture too far or become too provocative.

Anderson was also not, either temperamentally or intellectually, inclined to push sexual boundaries on the stage to such extremes. George Abbott characterized Anderson's demeanor thus: "On the surface Maxwell was a stolid, scholarly man, but inside he was all romance: he wished to ride a white steed over the mountains and carry off a beautiful maiden as much as the next fellow."[48] This romantic disposition reveals itself further in his devotion to verse drama, a form typically associated with grandiose characters and enriched emotions. Moreover, Anderson's depictions of women, even in his Jazz Age dramas, tend toward convention with respect to sex. The fates of his heroines exemplify this fact. Mary Kane dies at the hands of her husband for her defiance. Margaret dies mysteriously under the strain of male oppression. The instances of Bobby and Ellen are particularly telling. Though Bobby achieves her independence, she does so by adhering to monogamy, if not institutional marriage. Ellen, who is not monogamous commits suicide in the most frequently played Broadway version. Years later Anderson would publish a volume of essays elucidating his views on theatre. One such essay included the admonition that an audience would not accept female infidelity onstage.[49] Whether this was a reaction to the audience response to the original ending of *Gypsy* is unknown, but Anderson nevertheless tended toward monogamy for his female characters. Those who were not monogamous typically suffered negative endings. Empowering a woman with complete sexual freedom in the manner West did in *Sex* was simply not within the makeup of his character. Anderson did, however, invest his Jazz Age women with a measure of fortitude uncommon for most playwrights of the time. The reason for this fact may well lie, in part, in the personal experiences Anderson endured within his own marriage to Margaret at the time his playwriting career began.

Marriage and Maxwell Anderson

Unlike other theatrical luminaries such as Eugene O'Neill and Tennessee Williams, Anderson was not given to investing his dramas with personal details from his life. A colleague once asked Anderson about his reluctance to mine his personal experience when searching for dramatic material. Anderson replied that he wrote plays to escape the somberness of his past, not to relive it.[50] In fact, he was reticent about sharing personal information about himself at all. Burns Mantle[51] and Barrett H. Clark[52] discovered this fact on separate occasions when each applied to Anderson for biographical details for publication and received determined evasions. Anderson even rebuffed his own sister's request for his perspective on a family history she was compiling.[53] In examining his prominent work from the 1930s, one finds heavy doses of history, satire, and fantasy, but never anything inherently realistic. John Gassner strikes at this distinction when he pointed out that while O'Neill produced plays seemingly "wrung from [his] entrails," Anderson "seems rather academic.... More of an epigone than a trailblazer."[54] One must bear in mind, however, that Gassner bases this opinion on Anderson's Depression era work. Anderson's work in the 1920s teases a different perspective on his dramatic output. As early as 1920, signs were manifesting that Anderson's marriage to Margaret was failing.[55] These signs intensified throughout the ensuing decade.[56] The playwright's biographer, Alfred S. Shivers, speculates, in passing, that the timing of *Saturday's Children* appearing alongside his marital difficulties seems more than coincidental.[57] Though details are scarce, one can see a potential link between Anderson's own marriage and the pervasiveness of the marriage theme not only in *Saturday's Children*, but in all three of the other plays as well.

Two events in Anderson's life reveal the strain in his marriage to Margaret. By 1920, the Andersons had been married for nine years and Margaret had born two sons.[58] A third son would arrive in 1921.[59] One suspects the reality of Florrie's advice in *Saturday's Children* about how children can weigh a man down. Anderson seems to confirm this reality in an article he published in the *Freeman* on 22 September 1920.[60] In this article, which Shivers labeled "intensely personal,"[61] Anderson lays out, with remarkable candor, the impediment marriage bears upon personal freedom:

> Without the shadow of a doubt marriage and children, as we know them at present, constitute the most effective brakes on progress toward generally recognized ideals, the immovable barriers in the way of individual and industrial justice. If we were all celibates the present system would not last a fortnight. Our shares, large and small, in the good things of existing civilization, are necessary to us because we have dependents, and to keep those shares we must faithfully conform to the ideals and standards of life as it is being lived about us. A workman with only his living to make is practically impregnable beside the father of a family. Most of us have given hostages, not alone to fortune, but more particularly to the powers that be, and those powers are themselves no less committed to the schemes we all uphold.[62]

Anderson hardly sounds like a proud patriarch basking in the glow of a growing family. His tone comes off, rather, more like Rims or, even more closely, Mr. Halevy. Anderson's pessimism about marriage echoes sentiments at which radicals such as Emma Goldman, Charlotte Perkins Gilman, Floyd Dell, and Bertrand Russell were all driving. That marriage, as an institution, as a systemized way of life, represented little more than a social prison and a barrier toward individual freedom and felicity. This sentiment reverberates in the actions and expressions of so many characters from the plays examined. Mary, in *White Desert*, wondering why she should conform to marriage when doing so demands submission to her husband's dominance. The bigoted attitudes of the fisher-folk in *Sea-Wife* demanding a mock wedding to re-legitimize Margaret's union with her husband and to drive away supposed evil spirits on the island. Bobby's recognition of wanting a love affair rather than bills and dishes. Ellen's challenge to her friends as to why anyone should be required to limit their love affairs to one person just because society and tradition demands it. These are just a few cursory examples of how Anderson's thoughts about marriage emanate throughout his marriage dramas. These examples, taken in concert with the *Freeman* article and recognition of the state of Anderson's family life, further reinforce just how impactful the institution of marriage was upon his thoughts and his art in the 1920s.

Near the end of the *Freeman* article, Anderson mitigates his radical, anarchistic tone. He writes, without irony, that he means not for readers to take his words as "an indictment of the family."[63] Rather, his arguments pose "a more direct bearing on the problem of conscious evolution."[64] The current social structure, Anderson observes, finds itself bound not by any meaningful connection or loyalty to institutions, but rather only by "a taut thread of gold."[65] In other words, people do as they do, conforming to the current accepted institutions society exhorts, purely and simply out of economic necessity. A reframing of societal institutions is hampered by the fact that married men have dependents for which they must provide. "If it were not for the hostages we have given," Anderson declares, "we would have demanded a great remodelling (*sic*) long ago."[66] Interestingly, Anderson points to "the economic independence of women" as a primary means of shedding many social barriers.[67] We know that Margaret Anderson eventually subsumed her educational goals to her husband's, rendering Anderson the family's sole breadwinner. We also see questions of economic independence arising, most often, in *Saturday's Children*, but also bearing some weight in *Gypsy* wherein Ellen maintains separate finances and refuses her husband's efforts at reimbursing the cost of her abortion.

Anderson's strong, almost militant, stance against marriage in the beginning of the article only to soften the blow in the end stands in keeping with the attitudes of many radicals at the time. Many intellectuals who challenged traditional ideas of marriage, such as Judge Lindsey, often did so out of what they viewed as a need for accommodation. The 1920s brought significant social change in how men and women interacted. Women had increased their political power at the ballot box and their economic power in the workplace. Thus, marriage required modification in response to these evolving social conditions. Despite the fact that these intellectuals would often assail Victorian marriage with seeming iconoclasm, key tenets of traditional marriage, particularly monogamy, remained strong.[68] Anderson's mitigation of his tone at the end of the essay, therefore, reflects the upheaval taking place in 1920s America. It also demonstrates the power traditional marriage held. People may rail against it, but few were willing to completely obliterate its presence. Taken within this context, Mary's uncertainty in *White Desert* and Bobby's indecisiveness in *Saturday's Children* make more dramatic sense. Mary fully recognizes the burdens marriage will render upon her personal freedom, yet does not reject it. Bobby resists marriage, but eventually succumbs in order to legitimize her love affair. One could make a similar argument for Ellen in *Gypsy*. Marriage for her was more about the practicality of carrying on her sexual affair with David without social judgment.

Aside from the *Freeman* article, the second revelatory clue in Anderson's life in relationship to the plays is the playwright's sexual affair with the poet and novelist, Josephine Herbst. Significantly, Anderson initiated this affair in 1920, the same year he penned the *Freeman* article. The affair began innocently enough. Herbst was a friend of Anderson's wife. Margaret invited the young poet to their home for a weekend in February 1920. Anderson was charged with picking Herbst up at the train station and, in conversing with her on the way to his house, found they were both quite taken with each other. Herbst was young and exciting. Anderson, though still in his early thirties, seemed caught in a premature midlife crisis. He lamented to Herbst about how stagnant his life had become, finding himself suppressed under the weight of humdrum domesticity, his passion for life ebbing.[69] We see here, again, evidence of his life potentially impacting his dramatic works. His distaste for domestic life mirrors both Bobby and Ellen while his mournfulness over his lost youth echoes Mr. Halevy.

The enchantment between Anderson and Herbst extended well beyond the weekend visit. Anderson began sending her intimate notes and the two had lunch together on Herbst's twenty-eighth birthday. At that lunch meeting, they apparently negotiated a sexual affair. Herbst biographer, Elinor Langer, informs us that Anderson actually consulted his wife regarding his plans and that Margaret reportedly agreed "in principle" to the liaison.[70] Anderson and Herbst consented to an open sexual affair with no emotional attachments. Anderson was Herbst's first lover and, in spite of their arrangement, she seems to have fallen in love with him.[71] Langer describes Anderson's reaction to the affair as "a paroxysm of ambivalence" as he was often checking in with Margaret and hurrying home once their encounters concluded.[72] Such ambivalence once again demonstrates the dissonance between ideas and reality during the Jazz Age. Marriage may have represented a shackle upon individual freedom, but the weight of tradition proved difficult for Anderson to shake, just as it proved difficult for the characters in his plays to completely deny. The term "ambivalence" seems especially apropos. In all four plays marriage lingers like a shadow, but bears all the force of a freight train barreling down on its set, inevitable track.

Anderson's affair with Herbst comes to a sad end, which also provides potential insight into his marriage plays. Contrary to Herbst's growing affection, Anderson remained steadfast to his marital commitment. The tension boiled over into Herbst having an indignant confrontation with Margaret, which served to drive Anderson further away from Herbst and closer to his wife. By the summer of 1920 the affair was over.[73] That was not, however, the last of Josephine Herbst in Anderson's life. Their situation came to a head when Herbst realized she was pregnant with Anderson's child.[74] Herbst informed Anderson of her intention to keep the baby, but Anderson pushed for her to have an abortion because "the knowledge and responsibility [of a child out of wedlock] would weight him down."[75] Under pressure from Anderson, Herbst relented and aborted the pregnancy. Langer concludes, "nothing could illustrate better the state of relations between the sexes...than that both of them accepted as natural that his freedom was worth more than her maternity and that it was his welfare, not hers, that was at stake."[76] Anderson remained in his marriage until Margaret suddenly passed away in 1931.[77] By that time, the Stock Market had crashed, the Jazz Age was over, and Anderson had abandoned his artistic explorations of American marriage in favor of historical verse tragedy. His 1930 hit play, *Elizabeth the Queen*, would alter the tone and trajectory of his career for the next decade while suborning his work of the 1920s (save *What Price Glory*) to the dustbin.

In examining the life of any artist in relationship to their work one must always proceed with caution about drawing firm conclusions. Such conclusions are, more often than not, highly speculative. Nevertheless, the evidence demonstrates that the institution of marriage and its impediments on individual freedom were clear preoccupations in Anderson's life throughout the 1920s. He was, after all, married with three children. We know his relationship with Margaret bore the earmarks of a traditional marriage with her surrendering her ambitions while he assumed the sole-breadwinner role. We know that after nearly a decade of this arrangement, their marriage grew strained and that his restlessness led him into an extramarital affair with regrettable consequences. Given these experiences, it is not far-fetched to imagine that Anderson was influenced, if not motivated, somewhat by the realities of his life irrespective of the distaste he expressed for sharing personal information. It seems fair to say that every effective artist receives inspiration from the world around them. On this score, Anderson was no different, again despite his protests to the contrary. Brooks Atkinson offers some insight here. In his review of *Saturday's Children*, Atkinson wrote, "Mr. Anderson reveals a disquieting understanding of his innocent contemporaries in the first throes of married life."[78] Two years later, in reviewing *Gypsy*, Atkinson recalled *Saturday's Children* and stated that, in both plays, "Mr. Anderson writes with forthright honesty and considerable charm, and his candor about young married people has not deserted him."[79] In this same review, Atkinson criticized numerous other recent plays about marriage, calling them "wooden dances of angular, loose-jointed puppets" compared to the "decencies of truth in Mr. Anderson's sensitive characterizations."[80] In Atkinson's estimation, at least, Anderson offered far more thoughtful, effective commentary on the marriage issue than many of his contemporaries. It stands to reason that the playwright's personal experience colored, perhaps subconsciously, his honest, penetrating critiques.

However, one could not call any of these four plays autobiographical. Anderson seems to have deflected, again either consciously or subconsciously, his own experience onto that of his female protagonists. Mary Kane questions why a woman would seek marriage when she knows it will lead to humdrum domesticity. Michael could easily ask a similar question, yet he is not the focus of the drama. In *Sea-Wife*, Margaret struggles against traditional beliefs that have grown into irrepressible superstitions. Her husband also suffers, but again, the action revolves around Margaret's suffering. Likewise, in both *Saturday's Children* and *Gypsy* we see men suffering the burdens of marriage, yet Anderson places the crux of those dramas on the female experience. Bobby, in particular, adopts the views of her father, thus taking a masculine perspective on sexual affairs. Ellen's promiscuity also endows her with a more traditionally masculine persona. It seems doubtful Anderson consciously allowed himself to identify his experience through the guise of a female character. Again, Anderson was not a playwright with a propensity for allowing art to imitate life too closely. Moreover, while all four plays surely bear aspects of his personal experience in marriage, none of them are anywhere near the level of verisimilitude found in *A Long Day's Journey into Night* or even, for that matter, Tennessee Williams's *The Glass Menagerie* or Arthur Miller's *After the Fall*. Nevertheless, the personal touches that are present provide us with a radically different view of Anderson as a playwright, a view barely touched upon in previous scholarship. It seems his life at some level did, in fact, inform his art.

Summation

Plays depicting marriage during the Jazz Age ran the gamut between convention and revolution. *The First Year* may have been a phenomenon in its time, but its superficial treatment of its subject matter endowed it with little lasting value. Craven's play was safe, comfortable, and unlikely to provoke questions from its audience by holding a true mirror up to nature. *The First Year* reinforces gender stereotypes and conventional tropes associated with institutional marriage. *Sex*, on the other hand, confronted audiences with a starkness that eviscerated notions of traditional decency. West represented the consummate shameless iconoclast who delighted flying in the face of societal mores. It is telling that both Craven and West achieved long-running successes with these polar opposite works written only six years apart. Such was the dissonance of 1920s America.

There were, of course, other instances of playwrights attempting to push barriers without the confrontational model of Mae West. *Anna Christie* represents one such example. Like West, O'Neill centers his action on a prostitute, which was bold in and of itself. However, Anna finds redemption not because of her own agency, but rather through the benevolence of her lover, Mat Burke. In the finale of the play, Burke forces Anna to swear her loyalty to him on a crucifix as well as to promise him she will reform her ways. Anna agrees with childlike eagerness.[81] In effect, Burke rescues Anna with his love. Sidney Howard depicted a similar rescue in *They Knew What They Wanted*. Howard's heroine, Amy, bears the added disgrace of having conceived a child in an extramarital affair. Distraught and ashamed, Amy vows to leave her husband, Tony, to spare him further grief. Tony, however, refuses to accept her leaving. He demands that she remain with him, professes his undying love for her, and promises to raise the child as his own regardless of the social consequences. Moved by her husband's devotion, Amy agrees to remain.[82] Like O'Neill, Howard portrays a controversial situation, but does so with the primary agency resting upon the man. Each woman attains a happy result because, and only because, a man saw fit to demonstrate graciousness and mercy upon her. George Kelly's *Craig's Wife* represents an example of what typically happened when men were less than merciful toward women. Though not a promiscuous woman, Harriet Craig is nonetheless a domineering conniver who utilizes her wiles to manipulate and control her husband, Walter. When Walter finally realizes Harriet's game, he excoriates her behavior and proclaims, "I should be too embarrassed here, under your eye, knowing that you had no respect for [my] manhood."[83] He abandons Harriet[84] and Kelly clearly intends for the audience to view Walter's action as justified. Thus, a woman who fails to conform to feminine ideals as codified by the dominant culture must either rely on the forbearance of men or be ostracized. Even in plays such as these popular and critical hits, which depicted provocative female characters in controversial situations, the main agency centered upon men.

Anderson's plays by contrast, struck a more thoughtful artistic medium. Anderson's dramas were neither as superficial as Craven's nor as radical as West's. Nor were they as pandering as other critical and popular successes of the 1920s, for in all four of these plays Anderson centered his action, principally, upon the agency of the female protagonist. In so doing he crafted meaningful plays of both aesthetic and social merit that are more than worthy of reclamation as cultural documents of the ever-evolving issues pertaining to marriage and gender roles. At the same time, Anderson was no crusader for women's rights, either in his life or his art. Three of his four heroines remain sexually conventional while the fourth suffers suicide in the revised Broadway ending. Nevertheless, each character, in her way, strives against inequalities of tradition as manifested through institutional marriage. For Mary Kane that struggle is one of discovery. She enters marriage without a real understanding of why she should desire it. Marriage for her becomes an education leading to self-realization. In *Sea-Wife*, Margaret arguably suffers more than the others. Her martyrdom expresses itself through what is almost certainly mental illness precipitated by the loss of a child. She suffers in ways the men surrounding her cannot possibly fathom. Anderson's treatment of postpartum mental distress, though subtle, is nonetheless powerful. Bobby Halevy achieves the highest place in terms of asserting her own will. Similar to Mary, she enters marriage out of passion without a strong conception of its reality. She tries to play the game, but finds it rubs against the grain of her personality. Buoyed by the independent spirit of her father, Bobby, too, attains self-realization and, unlike Mary Kane, secures both her independence and her love affair. Ellen Hastings represents the woman closest to modernity. She is well-read, intelligent, and assertive. But she is trapped in a culture not conducive to women of her ilk. She represents a woman ahead of her time. The different endings Anderson created for the play allude to a sense of indecision on the part of the dramatist. This indecision may have stemmed from a dissonance in Anderson himself as Ellen Hastings ran too harshly against his more romantic idealizations of women. Ellen, in effect, proved so strong of a character and so out of place in her world that perhaps Anderson did not know quite what to do with her.

The influences upon Anderson's work appear both myriad and inscrutable. We see, for example, the possibility of his personal life impacting and informing his creative decisions. However, this was not something the dramatist himself would have acknowledged or admitted. Nevertheless, while Anderson was not as autobiographical as some of his more famous contemporaries, it is difficult to completely dismiss the notion that he was not influenced by life events given what we know of his life during the 1920s. We see, also, shades of Frederick Koch's folk elements. All four of these plays are set in distinctly American backdrops and all address themes unique to the American experience, be it historical or modern. Perhaps the most dominant influence in Anderson's work was a strident bent toward individualism. We find this theme most prominently in *White Desert*, which echoes the frontier theory of Frederick Jackson Turner. But individualism also manifests in the defiance of Margaret's husband in *Sea-Wife*, Mr. Halevy's *raisonneur* function and Bobby's self-assertions in *Saturday's Children*, and Ellen's fierce independence in *Gypsy*. Indeed, Anderson's philosophy in the 1920s seems motivated by a radical devotion to individual prerogative. We see this attitude evinced in his *Freeman* article, which rails against modern society's impairments upon personal freedom. This facet may best explain why Anderson endowed such strength and defiance in his female protagonists in an era where most playwrights, even ones as daring as O'Neill and Howard, remained essentially male-centric. For Anderson, it was not a question of feminism, but rather the oppression of an individual human being that was important. Anderson himself bore many of the same idealized prejudices toward women as did most men of his era and we see these biases in the plays, particularly with regard to sexual behavior. Yet his individualistic bent seems to have led him to create forceful women working against institutional oppression.

Maxwell Anderson's place in the American theatre canon remains stymied, in part, because of the preferred scrutiny critics and scholars devoted to his verse dramas of the 1930s, both in his lifetime and in the years following his death. But this focus fails to fully appreciate Anderson's true contributions. Most of his plays of the 1930s centered on real-life historical events or, in the case of *Winterset*, grew from contemporary themes that Anderson sought to universalize in the manner of classical tragedy. Moreover, though Anderson composed poetry throughout his life, both dramatic and lyrical, and though he published poems on occasion, his standing as a poet was never high. In an era that produced such poetic giants as Edna St. Vincent Millay, T.S. Eliot, and Langston Hughes, Anderson's achievements in poetry were meager at best. Indeed, many critics and scholars have questioned the vitality of his verse. John Gassner found Anderson's poetic efforts more literary than passionate.[85] Elmer Rice, Anderson's friend and professional associate in the Playwrights' Producing Company, tended to agree. Rice believed Anderson lacked the "poetic gift" and expounded upon this idea thus: "He had great command of language, great eloquence, and a scholarly understanding of prosody; but it seemed to me that his verse never took wings. In fact, I found it often turgid and rhetorical, and, when spoken on the stage, singularly undramatic."[86] Others have noted a certain clumsiness in Anderson's dramatic verse insofar as he fails to adhere to a strict meter, thus producing lines so irregular they often read like prose.[87] As Gassner observes, Anderson tended to employ "a loose iambic pentameter…which is neither good blank verse nor an autonomous meter."[88] Still others complained of Anderson's often blatant imitation of Shakespearean conventions as well as deriding his penchant for endowing modern lower class characters with flowery dialogue.[89]

All of these criticisms miss the true vitality of Anderson's contribution to American drama. By focusing on the 1930s and centering critiques on the quality and effectiveness of the verse tragedies, previous scholarship has narrowed Anderson's work to classical aesthetics rather than social commentary. In so doing, the value of his work has been misplaced. Whether or not the verse in *White Desert* or *Sea-Wife* is effective as dramatic poetry, whether the lines adhere to a strict meter or lift the passions to grand heights or not, is all irrelevant to the substance of what Anderson achieved in these plays. Anderson was not a great poet. But he was a keen observer and dramatic translator of his time. He understood the temper of the Jazz Age and its angst over the "marriage crisis." He was able to de-center these dramas away from a conventional male-centric perspective and endow these women with independence and agency uncommon for female characters on Broadway at the time. At the same time, the empowered women in Anderson's marriage plays are limited by his continued veneration of monogamy within relationships.

In this respect, Anderson's depictions were aligned with many of the marriage revisionists of the 1920s such as Judge Lindsey, who tended to reaffirm monogamy in marriage despite their radical critiques of Victorianism.[90] In the final analysis, Maxwell Anderson was more Shaw than Shakespeare; more satirical social critic than lofty poetic muse. He was much bolder than most playwrights of his era, yet careful enough to avoid provoking police raids. His heroines of the Jazz Age challenged audiences at the time and, to some extent, offered insight into the continued evolution of marriage and gender roles in American culture. These themes remain as relevant in the twenty-first century as they were in the 1920s and Anderson's importance in expounding upon these themes deserves re-framing and greater recognition.

Despite all fears to the contrary in the Jazz Age, marriage proved itself as durable an institution as any in American culture. Judge Lindsey noted "the stubbornness with which the human race clings" to marriage and observed, "[n]o amount of failure has ever been able to rob marriage of [its] prestige."[91] In the twenty-first century, marriage historian Stephanie Coontz has asserted that despite all cultural upheavals from the 1920s through the 1960s, "[marriage] remains the highest expression of commitment in our culture and comes packaged with exacting expectations about responsibility, fidelity, and intimacy."[92] Moreover, its presence on the stage has not wavered. From works as light as Neil Simon's *Barefoot in the Park* to more serious treatments such as Harold Pinter's *Betrayal* and Donald Marguiles's *Dinner with Friends*, playwrights throughout the twentieth century and into the twenty-first century continue to wrestle with questions of matrimonial relationships and gender roles. Marriage has evolved, but endured. The United States Supreme Court affirmed its "centrality," but also its malleability, in the landmark decision Obergefell v. Hodges (2015), which granted marriage rights to same-sex couples, a possibility unthinkable in the Jazz Age. The Court held, "The history of marriage is one of both continuity and change. That institution—even as confined to opposite-sex relations—has evolved over time."[93] As definitions of marriage evolve, as society continually redefines gender roles, so too must the American theatre canon broaden to include plays truly representative of these nuances and complexities of American culture.

Notes

1. Jesse Lynch Williams, *Why Marry?* (New York: Charles Scribner's Sons, 1918), 9.
2. Ibid.
3. Ibid., 13.
4. Ibid., 16.
5. Ibid., 55–57.
6. Ibid., 59.
7. *Brooklyn Dailey Eagle*, 27 December 1917.
8. *New York Times*, 26 December 1917.
9. *Best Plays of 1909–1919*, 602–631.
10. John Hohenberg, *The Pulitzer Prizes* (New York: Columbia University Press, 1974), 43.
11. Burns Mantle, *The Best Plays of 1921–1922* (Boston: Small, Maynard, & Company, 1922), 560.
12. Frank Craven, *The First Year* (New York: Samuel French, 1921), 15.
13. Ibid., Act I.
14. Ibid.
15. Ibid., Act II.
16. Ibid., Act III.
17. 21 October 1920.
18. 24 October 1920.
19. P.F.R., *New York Evening Post*, 21 October 1920.
20. *New York Times*, 31 October 1920.
21. Ibid.
22. *Brooklyn Daily Eagle*, 24 October 1920.
23. Woollcott.
24. *New York Evening Post*, 21 October 1920; *Brooklyn Daily Eagle*, 24 October 1920; *New York Times*, 31 October 1920.
25. 24 October 1920.
26. 31 October 1920.
27. Hohenberg, 50–51.
28. Zona Gale, *Miss Lulu Bett* (New York: D. Appleton, 1921), 177.
29. Ibid., 182.
30. Ibid.
31. Ibid., 159–162.
32. Hohenberg, 51.
33. Ibid., Act II.
34. Barrett H. Clark, *Drama* (April 1927); Joseph Wood Krutch, *Nation* (16 February 1927); George Jean Nathan, *American Mercury* 10 (1927): 503.
35. Mae West, *Sex* in *Three Plays by Mae West*, edited by Lillian Schlissel (New York: Routledge, 1997), Act I.

36. Ibid., Act II.
37. Ibid., Act III.
38. *New York Times*, 27 April 1926.
39. *New York Evening Post*, 27 April 1926.
40. *Brooklyn Daily Eagle*, 28 April 1926.
41. *Time*, 10 May 1926.
42. Quoted in Introduction to *Three Plays by Mae West*, 10.
43. Lillian Schlissel, Introduction to *Three Plays by Mae West*, 7.
44. Ibid.
45. Burns Mantle, *The Best Plays of 1926–1927* (New York: Dodd, Mead, and Company, 1927), 4–5, 536.
46. Ibid.
47. *New York Times*, 27 April 1926.
48. George Abbott, *Mister Abbott* (New York: Random House, 1963), 104.
49. Maxwell Anderson, *Off Broadway: Essays About the Theatre* (New York: William Sloane Associates, 1947), 26.
50. Shivers, *Life*, 262.
51. Burns Mantle, *American Playwrights of Today* (New York: Dodd, Mead, 1929), 70–71.
52. Clark, 3–4.
53. Letter to Lela Chambers, 26 March 1956 in *Dramatist in America: The Letters of Maxwell Anderson, 1912–1958*, edited by Laurence G. Avery (Chapel Hill: University of North Carolina Press, 1977), 277.
54. John Gassner, *Dramatic Soundings* (New York: Crown, 1968), 313.
55. Shivers, *Life*, 104.
56. Ibid., 104–105.
57. Ibid., 106.
58. Ibid., 354.
59. Ibid.
60. Maxwell Anderson, "An Age of Hired Men," *Freeman*, 22 September 1920, 31.32; Avery, *Catalogue*, 57. Though the article is unsigned in the publication, Avery confirms it was, in fact, written by Anderson.
61. Alfred S. Shivers, *The Life of Maxwell Anderson* (New York: Stein and Day, 1983), 104.
62. Anderson, "Hired Men," 31.
63. Ibid., 32.
64. Ibid.
65. Ibid.
66. Ibid.
67. Ibid.
68. Christina Simmons, *Making Marriage Modern: Women's Sexuality from the Progressive Era to World War II* (New York: Oxford University Press, 2009), 108.

69. Elinor Langer, *Josephine Herbst* (Boston: Little, Brown, 1984), 55–56.
70. Ibid., 56.
71. Ibid., 56–57.
72. Ibid., 57.
73. Ibid., 56–57.
74. Ibid., 60.
75. Ibid.
76. Ibid.
77. Shivers, *Life*, 120–121.
78. Atkinson, 27 January 1927.
79. Atkinson, 27 January 1929.
80. Ibid.
81. Eugene O'Neill, *Anna Christie* in *O'Neill: Complete Plays 1913–1920* (New York: Library of America, 1988), 1023–1024.
82. Sidney Howard, *They Knew What They Wanted* in *Sixteen Famous American Plays*, edited by Bennett A. Cerf and Van H. Cartmell (New York: Modern Library, 1942), 52–54.
83. George Kelly, *Craig's Wife* in *Three Plays by George Kelly* (New York: Princess Grace Foundation-USA, 1999), 394.
84. Ibid., 394–395.
85. John Gassner, *The Theatre in Our Times* (New York: Crown Publishers, 1954), 239.
86. Elmer Rice, *Minority Report: An Autobiography* (New York: Simon and Schuster, 1963), 394–395.
87. Bernard Dukore, *American Dramatists, 1918–1945* (New York: Grove Press, 1984), 90.
88. *Theatre in Our Times*, 291.
89. William E. Taylor, "Maxwell Anderson: Traditionalist in a Theatre of Change," in *Modern American Drama: Essays in Criticism*, edited by William E. Taylor (Deland, FL: Everett/Edwards, Inc., 1968), 57.
90. Simmons, *Making Marriage* Modern, 108.
91. Ben B. Lindsey and Wainwright Evans, *The Companionate Marriage* (Garden City, NY: Garden City Publishing, 1927), 71.
92. Stephanie Coontz, *Marriage, a History* (New York: Viking, 2005), 309.
93. Obergefell v. Hodges, 576 U.S. 644 (2015).

Index

A

Abbott, George, 7, 27, 31, 36, 52, 59, 64, 65, 169, 182
Addams, Jane, 9
Anderson, Alan, 38, 39, 41, 62–65
Anderson, Margaret Haskett, 22, 39, 170, 172–174
Anderson, Maxwell, 1, 11, 18–29, 33–41, 43–46, 50, 53, 55, 56, 59–65, 67–77, 80–82, 84, 87–92, 95, 97–118, 120–136, 139–142, 144, 146–148, 150–157, 159–162, 165, 166, 169–175, 177–180, 182, 183
  Elizabeth the Queen, 28, 39, 88, 174
  First Flight, 35, 36, 98
  Gypsy, 24, 29, 124, 129–132, 134, 137, 139, 141, 143, 147, 149, 151–157, 164–166, 169, 172, 173, 175, 178
  High Tor, 28, 39
  Mary of Scotland, 28
  Outside Looking In, 35, 36, 98
  Saturday's Children, 24, 29, 91, 97–99, 103, 114, 118, 121–131, 134, 140, 152, 161, 165, 166, 169, 170, 172, 175, 178
  Sea-Wife, 18, 21, 23, 24, 29, 49, 67–72, 76, 80–82, 88–94, 98, 99, 103, 104, 112, 120, 130–132, 152, 154, 166, 171, 175, 177–179
  The Buccaneer, 35, 36, 98
  What Price Glory, 24, 27, 36, 88, 98, 174
  White Desert, 21–24, 29, 37–42, 52, 56–65, 69–72, 74, 76, 80, 81, 83, 88–91, 98, 103, 104, 109, 112, 117, 120, 124, 130–132, 138, 140, 152, 154, 166, 169, 171, 172, 178, 179
  Winterset, 28, 35, 36, 179
Anderson, Sherwood, 20
Arnold, Matthew, 23, 70, 84, 92
  The Forsaken Merman, 23, 70, 92

INDEX

Atkinson, Brooks, 105, 123, 126, 128, 134, 135, 147, 151, 153, 154, 156, 157, 175, 183
Augustine, 131, 134
Avery, Laurence G., 34, 38, 61, 91, 154, 157, 182

B
Baker, George Pierce, 21
Beard, George M., 8
Benchley, Robert, 122, 128
Block, Anita, 46, 47, 59, 60, 63–65
Broun, Heywood, 39, 62
Brown, John Mason, 26, 35
Buhle, Mari Jo, 9, 32

C
Carb, David, 114, 123, 127, 146, 156
Chopin, Kate, 60
Cixous, Helene, 109, 126
Clark, Barrett H., 19, 34, 62, 65, 67, 69, 82, 91, 92, 114, 115, 121, 122, 127, 128, 170, 181, 182
Clayton-Bulwer Treaty, 40
Comstock Law of 1873, 27
Conrad, Joseph, 134
Coontz, Stephanie, 31, 40, 62, 64, 98, 125, 180, 183
Corbin, John, 59, 63
Cott, Nancy F., 6, 9, 31, 32, 117, 127
Craven, Frank, 18, 33, 84, 94, 122, 159, 162–164, 166, 168, 169, 176, 177, 181
 The First Year, 18, 19, 29, 33, 84, 112, 122, 124, 159, 162–166, 168, 169, 176, 181

D
Davis, Owen, 18, 33
 Icebound, 18, 33
Dell, Floyd, 4, 13, 30, 113, 127, 137, 155, 171
Dickens, Charles, 6, 31, 74, 93
Douglas, Ann, 10, 18, 25, 30, 32, 33, 35, 64
Dugan, William Francis, 19
 The Virgin Man, 19, 122
Dumenil, Lynn, 30, 76, 125

E
Eliot, T.S., 179
Ellis, Havelock, 6, 10, 31, 32, 44, 62
Emerson, Ralph Waldo, 7, 31
Erenberg, Lewis, 76
Erlanger, Abe, 17
Evans, Wainwright, 13, 30, 33, 63, 92, 125, 183
Exner, Max J., 7

F
Flexner, Eleanor, 147, 148, 156
Freud, Sigmund, 9, 10, 32, 147
Frohman, Charles, 17
Frost, Robert, 78, 93

G
Gale, Zona, 18, 33, 164, 165, 181
 Miss Lulu Bett, 18, 33, 164, 165, 181
Gassner, John, 28, 36, 170, 179, 182, 183
Gilman, Charlotte Perkins, 4, 8, 30, 53, 64, 138, 155, 171
Goldman, Emma, 9, 10, 32, 42, 43, 63, 101, 125, 171
Gordon, Ruth, 123, 124, 128
Groves, Ernest, 4–6, 12–14, 30–32, 40, 53, 62, 76, 85, 93, 94, 114

H

Hall, G. Stanley, 10
Hammond, Percy, 60, 64
Harding, Warren G., 3
Herbst, Josephine, 173, 174, 183
Hinkle, Beatrice, 4, 30
Hornblow, Arthur Jr., 19
　The Captive, 19, 122
Howard, Sidney, 18, 33, 176, 178, 183
　They Knew What They Wanted, 18, 33, 112, 176, 183
Hughes, Langston, 179

I

Ibsen, Henrik, 47, 60, 91, 117, 118

J

Jefferson, Thomas, 40
Johnston, William, 12, 32, 117, 127

K

Kelly, George, 19, 33, 176, 177, 183
　Craig's Wife, 33, 112, 176, 183
Key, Ellen, 9, 163
Kinsey, Alfred, 4
Klaw, Marc, 17
Klein, Alvin, 88, 92
Koch, Frederick, 21, 34, 39, 68, 89, 178
Krutch, Joseph Wood, 115, 121, 127, 128, 151, 157, 181

L

Langer, Elinor, 173, 174, 183
Lawson, John Howard, 11, 22
　Roger Bloomer, 22
Lewis, C.S., 138

Lindsey, Judge Ben B., 2, 3, 13, 14, 30, 33, 47, 53, 57, 63, 64, 69, 70, 73, 81, 83, 85, 92, 94, 97, 98, 114, 124, 125, 128, 136, 148, 172, 180, 183
Lindsey, Judge Ben B. & Evans, Wainwright
　The Companionate Marriage, 2, 13, 30, 33, 63, 81, 92, 97, 125, 183
Littledale, Clara Savage, 12, 32, 127
Locke, John, 40, 62
Lynd, Robert and Helen, 4, 70
　Middletown, 4, 30, 92

M

Manifest Destiny, 40, 41, 44, 48, 54, 62, 63
Mantle, Burns, 19, 33, 37, 59, 61, 62, 65, 125, 129, 130, 132, 151, 154, 157, 170, 181, 182
McClintic, Guthrie, 123, 124, 128
Merrill, Beth, 59
Meyer v. Nebraska, 40
Millay, Edna St. Vincent, 20, 44, 63, 179
Miller, Arthur, 175
Miller, Ruth Scott, 12, 32, 33, 66, 116, 127

N

Nathan, George Jean, 122, 128, 147, 156, 181

O

Obergefell v. Hodges, 180, 183
O'Neill, Eugene, 17, 18, 21, 28, 29, 33, 39, 59, 170, 176, 178, 183
　Anna Christie, 18, 33, 112, 176, 183

P

Parsons, Elsie Clews, 4, 30, 126
Pells, Richard H., 111, 126
Phelps, William Lyon, 164
Plato, 5, 31
Pollock, Arthur, 42, 59, 63, 65, 151, 157
Pomeroy, E.N., 88
Potter, Merle, 88–91, 94, 95
Pulitzer Prize, 14, 17, 19, 28, 33, 98, 161, 164, 165, 181

Q

Quinn, Arthur Hobson, 21, 34, 61

R

Rice, Elmer, 7, 31, 34–36, 179, 183
Riley, A. Dale, 67, 68
Rousseau, Jean-Jacques, 131, 134
Rudnick, Lois, 9, 31, 125
Ruhl, Arthur, 143, 151, 156
Russell, Bertrand, 4, 10, 13, 30, 69, 92, 171

S

Sanger, Margaret, 9
Schiff, Stacy, 74, 93
Shakespeare, William, 21, 56, 60, 65, 180
Shaw, George Bernard, 17, 29, 160, 180
Sherman, John K., 88, 92
Shivers, Alfred S., 22, 28, 29, 32–36, 61, 62, 68, 70, 92, 95, 154, 157, 170, 171, 182, 183
Shubert brothers, 17
Sievers, W. David, 147, 156
Simmons, Christina, 10, 11, 14, 32, 33, 182, 183
Skinner, R. Dana, 114, 122, 123, 127, 128, 147, 151, 156, 157

Socrates, 5
Stallings, Laurence, 24, 98
Stansell, Christine, 22, 34, 125
Susman, Warren, 6

T

Thoreau, Henry David, 115, 127
Treadwell, Sophie, 60, 84, 94, 152, 157
  Machinal, 60, 84, 94, 152, 153, 157
Turner, Frederick Jackson, 40, 62, 74, 93, 178

V

Victorianism/Protestant Victorianism, 5–12, 20, 45, 46, 50, 52, 56, 57, 60, 61, 76, 83, 98–100, 102, 104, 105, 114, 116, 119, 122, 141, 160, 162, 172
Victoria, Queen of England, 6

W

Washington, George, 6
Watson, John B., 10
Wells, Ida, 9
West, Mae, 19, 73, 122, 129, 159, 166–170, 176, 177, 181
  Pleasure Man, 129
  Sex, 11, 19, 29, 33, 53, 122, 124, 129, 159, 166, 168, 170, 176, 181
Williams, Jesse Lynch, 14–18, 159–161
  Why Marry?, 14–17, 33, 159–161, 163, 181
Williams, Tennessee, 39, 170, 175
Woollcott, Alexander, 163, 164, 181
Wyatt, Euphemia Van Rensselaer, 114, 115, 121–123, 127, 128

Printed in the USA
CPSIA information can be obtained
at www.ICGtesting.com
LVHW020719061023
760095LV00029B/449